THE NORDIC MODEL

CONTEMPORARY WORLDS explores the present and recent past. Books in the series take a distinctive theme, geo-political entity or cultural group and explore their developments over a period ranging usually over the last fifty years. The impact of current events and developments are accounted for by rapid but clear interpretation in order to unveil the cultural, political, religious and technological forces that are reshaping today's worlds.

SERIES EDITOR
Jeremy Black

In the same series

Britain since the Seventies
Jeremy Black

Sky Wars: A History of Military Aerospace Power
David Gates

War since 1945
Jeremy Black

The Global Economic System since 1945
Larry Allen

A Region in Turmoil:
South Asian Conflicts since 1947
Rob Johnson

Altered States:
America since the Sixties
Jeremy Black

The Contemporary Caribbean
Olwyn M. Blouet

Oil, Islam and Conflict:
Central Asia since 1945
Rob Johnson

Uncertain Identity:
International Migration since 1945
W. M. Spellman

The Road to Independence?:
Scotland since the Sixties
Murray Pittock

THE NORDIC MODEL

Scandinavia since 1945

MARY HILSON

REAKTION BOOKS

Published by Reaktion Books Ltd
33 Great Sutton Street
London EC1V ODX
www.reaktionbooks.co.uk

First published 2008

Printed and bound in Great Britain
by CPI Antony Rowe, Chippenham, Wiltshire

British Library Cataloguing in Publication Data
Hilson, Mary
The Nordic model : Scandinavia since 1945. – (Contemporary worlds)
    1. Consensus (Social sciences) – Scandinavia
    2. Scandinavia – Politics and government – 1945–
    I. Title
    320.9'48'09045

ISBN-13: 978 1 86189 366 6

Contents

Contents

Preface

I first encountered the concept of the Nordic model in September 1992 when I had the opportunity to study as an undergraduate exchange student at the Department of Economic History at Uppsala University in Sweden. Although I was unaware of it at the time, I now realise that I arrived in Sweden at the height of an economic and political crisis, when many elements of the Swedish model were being questioned and even rejected. Despite this, like many Britons with left-wing political sympathies, I still found much to admire in Sweden. I continue to do so, though I also hope I have developed a rather more critical perspective over the last fifteen years. And there are, of course, also some aspects of Sweden and its Nordic neighbours that I find less attractive. In particular it took me a long time to overcome my Anglo-Saxon prejudices against acquiring a state 'personnummer' after I moved to Sweden to undertake post-doctoral research in 1998.

This book, then, is an attempt to think critically about the meaning of the Nordic model, above all in its heyday of the period 1945–91. I have not confined myself entirely to this period. Chapter One includes a longer historical survey of the political development of the Nordic countries, and in chapters Four and Five I examine the debates of the 1990s on foreign policy and immigration. The book grew out of an undergraduate course on the Nordic model that I have taught at the Department of Scandinavian Studies, University College London, since 2000 (and I owe a special debt to all the students who have taken the course and debated these ideas with me), but it is also a result of dealing with some of the questions constantly thrown up by the institutional context in which I work: what exactly *is* Scandinavian Studies? What links these countries together? How far does the concept of Scandinavia/Norden stretch?

Sweden is the Nordic country where I have spent most time, and whose language I know best. This may be reflected to some extent in the sources I have used, but I have tried to avoid an overly Swedish bias. For the most part I have drawn on the very extensive international literature in the social sciences that deals with Norden or Scandinavia as a whole, supplemented where necessary with national studies. Unfortunately, my linguistic inadequacies mean that I have had to rely heavily on the English-language sources for Finland and Iceland, and Icelanders in particular may feel overlooked, for which I apologize. Unless otherwise stated, all translations from Swedish, Danish and Norwegian are my own.

You will ask, perhaps, why I wished to go further northward. Why? Not only because the country, from all I can gather, is most romantic, abounding in forests and lakes, and the air pure, but I have heard much of the intelligence of the inhabitants, substantial farmers, who have none of that cunning to contaminate their simplicity, which displeased me so much in the conduct of the people on the sea coast . . . The description I received of them carried me back to the fables of the golden age: independence and virtue; affluence without vice; cultivation of mind, without depravity of heart; with 'ever-smiling liberty', the nymph of the mountain.

Mary Wollstonecraft, *Letters Written during a Short Residence in Sweden, Norway and Denmark*, ed. Richard Holmes (London, 1987 [1796]), pp. 148–9.

The grounds for a unified treatment of the history of the North are, as stated, to be found in the very nature of the said history and the natural bonds that exist between the countries and their peoples. The effects thereof, and their influence upon the individual, may be supported by what are called Scandinavian sympathies. Such support is unnecessary; the historical interest alone will suffice. Indeed, it is fortunate that this is so, for after the bitter experience of our time it would seem that, as the evil spirit of discord in days of old, so in the present the frigid egoism and the narrow-hearted, myopic and heinous spirit of calculation shall prove the curse of the 'Scandinavian idea' and quell her with its might when she means to rise.

C. F. Allen, *De tre nordiske Rigers Historie under Hans Christiern den Anden*, Frederik den Første, Gustav Vasa, Grevefeiden, 1497–1536 (Copenhagen, 1864); cited and translated in Uffe Østergård, 'The Geopolitics of Nordic Identity: From Composite States to Nation-States', in *The Cultural Construction of Norden*, ed. Øystein Sørensen and Bo Stråth (Oslo, 1997), pp. 25–71: 40.

A homogenous people, with no racial conflicts, both the Swedes and the Norwegians are deeply rooted in an ancient culture. In this atmosphere social and economic forms have evolved with far less conflict than in the rest of the world. That is the essence of the Swedish story: there has been an opportunity for evolution. This evolution has occurred through the process of compromise and adjustment. Here, too, perhaps temperament, history, tradition help to explain why it has been possible . . .

[Sweden] was not Utopia. The objective was never in terms of an intellectual concept of perfection. The Swedes are too realistic for that, and too practical.

Marquis Childs, *Sweden: The Middle Way* (New York, 1948 [1936]), pp. vii, ix.

Introduction: The Historical Meanings of Scandinavia

For a small, sparsely populated region on the margins of Europe, Scandinavia seems to have generated an interest out of all proportion to its size. As the three short extracts cited above suggest, the region has been imagined in a variety of ways: extolled for the purity of the northern landscape, with its trees and lakes; the deep historical bonds between its peoples, stretching back to the Viking era; and the success (or occasionally otherwise) of the twentieth-century experiment in social policy. It has been more difficult to pin down a precise meaning for the term 'Scandinavia'. It first occurs in Pliny's *Naturalis Historia*, as the name for what is now the small Swedish province of Skåne (Scania).[1] By the eighteenth century, the meaning of 'Scandinavia' had become much broader. Diderot's *Encyclopédie* of 1765 described 'la Scandinavie' as '[a] large European peninsula, which the ancients believed to be an island, and which today consists of Denmark, Sweden, Norway, Lappland and Finland'.[2] 'Scandinavia' was thus distinguished from other parts of 'the North', which included the Slavic lands of Russia and Poland. When the Swedish kingdom was defeated by Russia in 1809, Finland became a grand duchy of the Russian Empire, and moved temporarily out of the Scandinavian sphere. 'Scandinavia' took on a new meaning derived partly from philology, which traced the roots of the Scandinavian peoples back to the common Old Norse language and literature of the Vikings. Briefly, during the mid-nineteenth century, Scandinavia was also associated with political ambitions to unite the three states – Denmark, Sweden and Norway – under a common crown.

By the end of the First World War, pan-Scandinavian dreams had given way to the much less ambitious aim of international cooperation between nations. Partly because of associations with failed ambitions, partly because of the need to incorporate linguistically different Finland into the Scandinavian sphere, the term 'Scandinavia' came to be replaced, during the inter-war period, by the alternative term *Norden* (literally, 'the North'). The adjective *nordisk* (Nordic) was used by the political leaders of the five countries concerned at a conference in Copenhagen in 1939, to demonstrate the unity of their countries on the outbreak of war.[3] The establishment of Nordic institutions after the Second World War, principally the Nordic Council, helped to establish the term as the preferred designation for the region: one that incorporated five sovereign nations – Denmark, Finland, Iceland, Norway and Sweden – and the autonomous island territories of Greenland, the Faroe islands and Åland.

Nevertheless, the term Scandinavia remains widely used today. For some, the term is purely topographical, referring to the large peninsula that makes up present-day Norway and Sweden. Many would add Denmark to this narrow definition because of the close cultural, linguistic and historical links between the three countries. Danish, Norwegian and Swedish are mutually intelligible, at least in their written forms.[4] In some quarters, not least in the university departments of Europe and the USA that teach the Scandinavian languages, it makes sense to include Iceland on philological grounds, even if that means hiving off Finland to a Department of Finno-Ugric languages.[5] Elsewhere, certainly in the English-speaking world, Scandinavia is used as a synonym for Norden to denote all five countries, although this usage is undoubtedly less popular within the Nordic countries themselves. In this book the terms are used interchangeably. In any case, Scandinavia has come to mean much more than the sum of its parts, generating a number of enduring myths and counter-myths: as socialist utopia or over-regulated night-mare, as haven of sexual libertarianism or stifled by collective conformity, as societies of exceptionally high standards of living or of exceptionally high rates of suicide. At the end of the twentieth century, in Britain at least, Scandinavia had come to stand for the epitome of 'cool', symbolized by the prominence and accessibility of designer consumer goods, while at the same time retaining its popular image of being cold, remote and extremely expensive.

This book attempts to explore the meaning of 'Scandinavia', especially within the context of the Scandinavian or Nordic 'model' of politics and policy since 1945. What were the main features of the model, and how have they changed during the last half century or so? What, if anything, was Scandinavian (or Nordic) about the recent history of Denmark, Finland, Iceland, Norway and Sweden, and does it make sense to write the history of these countries in this way? The emphasis is on Scandinavia as a *Geschichtsregion* or historical region, where examining the different countries within a common framework can help to reveal patterns of similarity and difference across national boundaries. A more detailed presentation of the different aspects of the model as they are covered in the individual chapters follows at the end of this introduction, but first a brief discussion of the concept of the *Geschichtsregion* is necessary.

SCANDINAVIAN HISTORY: SCANDINAVIA AS AN HISTORICAL REGION

There have, of course, been previous attempts to write the history of north-eastern Europe from a Scandinavian or Nordic perspective, although it has often been scholars from outside the region that have explored these common links most vigorously. As the cultural geographer Kenneth Olwig has commented, '[y]ou can experience and study Norden as a whole in America in a way that is difficult to do in Norden itself'.[6] This applies above all to the twentieth century, when the Scandinavian or Nordic 'model' of politics and social policy generated a substantial body of international literature within the social sciences. In contrast, the nationalist view continues to dominate history-writing within the Scandinavian countries. In the words of the distinguished Nordic historian Harald Gustafsson, 'It just about goes without saying in each Nordic country that history is best understood as Danish, Swedish, Icelandic etc.'[7] Nineteenth-century historians, following the Rankeian tradition, were pressed into the service of the nation state, demonstrating the distinctiveness of their particular countries.[8] The nationalist perspective dominated even to the extent that the medieval Kalmar Union between the monarchs of Denmark, Sweden and Norway was sometimes treated as an historical aberration (though, to be sure, the nineteenth-century pan-Scandinavian movement did inspire new interest in it). Even in modern historical research, attempts to write Scandinavian or Nordic history are often organized as 'anthology comparisons', where scholars from the various national academies contribute from their distinctively nationalist perspectives.[9]

This nationalist emphasis is surprising given that, before the twentieth century at least, it would be difficult to examine the history of one Scandinavian state without also considering that of its neighbours. The medieval Kalmar Union split into the two kingdoms of Denmark and Sweden in the early sixteenth century, but the Danish monarchy included Norway and Iceland within its territories, as well as, until 1658, what are now the southern Swedish provinces of Skåne and Blekinge. Iceland and Norway continued to exist as distinctive entities within the conglomerate Danish state, unlike Finland and Sweden, which were politically one and the same until 1809. By this criterion, of course, the early modern history of Scandinavia would also have to include Swedish and Danish territories on the southern Baltic coast and in northern Germany. Only after 1814 did the map of Norden begin to assume a shape that is more familiar today, coinciding with the era of nationalism.

Despite its national emphases, the existing historiography points to some shared historical experiences within this geo-political framework, which were common to the entire region, and thus could be described as 'Scandinavian'. These included the Viking Age and the Kalmar Union of the medieval period; the rivalry between the imperial states of Denmark and Sweden during the early modern period; and the political projects of pan-Scandinavianism and intra-Nordic cooperation during the nineteenth and twentieth centuries.[10] The two early modern states – Denmark-Norway and Sweden-Finland – were relatively similar in structure, characterized above all by the completeness of the

Reformation and the highly centralized nature of the state, which relied heavily on the Lutheran state church to exert its authority. The transition to modernity, economically, socially and politically, occurred at roughly the same time across the region, and took place with a relatively small degree of upheaval and violence, especially when compared to other parts of Europe.[11] At the same time, nineteenth-century Scandinavia remained overwhelmingly agrarian, sparsely populated and poor, forcing the emigration of many thousands of its peasant farmers to the New World.

Given these similarities, Scandinavia could function as a classic example of a *Geschichtsregion*, a concept that has its roots in the work of German historians on Eastern and Central Europe during the interwar period and afterwards. Historical regions are conceived not as being defined by clearly demarcated geographic borders, but as 'an abstract and oscillating space'.[12] The *Geschichtsregion* is thus not so much an object of study in its own right, but an heuristic concept for comparative analysis, a discursive construction fluctuating in space and time. It follows, therefore, that there are alternative ways of seeing the history of this part of northern Europe, of which the related but not identical concepts of *Nordosteuropa* and the Baltic are just two discussed further in the conclusion to this book.

However, as Stefan Troebst has pointed out, the historical region, even when intended merely as a category of analysis, is rarely neutral. Historical regions frequently overlap with those used in other spheres. These might include political concepts of the region as a target of geo-political aims and ambitions; representations of the region in the mass media and public discourse; and the region as it is imagined in the 'mental maps' of those living both within it and without it.[13] Scandinavia or *Norden* is no exception here, understood variously as the focus for pan-nationalist ambitions, as a geo-political bloc, and as the source of a cultural, ideological and political project. Perhaps this was never more true than during the period covered by this book, and one of the aims of the book therefore is to explore the meanings of Scandinavia in all these senses.

During the 1990s some scholars argued that the defining features of Nordic history were distinctive enough to amount to a Nordic

Sonderweg dating back to the eighteenth century or even earlier. Nordic exceptionalism, they suggested, was based on the successful reconciliation of the apparently oppositional Enlightenment traditions of equality and liberty.[14] National Romanticism had a relatively limited impact on the Nordic countries, allowing the liberal respect for individual liberty to flourish alongside peasant traditions of collectivism and community. This unique blend helped to explain why the Nordic transition to modernity was relatively peaceful and conflict-free. The enduring strength of Enlightenment rationalism in Scandinavia was attributable 'in large part to the powerful modifying presence of [Lutheran] Christianity'.[15] Common cultural influences across the Scandinavian states, the spread of which was facilitated by the presence of mutually comprehensible languages, linked the peculiarly Nordic experience of the Enlightenment with the development of the Nordic model in the twentieth century. Above all, Scandinavia or Norden came to be defined by its difference from the rest of Europe. It was non-Catholic, non-colonial and non-imperial, and for these reasons the Scandinavian states had actively tried to withdraw from involvement in major European conflicts from as early as the eighteenth century.[16]

As an attempt to trace the roots of the Nordic model in a long-term historical perspective, I find this approach rather teleological, and therefore not particularly helpful. There was no unbroken chain of events leading from the absolutist monarchies of the eighteenth century to the social democratic states of the twentieth. In Scandinavia, as elsewhere, historical change was contingent and unpredictable. The argument also conceals important differences between the Scandinavian states. Nineteenth-century popular democratic movements were, for example, much more oppositional in Norway, where they were associated with demands for national independence, than in Sweden, where they were not. The impact of liberal thought in Finland was limited in comparison to the other Scandinavian states, but the impact of revolutionary ideas, especially in the early twentieth century, was possibly greater.[17]

Despite its limitations, the explicitly Nordic and comparative focus of this work, like all transnational history, can help to illuminate links that are not always immediately apparent in a nationalist framework.

The roots of Scandinavia as a 'project' can indeed be traced before the twentieth century. Most importantly, it was associated with the ambition to unite Scandinavia under one crown during the nineteenth century. Like most nineteenth-century nationalist movements, pan-Scandinavianism was a complex phenomenon that cannot be attributed to one particular cause. As a political vision, it gained its strongest support among the student societies of the early nineteenth century, but there was more to it than this. For a time, it represented the main hope for liberal reform for those radicals who looked to the Norwegian constitution of 1814 as a model for the whole of Scandinavia, and for economic modernizers encouraged by the success of the German *Zollverein*. But pan-Scandinavianism was also influenced by National Romanticism, and in particular the enthusiasm that this inspired for discovering the common cultural roots of the Scandinavian peoples in the Old Icelandic language and literature of the Vikings. Despite this, or perhaps because of the diversity of its aims, the pan-Scandinavianist aspiration was never realized. Partly this was because Scandinavia lacked a Piedmont or a Prussia, a Cavour or a Bismarck, possessing the political will and military might to force through a project of unification. The state that might have achieved this was Sweden, but here there was too much divergence between the aims of the liberal nationalists on the one hand, and the foreign policy ambitions of the monarchy on the other. After 1848 Swedish liberals turned their attention briefly to Finland, and following the outbreak of the Crimean War in 1853, the possibility was mooted, briefly, of joining France and Britain to defeat Russia and reconquer Finland to revive a great northern power. These aspirations – laid conclusively to rest following the peace of Paris in 1856 – represented both a critique of tsarist absolutism, and also of the broadly pro-Russian foreign policy of the Swedish crown.[18]

The border with the Slavic east was clearly important in defining Scandinavia, but it was instead the border between Scandinavia and Germany that was to mark the final demise of aspirations for Scandinavian unity. Karl xv of Sweden's promise of 20,000 troops to help Denmark defend its southern border against Prussian aggression came to nothing very much, and proved of little consequence to Bismarck, who defeated Denmark and ignored Swedish promises of full diplomatic support to Denmark in the subsequent peace conference. After 1864 the dream of pan-Scandinavian unity gave way to the markedly less ambitious schemes for intra-Scandinavian cooperation between sovereign nation states. This cooperation continued to be influenced by a sense of cultural and linguistic unity, however, and it found expression in a considerable number of attempts to establish pan-Scandinavian institutions. The idea of Scandinavia provided a comforting sense of solidarity against the large states that now seemed to dominate the Baltic region: Russia in the east and a newly unified Germany in the south. Scandinavia was, moreover, defined partly in terms of its cultural and political differences from Russia: its Germanic culture and language contrasted with the Slavic one; its free peasantries contrasted with serfdom; its constitutional monarchy against tsarism. For much of Scandinavia, Germany never provided quite the same cultural counterweight, since many German nationalists looked to Scandinavia as the embodiment of the purest form of the common Germanic culture and, from the late nineteenth century, race. The exception to this was Denmark, following the defeat and loss of territory to Prussia in 1864.

Partly for this reason, when Germany did begin to pose a serious threat, ideologically and militarily, after the First World War, the idea of 'Norden' emerged as a term that was preferred over Scandinavia. It was also an acknowledgement that the Nordic family now consisted not only of the two 'old' Scandinavian states plus newly independent Norway, but also Finland, which had become independent from Russia in 1917. Unlike Scandinavianism, moreover, 'Nordism' never even hinted of supra-nationalist ambitions: it never amounted to more than 'a pooling of nationalisms'.[19] The Nordic aspiration for peaceful cooperation between sovereign nation states was embodied in the enthusiasm for the new League of Nations, and through the institutions established for intra-national cooperation in politics, such as the union of Nordic parliamentarians founded in 1907, and also of civil society. Many of these organizations, such as the Association for Nordic Unity founded in 1919, gained in popularity during the 1930s in the face of the twin threats of the USSR and the Third Reich.

It was during the inter-war period, however, and particularly during the 1930s, that another dimension of Nordic identity began to gain prominence internationally: the idea of the Scandinavian or Nordic model. Initially it was Denmark that attracted most attention, in particular its folk high school movement for adult education, and the agricultural co-operatives that seemed to offer a practical model for tackling some chronic agricultural problems.[20] From the 1930s the relatively swift recovery of the Scandinavian economies from the Great Depression, accomplished without the abandonment of parliamentary democracy as elsewhere in Europe, turned the attention of many towards the North. Much of this interest, initially at least, was directed towards Sweden rather than towards the Nordic countries as a whole, especially following the publication of the American journalist Marquis Childs's influential text *Sweden: The Middle Way*.[21] The success of the Nordic countries was attributed, above all, to the compromise their policy makers had made between liberal capitalism and state communism, a policy made possible by the achievement of a historic political settlement between working-class and agrarian interests. As Kazimierz Musał has pointed out, the emerging xenostereotype of the Scandinavian 'middle way' was matched, however, by an equally important autostereotype. The 1937 English-language volume *The Northern Countries in the World Economy*, sponsored by the Nordic governments, was influential in promoting the idea of a distinctive Nordic bloc that included both Finland and Iceland.[22] In early twentieth-century Sweden, modernizing nationalists such as Gustav Sundbärg spoke of the need to create a new 'great power' era for Sweden by reinventing the nation as the embodiment of modernity and progressiveness.[23] In the post-war era, the enduring concept of the Nordic model provided the means for northern Europe's small nations to avoid the image of small-state irrelevance.[24]

By the eve of the Second World War, therefore, Norden had become established in the minds of many in Europe and beyond as the source of radical new thinking on economic and social policy. Events after the war helped to consolidate this image of the region. The notion of the 'middle way' or compromise between socialism and capitalism sat conveniently with the perception of the region as a neutral but friendly bloc between the two superpowers, committed to the internationalism of the United Nations. Again, the extent to which this was at root a Swedish model, given that Sweden was the only Nordic country to maintain formal neutrality, deserves consideration. Even by extension, however, Norden or Scandinavia presented a powerful image of regional homogeneity to the outside world. Generally this was a positive image, of societies that were characterized by exceptionally high standards of living, though for a while during the 1970s this came to be replaced by a more negative portrayal of the region as an over-regulated, quasi-totalitarian nightmare, characterized by exceptionally high rates of suicide and drunkenness.[25] Scandinavia came to be best known for its welfare states, but its systems of politics and policy making, its economic policies, its industrial relations and culture of compromise, and its internationalist foreign policies also attracted much scrutiny.

Nordic distinctiveness in these fields was moreover strengthened by a number of powerful cultural stereotypes. Since the 'Modern Breakthrough' of the late nineteenth century, the Nordic countries have certainly produced their share of internationally acclaimed cultural figures, including the dramatists Henrik Ibsen and August Strindberg, the composers Edvard Grieg and Jean Sibelius, the artist Edvard Munch, the writers Knut Hamsun, Halldór Laxness and Karen Blixen, and the children's authors Astrid Lindgren and Tove Jansson, to name only a handful of the best known. Although some of these artists and their compatriots were influenced by National Romanticism, it would probably be more accurate to note the ways in which the outside world has received them as Scandinavian rather than identifying typically Scandinavian elements of their work. Moreover, the relative inaccessibility of the Nordic languages has inevitably meant that Nordic writers have been dependent on translation to reach a wider international audience, and for that reason some of the most prominent figures within the national contexts have had much less of an impact abroad. Examples might include the Swede Selma Lagerlöf, the Finn Väinö Linna and even the nineteenth-century Danish clergyman N.F.S. Grundtvig.[26]

For this reason it is perhaps those branches of the arts that do not rely on the written word that have contributed most to shaping the international image of Scandinavia in the second half of the twentieth century. Scandinavian popular music was important both culturally and economically, with artists such as Björk, A-ha, Sigur Rós, Europe and Roxette all enjoying commercial success abroad, though none quite as much as ABBA. Again, though, it would be hard to distinguish anything that was particularly Scandinavian about these groups, since most were influenced by American pop culture and produced much of their work in English. Even Björk, despite her use of images of the Icelandic landscape, had a style that could be described as eclectic and original, but could hardly be said to be 'typically' Icelandic (whatever that indeed might mean).[27]

Perhaps more important in this respect was film. Swedish and Danish filmmakers received international acclaim during the era of silent cinema, but during the post-war period Scandinavian culture – from an international perspective at least – came to be dominated by the towering figure of the Swedish director Ingmar Bergman. For many cinema-goers during the post-war era Bergman came to stand for the epitome of European art-house cinema, but as much as any other Scandinavian artist his work shaped Scandinavian cultural stereotypes with its treatment of themes such as the individual's fear of death in the face of a silent God (at a time of growing secularism), melancholy and loneliness, but also sexual permissiveness. From the 1990s Nordic cinema attracted new attention above all through the work of the Danish 'Dogme '95' school, dominated by Lars von Trier. If there were any continuities between Bergman and Dogme then they were to be found in the strong tradition of state support for the arts in general and cinema in particular, which allowed young, unknown artists producing work in a minority language to take artistic risks and establish themselves internationally.[28]

But if twentieth-century Scandinavian culture could be said to have its own aesthetic then it was expressed above all by the functionalist movement in architecture and design. Nordic functionalism, demonstrated to the world at the Stockholm Exhibition of 1930, shared with Le Corbusier and the Bauhaus school the concern to reconcile function and form and an interest in new materials such as tubular steel and reinforced concrete, but it came to mean much more than that. Above all, it implied a link between the aesthetic pursuit of architecture on the one hand, and practical social policy on the other. The new people's home was to be constructed not just metaphorically but literally, and the initiator of Swedish social democratic family policy, Alva Myrdal, collaborated with the architect Sven Markelius to design new types of social housing.[29] After the Second World War, the functionalist vision came also to embrace urban planning and the design of furniture and everyday objects. Stylistically, it was identified above all with clean, simple lines. Ideologically, it stood for the embrace of modernity and rejection of the past, demonstrated through hostility to the old bourgeois city centres, many parts of which were destroyed, and the construction of new 'forest suburbs' that were intended to promote closeness to nature.[30]

This was to some extent a Nordic phenomenon. Stockholm's first satellite town, Björkhagen, designed on functionalist principles and completed in 1948, was mirrored by Lambertseter in Oslo in 1951, though the redevelopment of the Norwegian capital was never quite as comprehensive as that in Sweden.[31] Finnish architects had already gained some prominence in the inter-war period as the constructors of monuments to the young nation, such as Eliel Saarinen's Helsinki railway station (1914–19) and the Olympic stadium designed by Yrjö Lindegren and Toivo Jäntti for the postponed 1940 games (they were eventually held in Helsinki in 1952).[32] The most dominant figure in Finland, however, was Alvar Aalto, who came to be known not only for his architecture but also for his designs for furniture and other household items based on functionalist principles. In Denmark, the design style known as 'Danish Modern' attracted widespread international attention, and came to be widely exported after 1945, with Hans J. Wegner's 'Round Chair' proclaimed as the world's most beautiful chair by Interiors magazine in 1950.[33] Even the famous Danish children's toy building blocks known as Lego could be seen as an embodiment of these principles. Alva Myrdal had also stressed the importance of children's play in the development of the rational citizen, and the name Lego was derived from the Danish 'Leg godt', meaning 'play well'.[34] In the early twenty-first century, the Nordic reputation for producing consumer goods that combine function, aesthetic desirability and democratic accessibility seems undiminished, with examples including Nokia's mobile phone handsets and, above all, the Swedish flat-pack furniture manufacturer IKEA, which makes explicit use of Scandinavian images in its marketing, despite its multi-national reach.

There is clearly a strong overlap between the popular and journalistic portrayals of the Nordic model, in which the Scandinavian countries are explicitly used as a model (or as a warning) for policy makers outside the region, and the concept of the Nordic model as it has developed within the academic social sciences. Many of the academics who have studied the Nordic region have done so from an explicit position of approval or admiration for societies that seem to differ in important ways from other parts of the world. Karl W. Deutsch's concept of the Nordic 'security community', Arendt Lijphart's 'consensual democracies', Christine Ingebritsen's characterization of the Nordic countries as 'norm entrepreneurs' in international relations, or the 'social democratic welfare state' theorized by insiders such as Walter Korpi and Gøsta Esping-Andersen, all cast the Nordic model as just that: a model that would bear emulation by other societies. There have been more critical or even hostile accounts, which emerged especially during the neo-liberal challenge to welfare capitalism during the 1970s and '80s. But the appeal of the Scandinavian utopia endured for academics, journalists and policy makers alike into the twenty-first century, bolstered by the frequent success of the Scandinavian countries in coming top of international surveys of welfare, standards of living, happiness and the like.[35]

This book examines different elements of the Scandinavian or Nordic model in turn. Chapter One scrutinizes recent claims that the Nordic political model of consensus and compromise can be traced to deep historical roots in the institutions of peasant democracy in the early modern period. An examination of patterns of political development in the Nordic region over a long historical period does indeed reveal some similarities, but there was nothing inevitable about the form that twentieth-century politics took. The chapter also examines the causes for the perennial question of Nordic political difference: the outstanding success of social democratic parties in Sweden, Denmark and Norway. Chapter Two deals with economic development, and examines the evidence for structural similarities between the small open economies of the Nordic region on the one hand and similarities in policy on the other. Chapter Three turns the focus to the epitome of Scandinavian distinctiveness: the welfare state. Here, the 'historic turn' in welfare state studies during the 2000s seems to erode the notion of a Nordic model, revealing instead important differences in the development of the Nordic welfare states over the twentieth century and its causes.

Given that Scandinavia also has some meaning within geo-politics, chapter Four considers international relations, both in the sense of the internal relations between the Scandinavian countries and the collective face that they have attempted to present to the outside world. The Scandinavian reputation for idealism and humanitarianism in international affairs seems to have become tarnished, partly because of evidence for rising ethnic tension and intolerance within Scandinavian societies since the 1990s. These matters are treated in chapter Five, where the apparently contrasting Danish and Swedish responses to mass immigration are compared in some detail. Finally, some consideration needs to be given to the future of Scandinavia as a region. Is the Scandinavian model still intact? Chapter Six considers the case for the continuing coherence of Scandinavia as a region, and the challenges and possibilities presented by new ways of looking at this part of northern Europe, including the Baltic and the north Atlantic.

Chapter 1

Consensual Democracies? The Nordic Political Model

The idea of the Nordic political model originated in the 1930s. In the face of threats to democracy across much of Europe, the example of the Scandinavian countries was widely cited as a cause for optimism, proof that parliamentary democracy could continue to function effectively even in times of severe economic difficulty. Scandinavian democracy was seen as a model for Britain in particular, because of the cultural similarities it shared with the Scandinavian countries.[1] Writing in *The Spectator* in 1938, Anthony Blunt commented: 'The Scandinavians are the very best sort of people, who seem to have all the advantages of being progressive without any of the unpleasantness. They have achieved real democracy of a kind, and one which is apparent at every step.'[2] Sir E. D. Simon, in a book written for the Left Book Club in 1939, pointed to the Scandinavian countries as a model for the defence of democracy against the 'terrific challenge' of the dictators in 'these dark days'. 'These small democracies are the most encouraging thing in the world today,' he wrote. '[T]he Scandinavian countries are the only countries in Europe which, since the war, whilst elsewhere the newer democracies have been destroyed and the older ones are on the defensive, have become steadily more democratic, steadily more prosperous and more contented.'[3]

The concept of a Nordic political model has continued to inform the self-identity of the Scandinavian countries in the period since 1945. The image of the Scandinavian countries as a 'specific egalitarian social democratic community of destiny' was contrasted against the capitalist and Catholic European continent, an imagined difference that continues to inform opposition to European integration in the Nordic countries today.[4] Moreover, the Nordic countries are often treated as a single block within the international political science literature, with scholars referring to a 'Nordic political model'. What seemed to distinguish the Nordic region was a political culture and political institutions that were characterized by collectivism and conformism, that had evolved peacefully without violent revolutionary upheavals, and that had been shaped primarily by the influence of the independent peasant farmers.[5] In contrast to states such as the USA and the UK, where political debate is more adversarial and there is more open conflict, the Nordic countries have been described as 'consensual democracies', where the political system has a high degree of legitimacy and support; where social divisions have been relatively mild; and where political deliberations aim to neutralize conflict and achieve compromise.[6] Other important features of the Nordic political model have included the electoral dominance of social democratic labour parties within multi-party systems, and the high levels of political participation and organization among citizens, with a tendency to favour neo-corporatist methods of decision making. The political influence of the farmers as a class waned during the second half of the twentieth century, though most would agree that agrarian parties were extremely important in shaping Nordic politics until at least the 1930s.

These similarities between the Nordic countries also conceal some important differences. Although social democratic parties were hegemonic in Norway and Sweden during the post-war decades, they never had an outright majority in Denmark, and were much less dominant in Finland and Iceland. Most importantly, the historical process of state-building differed markedly between the five countries. The main contrast was between the old imperial states of Denmark and Sweden, and the newer ones that gained full independence in the first half of the twentieth century (Norway in 1905, Finland in 1917 and Iceland in 1944). The notion of a path to modernity characterized by peaceful political evolution does not apply to Finland, which experienced a violent civil war in 1918. These differences have resulted in variations in the constitutional arrangements of the Nordic countries, with, for example, the presidential system in Finland contrasted with a greater role for parliaments elsewhere, leading some scholars to raise doubts about the existence of a Nordic model of parliamentarism.[7] Since the 1990s in particular these differences have become more apparent, and the extent to which the model may still be considered to exist is now a matter for debate.

HISTORICAL DIFFERENCES IN THE NORDIC POLITICAL SYSTEMS

There were some important differences in the historical processes of state-building in Scandinavia. The breakup of the medieval Kalmar Union and the sixteenth-century Reformation led to the establishment of Denmark and Sweden as two rival imperial states in the Baltic region, with the later territories of Norway, Iceland and Finland incorporated within their borders. These states were centralized monarchies. Patterns of land-holding and local administration were broadly similar across the whole of Sweden-Finland but there was more variation within the Danish state, not least the lack of a rural aristocracy and the dominance of peasant freeholders in Norway and Iceland.[8] Moreover, Sweden and Denmark also differed from one another in important ways relating to their trade networks, which in turn affected the development of the newly independent states from the early twentieth century. Of these, Norway and Iceland shared the status of 'seaward peripheries', but Finland's development before it became independent in 1917 was influenced by its position as a landward buffer at the western fringe of the Russian empire.[9]

As this suggests, there are alternative ways of comparing state formation within the Scandinavian region: 'west Norden' (Denmark, Norway and Iceland) versus 'east Norden' (Sweden-Finland); the old states (Denmark and Sweden) versus the new ones (Norway, Finland and Iceland); or even the Scandinavian 'core' monarchies (Denmark, Norway and Sweden) versus the two peripheral republics (Finland and Iceland). Despite this, the chronological pattern of development was broadly similar across the entire region. Although Scandinavia has been noted for the peaceful evolution of its political institutions, most of the major extensions of political rights came during periods of international crisis.[10] The Napoleonic Wars resulted in territorial upheavals and confirmed the reduced status of Sweden and Denmark as minor and neutral powers. Sweden ceded its Finnish territory to Russia and gained its present-day boundaries in 1809. The Danish state retained its north Atlantic island possessions (Iceland, Faroe and Greenland) and the duchies of Slesvig and Holsten, but lost Norway, which in 1814 became part of a monarchical union with Sweden.

These territorial changes were accompanied by political upheaval, though in no Scandinavian country were these upheavals revolutionary in the true sense. Although the new Swedish constitution of 1809 ended absolutism, it was by no means intended as a step towards parliamentary government. The Swedish state remained highly centralized and undemocratic, with power concentrated in the hands of a conservative elite including the monarchy, the upper civil servants and senior military officers. Following several decades of liberal agitation in the mid-nineteenth century, the four-estate Diet was replaced by a bi-cameral parliament in 1866, but it was elected on a very limited franchise, and conservative hegemony was retained in the form of an indirectly elected first chamber dominated by landowners, public officials and big business, and of a monarchy with revived personal ambitions. The Swedish state of the early twentieth century thus remained relatively authoritarian, such that one historian has described its Riksdag as 'one of the most reactionary of European Parliaments, surpassed only by the Prussian Landtag'.[11] But there was also growing pressure for reform, channelled through three popular movements – the free church movement, the temperance movement and the labour movement – which made common cause with liberal politicians in the Riksdag to campaign for universal suffrage during the 1890s and after. In the end, it was a conservative government that eventually passed a franchise reform in 1907, granting universal male suffrage for the second chamber, but also complying with the conservative demand for a new electoral system based on proportional representation.

The Liberal government that took office in 1905 was the first to do so on the basis of its parliamentary majority, but the principle of parliamentary government was challenged in 1914 when the king intervened over the question of naval defence, and in doing so brought down the government. The matter came to the fore again following a series of mass protests and demonstrations against the severe food shortages during the winter and early spring of 1917. There were some tense days of political unrest during the summer, but this was eventually channelled into a majority for the progressive parties during the parliamentary elections that autumn and the formation of a Liberal-Social Democratic ministry, which is generally accepted to mark the establishment of parliamentary government in Sweden. Reform of the parliamentary upper chamber and the introduction of universal suffrage followed. Parliamentary democracy had thus been established peacefully in Sweden without overthrowing the existing regime, but with more conflict than is sometimes acknowledged.[12]

In Denmark absolutism survived the upheavals of the revolutionary era intact, and endured until the new wave of European revolutions in 1848. The crown's success was partly due to its willingness to undertake reform, most notably with the 'great agrarian reforms' begun during the 1780s. Even so, the climate of public opinion was becoming an increasingly important influence on the regime.[13] The growth of liberal opposition from the 1830s, campaigning for economy in the state finances as well as the usual liberal demands such as freedom of the press, was linked to the emergence of liberal nationalism, especially in the duchies of Slesvig and Holsten. When the Holsten Liberals demanded new constitutions for the duchies during the European revolutions of March 1848, the National Liberals in Copenhagen presented their own demands for reform. The government resigned, and a new ministry was formed to oversee the introduction of a new constitution that was eventually ratified in June 1849, thus ending 188 years of absolutism. The monarchy survived but was now constrained by a two-chamber parliament partially elected by universal male suffrage. This was a remarkably democratic arrangement by the standards of its time, and one that survived moreover the period of reaction that followed the 1848 revolutions elsewhere in Europe.

As in Sweden, however, Danish politics during the last decades of the nineteenth century was dominated by a protracted and bitter struggle between Conservatives and Liberals over parliamentary democracy. The Conservatives had gained the upper hand in the wake of Denmark's military defeat by Prussia in 1864, and reformed the constitution to strengthen the Landsting (parliament) as a Conservative guarantee by changing the means by which it was elected. The so-called system shift came in 1901 when the Conservatives lost heavily in parliamentary elections and the first Liberal government was appointed on the basis of its parliamentary majority. Universal suffrage was introduced in 1915, but parliamentary democracy faced challenges from both the revolutionary left in 1917–18 and also from the renewed ambitions of the king during the so-called Easter Crisis of 1920. In the early spring of 1920 the Liberal-Social Democratic government found itself under severe pressure over the question of Denmark's southern border and lost its majority in the Folketing. The king asked the prime minister to resign, and when he refused took matters into his own hands by dissolving the government. The Social Democrats threatened a general strike against what they saw as an attempted coup by the monarch and his conservative supporters, and the king was eventually persuaded to back down and call a new election.[14]

For Norway, Finland and Iceland, constitutional reform was associated with the nationalist struggle for independence. Under the terms of the Treaty of Kiel in January 1814, Norway was transferred from the Danish to the Swedish crown. For a few months during the summer of 1814 it seemed that Norway would become an independent state, and 112 elected delegates assembled at Eidsvoll in May 1814 to draft a new Norwegian constitution. The document that they eventually agreed was, for its time, one of the most liberal constitutions in Europe.[15] It established a unicameral parliament (Storting) that possessed both tax-raising powers and a veto over the actions of the crown, elected by a democratic franchise that gave nearly half of adult male Norwegians the vote.[16] Norwegian independence was short-lived, however. Following the resignation of the Norwegian king, the Storting voted to enter into a union with Sweden, and to elect and recognize Karl XIII of

Sweden as the king of Norway. In doing so, the Storting was able to negotiate various concessions from Karl XIII's regent, the Crown Prince Karl Johan, with the result that Norway kept its liberal constitution and its council and Storting actually gained a stronger position than that originally envisaged for these institutions at Eidsvoll. For this reason, Norway came to be seen as a source of hope and inspiration for Swedish Liberals and constitutionalists, especially following the election of peasant majorities in the Storting in 1832 and 1836.[17] Swedish Conservatives, meanwhile, rallied to the defence of the union as a means of strengthening their interests in a strong monarchy and unreformed Riksdag. The conflict was sharpened when the radical politician Johan Sverdrup gained control of the Storting in 1882 and precipitated a constitutional crisis by removing leading ministers from office. The Swedish king was forced to concede to the demands of the Norwegian Liberals and accept the parliamentary principle in Norway. Universal suffrage was introduced in 1913.

In Iceland, as in Norway, constitutional reform was closely associated with the nationalist demands for independence.[18] And as in Norway, the parliament or Alþingi, revived in 1843, became one of the foremost symbols of national identity; indeed, it remained so throughout the second half of the twentieth century as well.[19] The island was ruled from Copenhagen as part of the Danish absolutist monarchy. Some Icelandic nationalists attempted to resist the introduction of the new Danish constitution to Iceland in 1849, but the upheavals resulted in a stalemate in Danish–Icelandic relations until the Status Act of 1871, which confirmed Iceland as an inalienable part of the Danish state, albeit one with special rights. A constitutional amendment in 1874 conferred legislative power on the Alþingi, shared with the Danish crown. Thereafter the nationalist campaign centred on the crown's exercise of its power through the minister for Iceland. Demands for parliamentary reform continued to go hand in hand with nationalism, and 1904 marked a turning point in both respects when a further constitutional amendment provided for the minister for Iceland to be elected by a parliamentary majority in the Alþingi. Universal suffrage followed in 1915. The so-called Home Rule period lasted until 1918 when Iceland became a separate state within a personal union with

Denmark. Full independence and the establishment of the republic came in 1944, precipitated by the Nazi occupation of Denmark.

Finland differed from the other Nordic countries in that its path to independence and parliamentary democracy involved a violent civil war in 1918. As a grand duchy of the Russian empire, Finland was allowed a greater degree of administrative autonomy after 1809 than that experienced elsewhere in the empire, although it was in no sense a democracy. From the 1890s, however, the Russian emperors sought to impose a more direct rule, driven partly by security policy concerns following the rise of Germany. Nonetheless, they could not prevent Finnish manifestations of the revolutionary pressures felt elsewhere in the empire, and the first major democratic reform came in response to a general strike in the revolutionary year of 1905, when the four-chamber estates were replaced with a single-chamber parliament (Eduskunta), elected by universal male and female suffrage. The first elections in 1907 resulted in a victory for the Social Democrats, which now became the largest party, though the tsar retained his veto over the legislative process. Full independence was declared by a Conservative government in the wake of the revolutionary turmoils of 1917, with the new Bolshevik government in Russia being the first to recognize the new country. In the context of serious food shortages and unemployment, however, the radical wing of the Social Democratic Party gained an internal majority in support of its programme for a revolutionary takeover of the government, and in January 1918 its armed Red Guards proclaimed a new government, having attacked and taken control of the four largest cities. This action was resisted by hastily assembled government forces assisted by some German troops, and there was full-scale civil war from February 1918. The period of hostilities was relatively short – the Reds surrendered in May 1918 – but the conflict was divisive and bloody, with more than 27,000 deaths on the Red side.

Despite these differences in the Nordic paths to statehood and parliamentary democracy, there were also some important similarities between the Nordic countries. Some scholars have suggested that these are even distinctive enough to constitute a Nordic *Sonderweg*.[20] They may be summarized as follows. First, the Nordic path to parliamentary democracy was, with the partial exception of Finland, remarkably

peaceful. The Scandinavian countries were affected by the revolutionary currents of 1789, 1830, 1848 and 1917–18, but the political demands
of newly mobilized social groups were accommodated through a series
of political compromises and reforms, obviating the need for a violent
or revolutionary overthrow of power. Secondly, the state helped to
guarantee its own survival by carrying out social, economic and political reforms from above. Examples of this might include the Danish
monarchy's agrarian reforms in the 1780s, the Danish constitutional
reform of 1849 and the Swedish parliamentary reform of 1866. This
helped to foster a view of the state as a benign institution capable of
acting in the best interests of society, especially when combined with
an emerging sense of national identity. State nationalism in
Scandinavia was thus above all an educational project aimed at turning
peasants into citizens.[21] Thirdly, the salient feature of nineteenth-
century Scandinavian politics was its agrarian character. Following
the eighteenth-century agrarian reforms – in Sweden as well as in
Denmark – the self-owned family farm became ever more dominant in
rural society and the independent peasant farmers became the principal political class. Nineteenth-century political mobilization was also
largely a rural phenonemon, even in the labour movement where
urban workers made common cause with agrarian labourers, smallholders and fishermen. The farmers' parties formed the backbone of
nineteenth-century liberalism and the main political groupings within
the respective parliaments.[22]

Scholars have debated the reasons for the relatively peaceful and
consensual nature of political development in the Scandinavian countries and the apparent lack of violent upheaval. Until recently, the
twentieth-century Nordic political culture of consensus was generally
attributed to the political compromises of the 1930s and the
'Red–Green' coalitions negotiated between social democratic and
agrarian parties that resolved the political class conflicts prevailing at
the time. Since the 1980s, however, Swedish historians in particular
have suggested that the consensual political model should be understood instead in terms of its deep historical roots in the political
institutions of the early modern period. According to the distinguished
early modernist Eva Österberg, the consolidation of central state power

in the sixteenth and seventeenth centuries led to the development of local political institutions – above all the *sockenstämman* or parish council – which provided a forum for peasants to articulate and receive redress for their grievances, and thus became an important arena for political interaction between different social groups, and between the central state and the local community.[23] The survival of these institutions and the continuity in political culture that they represented explained why '[b]loody rebellions, wildcat strikes and coups d'état have for centuries not been the normal way for Swedes'.[24] From his study of three parishes in early modern Småland, Peter Aronsson concluded: 'it seems clear that many aspects of the modern Swedish model – the relatively peaceful institutional means of solving conflicts, with the participation of the broad mass of the population – are not historical accidents'.[25]

These conclusions seem to support social scientists' attempts to apply Barrington Moore's modernization theory to the Scandinavian case, which suggests that the relatively strong political position of the peasantry during pre-industrial times was crucial in determining the consensual nature of twentieth-century Scandinavian politics.[26] But from an historical perspective, the thesis of long-term continuity is less satisfactory. First, as Börje Harnesk has pointed out, the argument suggests a Swedish *Sonderweg* that has still not been adequately tested by empirical comparative analysis. In fact, evidence suggests that there were no fewer peasant revolts in early modern Sweden than in many other parts of Europe, and that there were also many instances where peasants enjoyed a similar level of local access to the central state.[27] Secondly, the argument is a teleological one that interprets the early modern past in the light of assumptions about the present. Indeed, there would be a strong case for suggesting that the history of political consensus has the status of a Swedish 'Whig' history. As Patrik Hall has shown, the Swedish 'story' of consensus between the independent peasantry and the benign central state has its own long tradition within Swedish historiography, found, for example, in Erik Gustaf Geijer's *Svenska folkets historia* of the 1830s.[28]

Similar points could be made about the other Scandinavian countries. In Norway, the institutions of 1814 – the constitution and the

Storting that it established – took on an iconic status in the political struggles of the later nineteenth century. Icelandic nationalists made similar claims about the historical legitimacy of their parliament as an institution that had been founded during the period of the medieval commonwealth, and in this they were perhaps helped by the enthusiasm of Victorian antiquarians in Britain for what they regarded as a particularly pure form of democracy.[29] Meanwhile, in Denmark the independent peasant farmer took on an iconic national status after the land reforms of the late eighteenth century, although the 'farmer interpretation of Danish history' was problematic in that it seriously underestimated the complexities of rural society.[30]

The point here is not to challenge or deny the validity of claims about the nature of Scandinavian politics in the early modern period, but to question the assumption of an unbroken link between the seventeenth-century parish assemblies and the 'consensual democracies' of the twentieth century. A closer analysis of the political history of Scandinavia in the late nineteenth and early twentieth centuries suggests that there was nothing inevitable about the Scandinavian transition to democracy.[31] Indeed, for a while it seemed that the potential for more violent outcomes was never very far away. This is particularly true viewed from the vantage point of the 1920s. By the start of the decade parliamentary democracy had been established in all the Scandinavian countries, but the problem remained of how to make it work effectively.[32] Few governments were able to achieve a workable parliamentary majority in the inter-war period, with the consequence that many were unstable and short-lived: there were twelve different governments in Sweden alone between 1920 and 1932. Moreover, liberal democracy seemed totally unable to offer any convincing solutions to the problems of economic instability and high unemployment, and in the face of this impotence there was no shortage of voices advocating a more extreme political response. While the social democratic labour parties of Denmark and Sweden had since 1917 committed themselves to the parliamentary route to socialism, under the reformist leadership of Thorvald Stauning and Hjalmar Branting respectively, the Norwegian Labour Party had taken the opposite course. Alone among the pre-war European social democratic parties it joined the Communist International in 1919, and continued to advocate socialist revolution for the next decade. As we have already seen, the revolutionary wing of the Finnish Social Democratic Party went even further, instigating an armed attempt to overthrow the government in 1918.[33] Meanwhile, the anti-parliamentary right was also represented in Scandinavia, and some attempts were made to found proto-fascist organizations among the farmers.[34] The most significant of these was the Finnish Lapua movement, which drew its core support from rural Ostrobothnia in the north of the country and attempted – unsuccessfully – an armed revolt against the government in 1932. A comparable movement in Denmark was able to mobilize 40,000 farmers in a march to Copenhagen in 1935.

Given these challenges, the survival of the Scandinavian parliamentary democracies during the inter-war period must be attributed to a large extent to the events of the 1930s, and the success of the social democratic parties in negotiating coalitions with the agrarians. The pattern was established by the so-called Kanslergade Agreement in Denmark, named after the prime minister's residence where the negotiations took place. The agreement was concluded in January 1933, just one day before Hitler came to power in Germany. The agreement, for which the immediate trigger was the need for consensus on the devaluation of the krona, guaranteed a parliamentary majority for the Social Democrats through the support of the Social Liberals (Radikala Venstre, RV) and the Agrarian Party (Venstre). In return, the Social Democrats agreed concessions on devaluation and agrarian price support to help the farmers. The Agreement was observed with great interest in the rest of Scandinavia and provided a model for a similar arrangement negotiated between the Social Democratic Labour Party (Sveriges Socialdemokratiska Arbetareparti, SAP) and the Agrarian Party in Sweden in May 1933. Similar agreements were negotiated in Norway in 1935, perhaps more unexpectedly given the Labour Party's previously uncompromising stand toward cooperation with bourgeois parties, and in Finland in 1937. Here, the 'red-earth' coalition negotiated between the Liberals, the Agrarians and the Social Democrats was significant in that it bridged the post-civil war divide between the Social Democrats on the 'red' side, and the bourgeois or 'white'

Agrarian Party. As such it laid the foundations for a political cooperation that was to endure for half a century, though the Social Democrats
never achieved the position of dominance within the coalition that
they did elsewhere in Scandinavia. Finally, the pattern was also
repeated in the 'Government of the working classes' formed between
the liberal-agrarian Progressive Party and the Labour Party in Iceland
in 1934, though here the Labour Party remained the junior partner.

SCANDINAVIAN POLITICS SINCE 1945

The crisis agreements of the 1930s were important in that they set the
pattern for Scandinavian politics during the post-war era. Indeed, the
upheavals of the war itself served not so much as to disrupt this pattern
as to consolidate it. This was certainly true for Norway and Sweden,
where the Labour and Social Democratic parties respectively emerged
from the war on a wave of popular support that was translated into
electoral dominance for at least two decades after 1945. The Swedish
Social Democratic Party was associated with the successful defence of
the country's neutrality policy, and the prime minster and party leader
Per Albin Hansson was regarded with great affection. In Norway,
prominent Labour politicians such as Einar Gerhardsen could claim
active involvement in the resistance movement. The situation for the
Danish Social Democrats was trickier, since they had participated in
the coalition government that had cooperated with the Nazi occupiers,
and this was reflected in a surge of support for the Communists during
the first post-war elections. But the main point is that all the
Scandinavian countries emerged from the war with their political
systems intact. Indeed, Finland was alone among the post-1918 successor states in the survival of its democratic constitution and political
institutions, despite the experience of fighting and losing two wars
against the Soviet Union between 1939 and 1944. Nor was there a
sudden and dramatic shift in political opinion as a result of the war, as
some historians have suggested there was in Britain, for example.[35]

The political arrangements of the 1930s endured therefore, and such
was their stability that they are often described as 'frozen' during the

period c. 1930–70. There were two main features of this model: first, the dominance of social democratic parties within a multi-party system, governing either alone or through stable coalitions with other parties of the left or centre. Secondly, the Scandinavian democracies were described as 'consensual democracies', where broad consensus-building mechanisms were favoured over majority rule and adversarial politics, and social divisions were neutralized by 'over-arching sentiments of solidarity'.[36] This was partly because all the Scandinavian countries had electoral systems based on proportional representation, which made one-party majority governments unlikely. In Sweden, Denmark and Norway, the usual pattern was for the largest party – until the 1970s this was usually the Social Democrats – to form a minority government supported by one or more parties in parliament. In Finland, where the left was divided between the Social Democrats and the Communists, broad coalition governments involving several parties were more normal, and the Agrarian/Centre Party remained an influential force for much longer after 1945. But even here, where the Social Democrats did not achieve the hegemonic status of their counterparts in Sweden and Norway, the party was consistently the largest both in terms of the popular vote and the distribution of mandates in the Eduskunta. In Iceland, post-war governments were dominated by the centre-right Independence Party, though it too had to govern with the support of other parties, and formed an enduring coalition with the Social Democrats during the years 1959–71.

The Scandinavian party system that existed until the 1970s consisted of five or six parties (four in Iceland). These parties were commonly divided into two blocks: the socialist or non-bourgeois block consisting of the social democrats and the communists, and the bourgeois or non-socialist block consisting of the liberal, agrarian and conservative parties. (The historic party system is illustrated in Table 1 in the Appendix) The parties could be aligned fairly neatly on a left–right axis, with the main split being between the social democrats and communists on the left, and the liberals, agrarians and the conservatives on the centre and right. The basic attributes of the Scandinavian party system were already in place before the 1930s, and most of the parties emerged – in common with the rest of Europe – during the period of the establishment of parliamentary democracy in the late nineteenth and early twentieth centuries. Political scientists have suggested that the emergence of political parties reflected dominant social cleavages in the late nineteenth century, and that this was carried over into a strong correlation between class affiliation and party affiliation.[37] In Scandinavia, the main social divisions were twofold: between workers and capital, reflected in the emergence of social democratic labour parties and conservative parties defending the interests of big business; and between town and countryside, reflected in the emergence of the agrarian parties. Moreover, the absence of significant religious or ethnic cleavages in Scandinavian countries obviated the need for confessional or ethnic parties, the only historic exceptions being the Norwegian Christian People's Party, founded in 1933, and the Swedish People's Party in Finland, founded in 1906, neither of which, however, gained significant parliamentary support.

One of the more distinctive features of the Scandinavian party system was the phenomenon of the agrarian party, which emerged as an electoral force in response to the economic difficulties faced by the farmers during the early twentieth century, and remained influential until the 1950s or even 1960s. The strength and influence of these parties during the inter-war period reflected the continued significance of agriculture in the Nordic region and the growing gulf between urban consumers and rural producers that was exacerbated by the food crises of the war.[38] The economic difficulties of the 1920s and '30s affected farmers badly: declining commodity prices and the shrinking of export markets forced many into bankruptcy. Unlike the peasant parties of Eastern Europe, however, the Nordic agrarian parties represented mostly independent family farmers, not agricultural labourers or small subsistence farmers, and they were mainly concerned with the economic interests of farmers as a corporate group rather than the defence of farming as a way of life.[39] Indeed, none of the Scandinavian agrarian parties was ever able to command the exclusive support of all rural dwellers. In Sweden and Norway, the social democratic parties made concerted and successful efforts to win the support of smallholders and agricultural labourers, while in Denmark the nineteenth-century agrarian party split into two in 1905: the farmers' party, Venstre, and

De Radikale Venstre (usually translated as the Social Liberals), which drew its support from urban intellectuals and rural smallholders.

If the influence and success of the Scandinavian agrarian parties is to be measured through participation in government, then the Finnish and Icelandic parties stand out. Indeed, the Finnish Agrarian Party had some claim to be considered a party of the establishment equivalent to the social democrats in the other Nordic countries, by virtue of its participation in many coalitions and its close links with the long-standing president Urho Kekkonen.[40] Nonetheless, faced with the long-term decline in the importance of agriculture in the economy, the depopulation of rural communities and a corresponding electoral decline, all the Scandinavian agrarian parties found it necessary to adapt their political appeal in the post-war era. Beginning in the 1950s, the agrarian parties in Sweden, Finland and Norway attempted to rein-vent themselves as centre parties, appealing to new constituencies such as small business owners. In fact, under its new name the Norwegian Centre Party made more effort to attract the support of small farmers that had traditionally voted Labour and thus become more of an exclusively rural party. It was to gain a new lease of life through its opposition to Norway's EEC membership.[41]

The second distinctive feature of the party political system in Denmark, Norway and Sweden was the dominance of social demo-cracy. The Scandinavian social democratic parties belonged to the European family of mass working-class parties that emerged during the late nineteenth century and were influenced to a greater or lesser extent by the Marxist critique of industrial capitalism. In Scandi-navia these parties could be considered the first truly mass parties with extensive extra-parliamentary organizations linked closely to the emergent trade union movements. The social democrats made common cause with the liberals in campaigning for suffrage reform before the First World War and were able to form minority govern-ments for the first time in 1920 (Sweden), 1924 (Denmark) and 1928 (Norway). These and subsequent governments were short-lived, however. The major breakthrough came, as we have seen, during the 1930s, when the social democratic parties were able to negotiate crisis agreements with the agrarian parties to provide them with a parliamentary majority. Since 1945 these parties have been extraordinarily successful in comparison to their sister parties elsewhere in Europe, as Table 1.2 illustrates. The Swedish Social Democratic Party, as is well known, enjoyed an unbroken run of 44 years in office between 1932 and 1976. The party governed alone during the period 1945–76, with the exception of 1951–7, when a coalition was formed with the Agrarian Party. The Norwegian Labour Party was in government continuously between 1945 and 1965, and the Danish Social Democrats were in government (albeit usually in coalition) from 1947 to 1968, with the exception of a brief period out of office in 1950–53.

Why have the Scandinavian social democratic parties been so successful, at least in Norway, Denmark and Sweden? The question has been pursued with particular interest in Sweden, given the status of the SAP as perhaps the most successful political party, measured by any criteria, in the western democracies.[42] For some scholars the main explanation has been sociological. The Scandinavian working classes were unusually homogeneous, lacking significant ethnic or religious cleavages, and they were also highly organized. In 1980, 78 per cent of Swedish wage earners were unionized; the corresponding figures for the other Scandinavian countries were Finland 70 per cent, Denmark 76 per cent and Norway 56 per cent, which was considerably higher than most other western countries (see Table 5).[43] The Scandinavian social democratic parties seem to have been conspicuously successful in mobilizing their 'natural' constituency within the working class. Indeed, until the 1970s Scandinavian politics was notable for the consistency of class-based voting patterns and the lack of supposed 'anomalies', such as the strong working-class support for the British Conservative Party, for example.[44]

Nonetheless, no social democratic party could base its success on the support of the working class alone. Many scholars, therefore, have pointed to the social democrats' ability to mobilize supporters from other social classes, and to create a broad social consensus in support of their policies. According to Gøsta Esping-Andersen, Scandinavian social democracy 'distinguished itself by the decision to subordinate class purity to the logic of majority politics. The organization moved from "working-class party" to "people's party", its platform addressed the "national interest" rather than the "proletarian cause".[45] Of the Scandinavian parties, the SAP was perhaps the most successful in broadening the class base of its support and creating 'a broad wage-earner coalition of blue- and white-collar workers'.[46] There were several reasons for this success. The first was the high level of union-ization among white-collar workers and the SAP's success in institutionalizing its own power base among this group by introduc-ing economic policies designed to benefit all wage earners. The second was the 'popular' (*folklig*) character of the Scandinavian labour move-ments, which had developed as part of the nineteenth-century popular movements, most importantly the free church and the temperance movements.[47] Particular characteristics of these movements included their inclusive and democratic organizations, and their emphasis on awakening, education and self-improvement. During the late nine-teenth century the labour movement made common cause with temperance societies and other popular movements to campaign for democratic rights, with the result that Scandinavian social democracy developed an ideology that owed as much to the inclusive and demo-cratic idea of the *folk* or people as to a Marxist analysis of class conflict.[48] This allowed even the most unequivocally radical and Marxist of the Scandinavian social democratic parties, the Norwegian Labour Party, to broaden its electoral appeal to include peasant farm-ers, fishermen and small traders – the little people or *småfolket* – during the inter-war period.[49]

Indeed, it is the ability to make ideological compromises and form electoral coalitions with other political parties that might be seen as the defining feature of social democratic success in Scandinavia. This was partly driven by the existence of an electoral system based on proportional representation, but it is not the whole story. The success of the Scandinavian social democratic parties was partly the result of their ability to 'institutionalise mechanisms for collaboration between social groupings' through a corporatist approach to policy making, an arrangement that allowed social democratic governments to govern effectively even where they lacked a parliamentary majority, as in Denmark, for example.[50] In practice, this was achieved through the use of state commissions of inquiry to thrash out the details of new policies before they were presented to parliament, and by negotiations between the representatives of the major interest groups: the trade union federations, the employers' federations and the farmers. In Sweden the term 'Harpsund democracy' was coined to describe the practice of agreeing important matters of policy through informal negotiations between the leaders of the trade unions, the employers and the government, which took place at the prime minister's official country residence at Harpsund. These meetings were hailed as an example of the new spirit of cooperation between labour and capital that prevailed at the time, though they were also criticized for excluding the opposition parties.[51]

An important example of the social democrats' apparent ability to generate consensus, often seen as a major turning point, was the debate over supplementary pensions (*Allmänna tilläggspension*, ATP) in Sweden during the 1950s. The eventual adoption of the SAP/LO (Landsorganisationen: trade union federation) proposals for a supplementary pension scheme based on compulsory contributions to a large state fund, in the face of fierce opposition from the non-socialist parties, could be read as an example of compromise and the SAP's ability to consolidate a broad base of support. By making the supplementary pensions compulsory, the reform gave the new middle strata of society a direct material stake in the welfare state and thus secured their support for it. The ATP reform was thus seen as significant in the further transition of the SAP from people's party to wage earner's party and the institutionalization of its power base.[52]

The consensus over ATP should not be over-stated, however. In fact, the issue were one of the most controversial in post-war Swedish politics. The early 1950s were marked by a period of ideological revitalization on both left and right. The SAP suffered an electoral setback in 1956 and stood accused by its critics of having become 'the contented party' (*det belåtna partiet*), content merely to manage capitalism without seeking to reform it further. The party's response, expressed in a speech in 1956 by the prime minister and party leader Tage Erlander, and in the pamphlet *Framstegens politik*, was to suggest a new and ambitious role for the welfare state to satisfy new demands for affluence, rather than seeking merely to alleviate poverty through the provision of a basic safety net. Against this the bourgeois parties argued that affluence should make it possible to reduce dependence on the state and to create an 'ownership democracy' where freedom of choice was paramount. The reconciliation of this ideological divide was accomplished not so much through the negotiation of compromise as through adept political manoeuvring on the part of the Social Democrats. The opposition parties put forward counter proposals for a voluntary supplementary pension scheme and demanded, moreover, that the matter should be put to a referendum. This took place in 1958 but the results were inconclusive, partly because of the split between the Conservatives and Liberals on the one hand and the Agrarians on the other. The referendum did, however, force the government to resign. A new minority SAP government was formed, without the support of the Agrarian Party, but when it failed to secure agreement with the other parties to provide the necessary parliamentary majority for its ATP legislation, the prime minister dissolved parliament. The 1958 election produced a parliament divided exactly evenly between the bourgeois and non-bourgeois parties, but the deadlock was finally resolved when the Liberal Ture Königsberg announced his intention to abstain, and the SAP's ATP proposal was passed.

The ATP affair can thus be seen as a good example of the limits of consensus in post-war Swedish politics. The bourgeois parties were fragmented and unable – or unwilling – to mount a serious challenge to the prevailing social democratic consensus.[53] Viewed from a more critical perspective, it has been suggested that it is more appropriate to speak of hegemony rather than consensus. The success of the SAP was, according to Hugh Heclo and Henrik Madsen, attributable to the organizational capacity of the Swedish labour movement and its ability to create what amounted to a state within a state.[54] The structures of policy making – the reliance on structured consultations through commissions of inquiry and the corporate representation of different interests within these commissions – helped to channel and neutralize conflict in predictable ways, but not necessarily to achieve true consensus. According to Heclo and Madsen, 'hegemony does not eliminate disagreement but channels and at times suffocates it ... [c]onsensus is often a surface phenomenon produced by Social Democra[tic] hegemony'.[55] Moreover, the the transfer of power under the corporatist system to bureaucrats and powerful interest groups also undermined the role of the Nordic parliaments, to the extent that the Norwegian Storting, for example, had by the 1970s become 'virtually irrelevant ... an an[a]emic version of its former self'.[56]

How fair is this assessment? Could the SAP – and the other Scandinavian social democratic parties to a lesser extent – be described as hegemonic in these terms? Some of the more critical accounts of SAP dominance – perhaps most notoriously Roland Huntford's depiction of Sweden as a socialist dystopia where the Swedish population had consented to its state of servitude – were inevitably coloured by the ideological divisions of the Cold War.[57] The term hegemony is used here in Gramsci's sense of 'direzione intelluttuale e morale': 'an order in which a common social-moral language is spoken, in which one concept of reality is dominant, informing with its spirit all modes of thought and behaviour ... predominance obtained by *consent* rather than force of one class or group over other classes.'[58] In Sweden, the term 'problemformuleringsprivilegium', expressed rather awkwardly in English as 'privilege of formulating problems', has been coined as a description of SAP hegemony, though as Åsa Linderborg points out, it cannot be assumed that SAP parliamentary and organizational dominance equates with ideological dominance, implying – as Heclo and Madsen suggest – the unconscious adoption of social democratic ideas among the population. Rather, one must also take account of the strong and well-organized business sector, which provided a counterweight to the political dominance of the SAP.[59] Indeed, Linderborg seems to be suggesting that the SAP has been markedly unsuccessful as a counter-hegemonic party in the Gramscian sense, in other words as a party that was able to replace the dominant bourgeois world view with its own socialist one. Instead, the party's success can be explained by the SAP's ability to assimilate its ideology into a greater bourgeois hegemony, and thus to identify itself with the national interest.[60]

Social democratic dominance was above all a Swedish story; it did not apply to all of the Nordic countries. Indeed, the only truly comparable case was Norway, where the Labour Party emerged from the war with a level of popular support that kept it in power for two decades.[61]

The party that only a generation before had espoused revolutionary socialism now became associated with ideological pragmatism and an impetus to forge cross-class consensus on economic and social policy. Elsewhere in the Nordic countries the influence of social democracy was more limited. In Denmark, the Social Democratic Party was able to remain consistently in government after 1945, but always did so in coalition with non-bourgeois parties. The Danish Social Democrats did, however, retain a majority within the labour movement itself, which was not the case in Finland or Iceland. Here, there was much stronger support for the Communists, both elec-torally and within the trade unions, which precluded the possibility for social democratic hegemony, and frequently produced outbreaks of industrial unrest, notably a general strike in Finland in 1956. In Iceland, therefore, it was the centre-right Independence Party that came to be identified most strongly with the national interest. In Finland, that role could possibly be attributed to the Agrarian Party, reflecting not only the greater strength of the farming sector in Finland but also the influence of its leading politician Urho Kekkonen, president from 1956 to 1981.

CONSENSUS AND CONFLICT: PARTY SYSTEM CHANGE
SINCE THE 1970S

Mixing their meteorological metaphors somewhat, political scientists agree that the 'frozen model' of Scandinavian politics was 'thawed' in a series of 'earthquake elections' during the early 1970s.[62] The first of these electoral earthquakes is described as happening in Finland in 1970, when the Finnish Rural Party (Suomen maaseudun puolue or SMP) took a 'sensational' 10.5 per cent of the popular vote and increased its representation in the Eduskunta from one to eighteen seats.[63] Formerly a party purporting to represent smallholders, the SMP was an attempt to found a new populist party that defined itself above all by its protest against the political establishment. It was followed by the emergence of the Progress Party (Fremskridtspartiet) in Denmark and 'Anders Lange's Party for a Drastic Reduction in Taxes, Rates and State Intervention' in

Norway, both of which made significant electoral breakthroughs in 1973. All three parties shared a similar political platform as 'anti-establishment' parties, defined by their opposition to the high taxes and welfare consensus that had dominated post-war Scandinavian politics, and they seemed to gain votes in particular among the traditional working-class constituencies of the Social Democrats. No similar party emerged in Sweden, but the country experienced its own electoral 'earthquake' in 1976 when the Social Democratic Party lost power to a coalition of the three traditional bourgeois parties, bringing to an end an unbroken run of 44 years in government. Finally, Iceland during the 1970s also experienced a period of frequent elections and greater political instability following the election of the opposition parties to a 'broad left' government in 1971.

The electoral breakthrough of these parties can be seen as part of an ideological backlash against the Social Democratic welfare state. This was also expressed in the emergence of Christian parties concerned with what they perceived as moral decline associated with the values of the permissive society, and which campaigned on issues such as religious education, abortion, the family and pornography.[64] Although in Denmark, Sweden and Finland these adopted the name 'Christian Democrats', they were very different parties from the traditional Catholic Christian Democrats of central Europe. Free church revivalism had been an important popular movement campaigning for democratic reform in nineteenth-century Scandinavia, but only in Norway did this result in the formation of a Christian People's Party (Kristelig Folkeparti, 1933) before the Second World War. Until 1945 and even after this was mainly a regional party associated with the so-called counter-cultural *nynorsk*-speaking region in the south-west of the country, where evangelical Protestantism was strong, but it subsequently formed the model for the formation of similar parties in Finland (Kristillisdemokraatit/Kristdemokraterna, 1958), Sweden (Kristdemokraterna, 1964) and Denmark (Kristendemokraterne, 1970).

The challenge to political consensus came not only from the right, however, but also from the left. In common with many other Western European countries, from the 1960s the Scandinavian countries experienced a surge of concern over and protest against the effects of sustained economic growth on the environment. Generally, the new politics took the form of extra-parliamentary protest movements, but in Finland and Sweden environmentalism coalesced into Green parties that won parliamentary representation from the 1980s. In Sweden, the catalyst for this change was the intense public debate over nuclear power during the 1970s, which contributed to the Social Democrats' electoral defeat in 1976 and was the subject of a referendum in 1981. During the period 1998–2006 the ruling Social Democratic Party relied on the support of the Greens, along with the Left Party, in parliament. In Finland, the Green Party, formed from a disparate group of various social and protest movements, achieved parliamentary representation in 1983, and became part of Paavo Lipponen's 'rainbow coalition' in 1995.[65]

A further element was feminism, and the 'new wave' women's movement that made an international impact from the early 1970s. Despite the historically high levels of female representation in Scandinavian politics, many Scandinavian feminists remained critical of what they perceived as the failure of the political system to address gender inequality. The women's movement of the 1970s was, like its counterparts outside Scandinavia, largely an extra-parliamentary movement, based on a disdain for conventional politics and calls instead to politicize new areas of social life. But this also resulted in a development that was unique to Scandinavia: the formation of a new feminist party, the Icelandic Women's List, founded in 1981. After an initially discouraging start, the Women's List put up three candidates for election in 1983, and won all three seats, increasing its representation substantially in 1987.[66] It subsequently declined and became subsumed into a wider leftist alliance, but remains unique as a successful attempt to seek parliamentary representation on a purely feminist platform. The Icelandic Women's List was followed in 2005 by the foundation in Sweden of a new party called Feminist Initiative, under the leadership of the former Left Party leader Gudrun Schyman. The new party initially performed very well in opinion polls, but shortly afterwards crumbled amid internal disputes, and had all but disappeared by the time of the parliamentary election in 2006.

The wave of student protests in 1968 also affected Scandinavia and had some impact on the universities, though the long-term political effects were perhaps less significant.[67] But by the mid-1960s, the Scandinavian social democratic parties found themselves in a paradoxical position: presiding over record levels of economic growth and prosperity, but at the same time facing growing criticism from left-wing opponents who argued that the parties had abandoned their ideological commitment to socialist reform and were content merely to manage capitalism rather than to reform it. The social democratic labour movement had become part of the political establishment, its leaders alienated from the grassroots concerns of ordinary trade unionists. When miners employed by a state-owned company in Swedish Lapland came out on a wildcat strike in December 1969, it was interpreted as a warning to the social democratic hierarchy that could not be safely ignored.

The impact of the 'new left' on the social democratic parties of Scandinavia was determined above all by foreign policy issues, however. In Denmark and Norway, the coming of the Cold War had initially helped to cement the reformist and pragmatic outlook of the social democratic parties in opposition to communism.[68] But opposition to NATO membership was growing from the 1950s, and, in the wake of the upheavals in international communism in 1956, it became one of the main driving forces behind the emergence of new left-wing parties in both Denmark and Norway.[69] In Denmark, the former communist Aksel Larsen formed a new Socialist People's Party, which replaced the Communist Party as the representative of the far left in parliament in 1959. In Norway, a group on the left wing of the Labour Party split in 1961 to form their own party, which later aligned itself with the euro-communist wing of the Communist Party to form the Socialist People's Party. Here, not only the NATO question but also opposition to membership of the EEC was to have a catalytic effect on the left, splitting the Labour Party and contributing in 1973 to its worst electoral defeat since 1930 with the loss of grassroots support to the anti-EC Socialist People's Party.

In Sweden, however, the unbroken consensus on Swedish neutrality allowed Palme to build his radical reputation partly on foreign policy, not least through his outspoken criticism of the American involvement in Vietnam, and the Swedish Social Democratic Party was thus the most successful at absorbing these changes.[70] In 1967 the Communist Party had forestalled moves towards the formation of a new leftist party like those already existing in Norway and Denmark by changing its name to the Left Party Communists, aiming to absorb some support from the new grassroots protest movements emerging at that time. But the following year the Social Democratic Party achieved a record electoral success, winning over 50 per cent of the popular vote for only the second time in its history. Under its new and youthful leader, Olof Palme, the party embarked on a period of ideological renewal, the best-known and most controversial example of which was the proposal for wage-earner funds intended to promote industrial democracy.

The Danish and Norwegian social democratic parties followed their Swedish counterparts in making similar turns to the left during the 1970s. Following its shock electoral defeat in 1973, the Danish Social Democratic Party introduced a new party programme in 1977 that was remarkable for its use of Marxist vocabulary and emphasis on equality. The party's shift to the left had shattered the traditional electoral alliance with the Social Liberals (RV) and led to the secession of a moderate faction, the Centre Democrats, from the party in 1973. Meanwhile, the Norwegian Labour Party also turned explicitly to the left under the leadership of Oddvar Norli. It too adopted policies intended to promote industrial democracy, but also made an ambitious attempt to democratize the Norwegian banking system.[71]

The electoral breakthrough of new political parties during the 1960s and afterwards, and the corresponding losses for the traditional parties, especially social democracy, do indeed appear to mark the first major challenge to a party political system that had remained intact since the inter-war period. But the apparent suddenness of this change should not be over-estimated. As we have seen, the Scandinavian agrarian parties had changed their names and programmes as early as the 1950s in an attempt to broaden their appeal in the face of the continued decline of their traditional constituencies after 1945. Indeed, the earth-quake metaphor conceals important continuities in the evolution of Nordic politics on both the left and the right since the Second World War, and, in turn, the existence of these continuities may also cast doubt on the extent of consensus in Scandinavian politics during the two decades or so after the war.

Moreover, the political changes in Scandinavia must be seen within a wider international context, though there were also elements that were nationally specific. This is especially true for the politics of the left, which was profoundly shaken up by the events of 1956 and 1968, but the changes on the political right also paralleled developments elsewhere. Broadly, this could be understood – paradoxically – in terms of both the retreat from but also the return of ideology in party politics from the late 1960s, as the established parties moved towards the middle ground but were in turn succeeded by new groupings on either end of the political spectrum. Above all, it marked a generational shift, as the so-called 'baby boomers' (in Swedish known as the *fyrtiotalister* or '40s generation) reached maturity, and engaged in new types of political activism unmarked by their parents' memories of the ideological polarization and turmoil of the inter-war period.

These international influences on Nordic politics remained important after 1970. The further efforts of the social democratic parties to reform their ideology and to establish a 'third way' during the 1980s must be seen in the context of similar debates on the left in other European countries – Britain, Germany, France – at the same time.[72] Conversely, the neo-liberalism espoused by right-wing politicians such as Ronald Reagan and Margaret Thatcher had less of an impact on Nordic conservatives, with the possible exception of Denmark, at least during the 1980s. From the 1990s, two international issues in particular have had a profound impact on Nordic politics. The first was the question of European integration, which dominated Nordic political debate especially during the first half of the 1990s.[73] European Union scepticism was generally a phenomenon of the left in Scandinavia, which partly explains the revived fortunes of parties such as the Swedish Left Party and the Norwegian Socialist People's Party during the 1990s. But it also cut across the traditional party divides, giving rise to a number of diverse groupings united only by their opposition to the EU, which confined themselves to campaigning in European parliamentary elections and referenda on EU matters.

The European integration debate was also coupled to the second phenomenon, namely nationalist opposition to mass immigration.[74] This breathed new life into the anti-establishment, right-wing populist parties that had seen their support decline since the 1970s. In Denmark, the moribund Progress Party was revived during the mid-1990s as the Danish People's Party under the leadership of Pia Kjærsgaard, and achieved over 12 per cent of the vote in 2001. Its progress was mirrored by the successes of similar parties in Finland and Norway, the True Finns and the Progress Party, respectively. No party had become a member of a governing coalition by 2007, but all were able to use their parliamentary strength to pursue their political agenda. Sweden, meanwhile, seemed to lack an equivalent movement, following the demise of the New Democracy Party, which gained parliamentary representation for a short while during the early 1990s. A right-wing populist anti-immigration party – the Sweden Democrats – did make substantial gains at the 2006 general election, though not enough to reach the 4 per cent threshold required for parliamentary representation.[75]

CONCLUSION: IS THERE A NORDIC POLITICAL MODEL?

Nordic politics never existed in isolation, of course. The party political systems of the Nordic countries were always influenced by, and in turn helped to shape, political currents in Western Europe and beyond. But the extent of the changes since the 1960s, and, moreover, their transnational nature, might be interpreted as presenting a challenge to the notion of a distinctive Nordic model. Nonetheless, the consensus among political scientists seems to support the case for limited change in the Nordic political systems since the 1970s. A comparative study of Sweden, Denmark and Norway in the 1980s found that they could still be described as consensual democracies in terms of three criteria: low levels of opposition to the rules and regulations for the conduct of politics; low levels of conflict about the exercise of power; and a high degree of concertation in public policy making.[76] Studies published during the 1990s and afterwards concurred with this assessment.[77] Moreover, the main party divisions endured despite rapid social changes that might have been thought to undermine them, especially in Finland, which industrialized rapidly from the 1960s.[78]

More significant was the change in the ways in which the parties worked together to build coalition governments: stable coalition arrangements between the major parties were replaced by minority governments based on ad hoc deals between two or more political parties.[79] This gave an opportunity for the new parties to enter government, or even to influence government policy, without holding positions in government, something that the right-wing populist parties in Norway and Denmark were particularly adept at doing. That said, the traditional block divisions seemed to hold true to a certain extent into the early twenty-first century, with the parties of the left seeking to defend the generous welfare systems, and the other parties seeking economic deregulation and liberalization. Knut Heidar's 2005 assessment of Norwegian politics found that 'old politics' and the traditional left–right ideological divide remained important in defining the position of political parties, despite changes in party organization and membership.[80]

Similarly, political culture in Scandinavia seemed to retain some of its former distinctive characteristics into the twenty-first century, though here too there were signs of change. Perhaps most distinctive was the historically high level of female participation and representation in the Nordic parliaments and Nordic governments.[81] Levels of political participation and engagement remained relatively high with turnout in national elections around 80 per cent, though it was much lower for European parliamentary elections. Although membership of trade unions remained unusually high in comparison with other European states, the close identification between collective organizations and political parties declined substantially. This also had an impact on the process of policy making, with a decline in the institutions of structured corporatist consultation and their replacement with parliamentary lobbyism.[82] The Nordic parliaments may have gained power, due to the preponderance of weaker minority governments since the 1970s.[83] Nonetheless, in the early twenty-first century there were also fears about the challenges to parliamentary democracy presented by voter alienation and declining political participation. The Norwegian Study of Power and Democracy, which submitted its final report in 2003, concluded that 'rule by popular consent is distintegrating before our eyes'.[84] Political parties, in turn, turned away from their core grassroots support, adopting new methods of campaigning and communication to win over an increasingly volatile electorate. Inevitably, this meant a higher profile for the party leader, and more emphasis on the personal appeal of individual politicians. Traditional parties from both sides of the political spectrum turned to younger, supposedly more dynamic and charismatic leaders to boost their appeal. Generally, the levels of trust in Scandinavian politicians remained higher than elsewhere in Europe, despite some high-profile scandals.[85] But there was also evidence for political alienation among some voters on certain 'critical issues', notably those to do with questions of national sovereignty, such as European integration and immigration.[86]

The international reputation of the Scandinavian countries as consensual democracies was challenged by several events in the late twentieth century. The most shocking of these were two public assassinations in Sweden, of the Prime Minister Olof Palme in 1986 and the Foreign Minister Anna Lindh in 2003. These events were unrelated, although they took place in similar circumstances, but the impact was the same: both came to be perceived both at home and abroad as a challenge to the tradition of openness (or naivity) in Swedish politics, where politicians were able to behave more or less like ordinary citizens. Other events, in particular the Mohammed cartoons affair in Denmark in 2006, seemed to provide further evidence for the break-down of consensus and question popular perceptions of the Scandinavian democracies as being somehow different from the rest of Europe. As a result, if consensus did continue to exist, it did so as a consensus about the past: a collective nostalgia for an era when the Nordic model really did seem to exist and really was different from the rest of Europe. By the 2000s this had formed part of the political discourse of both the social democratic left and the populist right in their articulation of 'welfare nationalism'. As we have seen, although there were some important similarities between the political history of the Nordic countries in the inter-war period, there were also many important differences that worked against the concept of a Nordic model in institutional terms. But as a trope of Nordic identity, and as a utopia or indeed dystopia for outside observers, the Nordic model remained a powerful reality throughout the period.

Chapter 2

The Nordic Economies

Is there a Nordic economy? Since the pan-Scandinavian movement of the mid-nineteenth century there have been various attempts to promote Scandinavian economic integration modelled on the German *Zollverein*.[1] There were some enduring successes, such as the creation of a passport union and a common Nordic labour market in 1954, but the aspiration for a full customs union was never realized. The Nordic countries always traded with each other, but the small size of the Nordic markets meant that external trade was more significant, and each country continued to manage its affairs autonomously from its neighbours. By the turn of the twenty-first century there was, for example, no Nordic central bank and no formal mechanisms for co-ordinating interest rates or other economic policy, and the region still had five different currencies. Moreover, there was some marked divergence in the economic performance of the Nordic countries in the period since the early 1990s. Sweden and Finland experienced a very severe recession during the early 1990s, followed by recovery based on a fairly drastic restructuring and reorientation of policy. In Denmark, the economy was less severely affected by the 1990s recession, having already undergone a period of decline and restructuring following the oil shock in the early 1970s. Meanwhile, the discovery of North Sea oil had a profound effect on Norway, making it a very unusual economy in European terms. Finally, European integration threatened to pull the Nordic block apart: by 2007 Finland alone had adopted the single currency, while Sweden and Denmark were members of the EU but remained outside the euro-zone, and Norway and Iceland remained outside altogether.

Despite this divergence, there were also some important shared characteristics in the economic history of the Nordic countries. Above all, during the late nineteenth and twentieth centuries all five countries underwent an exceptional transition: from being relatively poor societies, where many rural districts were still blighted by poverty, disease and heavy emigration until the early twentieth century, to becoming some of the most prosperous and stable economies in the OECD.[2] The Scandinavian economies grew rapidly after the Second World War, and by the end of the twentieth century were known for their exceptionally high standards of living. This growth was combined with the maintenance of a comprehensive welfare state and a high level of government intervention in the economy, though it was a particular type of intervention, as we shall see. Indeed, as early as the 1930s foreign observers suggested that the Scandinavians had managed to achieve a successful compromise between capitalism and socialism, combining social redistribution with a vigorous private sector, and the idea of the Scandinavian middle way was born.[3] Many observers have continued to admire this system as an effective means of running a capitalist economy, while others have argued that it concealed some deep problems in the Scandinavian economies that are only now being addressed.

To these broad patterns in long-run economic development and policy might be added some structural similarities between the Nordic countries. Most importantly, all of them were historically small and relatively open economies.[4] The restricted size of the domestic market meant that the export sector was always important in stimulating economic change. Historically, exports were based on raw materials, with which the Nordic countries were relatively well endowed. Sweden exported high-quality iron for several centuries, and both Sweden and Finland exploited their vast forests for tar, timber, pulp and paper.[5] Forestry was important too in Norway, as was fishing and, from the late nineteenth century, the development of a heavy engineering industry driven by hydro-electric power. Since the 1970s, however, all of these faded into insignificance besides the oil and gas reserves of the North Sea. Iceland relied very heavily on its fisheries, though in the late twentieth century it also began to exploit its geo-thermal energy reserves. Finally, the Danish economy was historically dominated by its agricultural exports, especially processed livestock goods such as bacon and butter.

These traditional industries declined in the late twentieth century, but since the 1990s the Scandinavian economies have established a reputation as leaders in the information and communications technology (ICT) sector, led by well-known companies such as Nokia and Ericsson. They had also developed their reputation for innovative and ultra-chic design in consumer goods such as furniture and other household items, including products for the mass market (IKEA) and more exclusive ones. There were various reasons for the success in ICT, but it may indicate another shared characteristic of the Scandinavian economies, namely the existence of a highly skilled labour force created by active labour market policies and substantial investment in state education. For much of the period since 1945 the Scandinavian countries experienced a labour shortage, and from having been major exporters of labour for much of the nineteenth century they became countries of net immigration. Here the experience of Finland and Iceland lagged behind the other Scandinavian countries, as they remained countries of net emigration until the 1970s at least; indeed, several hundreds of thousands of Finnish workers found employment in Sweden.[6]

Is there then a Scandinavian economic model? Two aspects of this question will be explored in this chapter. First, to what extent is it possible to distinguish a common pattern of economic development shared by the five Nordic countries, and what, if anything, makes this experience different from that of the rest of Western Europe during the same period? Secondly, if there are common patterns of economic development, then to what extent can these be attributed to a Scandinavian model of economic policy? Most observers point to some similarities in the way in which the Scandinavian economies are run, including the combination of state regulation and intervention with private enterprise. How much of the Nordic economic success could be attributed to government policy and how much was accounted for by favourable external circumstances? In what ways do the Nordic countries differ from one another and in what ways are they similar? Above all, it has been the 'Swedish model' of economic policy that has attracted international attention, and this is also discussed. Finally, there is a brief discussion of recent attempts to restructure the Nordic economies in response to economic difficulties, and of whether there can still be said to be a Nordic model.

ECONOMIC DEVELOPMENT SINCE 1945

The economic history of Western Europe since 1945 can be divided into three periods: first, the post-war period of reconstruction, 1945–c. 1950; secondly, the 'golden age' of high and steady economic growth, full employment, low inflation and general prosperity during the period c. 1950–70; and thirdly, a period of instability following the first OPEC oil shock in 1973, and the structural transformation of the European economies sometimes described as the third industrial revolution.[7] For the most part the Scandinavian economies conformed to this pattern of economic development, though there were also some important deviations both from the wider European picture and between the five Nordic countries.

1. Post-war adjustment and reconstruction

The Nordic countries shared the economic problems that beset interwar Europe. The speculative boom during the First World War produced high levels of inflation and shortages of many commodities including basic foodstuffs, and this was followed by declining commodity prices, recession and unemployment during the 1920s, culminating in the Great Depression. For many, the main experience of the period was unemployment, which affected nearly a third of the entire workforce in Denmark and Norway in the early 1930s. It was lower in Sweden, peaking at 23.7 per cent in 1933, and lower still in

Finland, where according to one estimate it peaked at 6.2 per cent in 1932. These national rates may, however, have concealed wide variations by industry and region: for example in 1932 as many as 45 per cent of Helsinki construction workers were out of work.[8] Given the apparent failure of orthodox liberal economic policy to cope with these problems, there were many, in Scandinavia as elsewhere, who were willing to abandon a rather fragile parliamentary democracy in favour of more authoritarian politics. But the 'Red–Green' coalitions negotiated between the social democratic and the agrarian parties in all the Nordic countries in the 1930s gave the social democratic parties the parliamentary majorities they needed to introduce economic crisis programmes, which in Sweden and Norway included innovative counter-cyclical fiscal policies to stimulate demand. Economic historians now argue that the relatively swift Scandinavian recovery from the Depression was due largely to structural reasons, including favourable export markets for Nordic goods, but many contemporaries attributed the Nordic success to the policies of the new Red–Green coalition governments.[9]

By the outbreak of the Second World War, therefore, the Nordic countries had gained some degree of international celebrity as model examples for how economic stability could be achieved without compromising democracy. The British Labour politician Hugh Dalton wrote enthusiastically in 1936 that the Swedish recovery from the Depression had been 'sensational' and nothing short of 'an economic miracle'.[10] Particularly influential was the book by the American journalist Marquis Childs, Sweden: The Middle Way (1936), which extolled the idea of the Swedish and Scandinavian compromise between free market capitalist democracy on the one hand, and fascist or communist totalitarianism on the other.[11] By 1937 the Nordic governments were themselves responding to this international interest with the publication of The Northern Countries in the World Economy, intended to demonstrate 'the spirit of co-operation among the northern Nations' and to promote the Nordic region more widely as a model for future economic cooperation.[12]

The enduring success of the political arrangements established in the 1930s suggests continuities in Scandinavian economic development and economic thinking from the 1930s into the post-war period. In this interpretation, the Second World War can appear as a temporary and unwelcome distraction from the main business of constructing the Nordic 'model'. The emphasis on continuity is indeed justified, to an extent. The Red–Green coalition arrangements brought the social democratic parties into government with working parliamentary majorities, which allowed them to adapt socialist principles into concrete and pragmatic proposals for reform. The experience of the 1930s undoubtedly established a *direction* in economic policy that could be built upon after the war. But there was never a detailed blueprint for how the post-war economy should be managed, either within the social democratic parties or among their bourgeois opponents, and the experience of the war was to throw up new obstacles and new opportunities alike. This was even the case for Sweden, despite its neutral status and non-participation in the war.

Nonetheless, it should be acknowledged that although the problems facing Scandinavia in 1945 were the same as those affecting the rest of Europe – shortages of all the basic commodities including food and raw materials, destruction of infrastructure, indebtedness and the collapse of international trade – these problems were generally less severe in Scandinavia than they were in the rest of the Continent. Sweden, as a non-belligerent neutral country, was in a particularly strong position. The economy had recovered rapidly from the Great Depression, to the extent that during the two decades before 1950 the Swedish economy exhibited some of the highest growth rates in the world.[13] Transport, industry and the public sector expanded particularly rapidly. Critics could note that this growth was perhaps morally dubious, given that many Swedish products and particularly high-quality iron ore were exported to Germany and thus supported the Nazi war effort. Nonetheless, the country had kept its neutrality intact, and later the years after 1945 would come to be seen as 'harvest time' (*skördetiden*): a period when the economic troubles of the inter-war period, and the accompanying poverty and social divisions, could at last be left behind. This was not necessarily how contemporaries saw the situation, however. The Social Democratic Party's initial proposals for post-war economic policy, presented in 1944, were devised in the expectation that the cessation of hostilities would lead to a recession, as indeed had been the case after the First World War.[14]

The governments of Denmark and Norway, as the two Scandinavian countries to have experienced Nazi occupation, faced the daunting task of trying to stabilize and readjust their economies after liberation, though neither country was in anywhere near the state of utter devastation found in other parts of liberated Europe. Denmark, in fact, had experienced very little destruction of its infrastructure, though the important agricultural sector suffered from the loss of its export markets, and this in turn created severe balance of payments problems. These were exacerbated by difficult climatic conditions in 1947, which produced a poor harvest. For the Agrarian-led government elected in 1945 the priority therefore was to re-establish trade. It did this by pursuing a bilateral agreement with Britain, which provided for the export of Danish agricultural products almost exclusively to the British market.

Norway was worse off. Heavy fighting in the north of the country had caused widespread destruction in Finnmark and Nord-Troms: 12,000 private dwellings and most public buildings such as churches and schools had been destroyed; the transport infrastructure was in ruins, with most of the main bridges down; more than 100 electric power stations were out of action. The damage to this region accounted for nearly one third of Norway's total war losses, the rest including the loss of half of the merchant and fishing fleets.[15] In 1945 two Norwegian economists estimated that the country's industrial production stood at only half its pre-war level.[16]

The worst affected of all the Nordic countries was Finland. Here, the fighting itself had cost the lives of 90,000 Finnish citizens and seriously disrupted economic production, but graver still were the consequences of defeat. In the first place, the territorial losses to the USSR amounted to about 10 per cent of the country's total area, including some of the best agricultural land on the Karelian isthmus and Viipuri (Vyborg), Finland's second largest city. The loss of eastern Karelia also displaced about 400,000 refugees (approximately 11 per cent of the total Finnish population), who needed to be resettled.

Secondly, under the terms of the peace treaty with the USSR, Finland was committed to paying substantial war reparations of $300 million at 1938 values. This was the equivalent of one and a half times the value of Finnish exports in 1938 and was estimated to be worth more per capita than the reparations imposed on Germany at the Treaty of Versailles.[17] The total was reduced in 1948, but nonetheless remained a substantial burden for a small war-torn country, amounting to 4.5 per cent of Finland's GDP annually for the years 1945–7.[18]

One big advantage in overcoming all these difficulties was that the legal and constitutional machinery of government had remained intact in all the Scandinavian countries. The Finnish government faced social instability and the threat of a communist takeover, but the civil service, the law courts, the army and the police were unchanged from before the war.[19] The wartime exile of the Norwegian king, government and Storting in London also preserved constitutional continuity, and enabled the government – by means of the Lex Thagaard promulgated in London on 8 May 1945 – to assume almost dictatorial powers over the economy, to a degree perhaps unmatched elsewhere in Europe, and to impose tight controls on private sector prices, profits, rents and dividends. Wages were left to voluntary agreements between the trade union federation (LO) and the Norwegian Employers' Association (NAF). The aim of these measures was to try to stabilize the monetary system and counter the inflationary pressures arising from the huge expansion in circulating cash during the war. The government also ran a substantial budget deficit during 1945–6 in order to promote record levels of investment.

Despite these measures, and the impetus of the initial wave of optimism immediately after the end of the war, by 1947 there were signs that the recovery was losing its momentum.[20] Denmark and Norway both faced problems of sharply increasing foreign debt and trade deficits, and shortages of both raw materials and basic consumer supplies. Like Britain, Norway continued to ration food, clothes and luxury goods until well into the 1950s, longer than any other country in Western Europe.[21] What ultimately rescued the faltering recovery efforts in these countries was, of course, the Marshall Plan. For the Danish government the decision to accept

Marshall aid was uncontroversial, and the country received $236 million in grants and $42 million in cheap loans.[22] The Norwegian government initially hesitated over whether to accept Marshall aid. Many within the Labour Party were suspicious of the plan as a tool to promote American capitalism, and were reluctant to tie the country so firmly to the Anglo-Saxon west at a time when it was seeking to pursue a bridge-building strategy in its foreign policy. But the mounting tensions in international relations that brought Norway into NATO in 1949 helped to change that, as did the communist coup in Czechoslovakia, which raised fears of a similar challenge in Norway. Norway received $400 million in the years up to 1952, of which $350 million were paid as direct grants.[23]

Despite its neutrality, Sweden accepted loans through the Marshall Plan.[24] Likewise, although the Finnish government had no option but to decline Marshall aid in order to avoid antagonizing the Soviet Union, it did nonetheless receive $70 million in loans from the USA by 1947, granted on condition that these were not to be used for reparations payments.[25] Like the other Nordic countries, Finland also benefited indirectly from the swift recovery of the rest of Western Europe that the Marshall Plan promoted, and the growing demand for Scandinavian exports that came with it. For Sweden, Denmark and Norway, the development of these new markets marked a re-orientation away from central Europe and Germany as the main trading partners towards the Anglo-Saxon west. Norway in particular became closely aligned with Great Britain after 1945. This economic re-orientation was also matched by a cultural one: English replaced German as a second language in the Scandinavian countries and the Scandinavian populations came to exhibit the same fascination with American consumer culture that characterized all of Western Europe in the post-war period.

Moreover, for Denmark and Norway the Marshall Plan was also very important in helping to maintain political stability in the turbulent post-war years. For Denmark, Marshall aid provided the 'critical margin' the government needed in order to avoid having to introduce austerity measures, a situation that would no doubt have been exploited by the resurgent Communist Party.[26] In Norway, about 40 per cent of Marshall aid was used to import scarce consumer goods such as corn, flour, textiles and tobacco, to the extent that some of the government's critics in the Norwegian Employers' Association went so far as to suggest that the Americans had helped to save the Labour government with their intervention.[27] Equally importantly, the Marshall Plan's demands for international economic trade and cooperation, and for long-term domestic planning of the economy, chimed with the emergence of similar thinking within the governing social democratic parties, and thus contributed to the establishment of a new consensus on economic policy for the post-war period.[28]

2. The Golden Age? c. 1950–70

With hindsight it is easy to view the two decades or so after c. 1950 as a golden age in European economic history. The problems of the interwar period – hyper-inflation, falling commodity prices, depression and mass unemployment – seemed by the 1960s to have become no more than a bad memory, and the stability of the years 1950–70 stands in stark contrast to both the earlier period and the more difficult and unsettled years that came after 1973. Viewed from the perspective of the uncertain post-1973 world it is easy to see how the idea of the golden age came to take on something of a mythical quality, but this should not be allowed to conceal the patterns of divergence and fluctuation that continued to characterize economic development in these years.

The Scandinavian countries shared the characteristic features of economic development across Western Europe: high and stable levels of growth, full employment, low inflation and expanding international trade assisted by international agreements such as the GATT and the EFTA. Within this general model there were, however, some important examples of divergence, both from the Western European pattern as well as from a more specifically Nordic one. With the exception of Finland, growth rates for the region were generally below the OECD average, especially during the 1950s, when they were 1.25–1.5 percentage points lower (see Table 2 in the Appendix).[29] The exceptionally high rates of growth in Finland – the annual average growth rate was over 5 per cent for the period 1946–70 – were mostly accounted for by the relatively late structural transformation of the Finnish economy in a country where in 1950 nearly half the population (46 per cent) was still employed in agriculture.[30] Despite slightly lower growth rates, Norway and Sweden were distinguished by the virtual absence of cyclical fluctuations and more or less continuous full employment.[31] Denmark, where balance of payments constraints forced the government to adopt more of a conventional stop–go policy, experienced much higher levels of unemployment during the 1950s.[32] In all the Nordic countries, however, full employment was generally given a high priority as an economic policy goal. The cost of this was higher than average levels of inflation, but in the mainland Scandinavian countries this never reached the exceptionally high levels found in Iceland for most of the period, which forced repeated devaluations of the Icelandic króna to keep exports competitive. The average annual rate of inflation for Iceland during the period 1944–70 was 7.8 per cent, but prices increased by over 21 per cent in the worst years, 1950 and 1951.[33] The reason for this was mainly Iceland's heavy reliance on fish exports, and the fluctuating international prices for fish and fish products, but it was also a result of the negative interest rates prevailing for much of the period and the practice of index-linking wages until 1983.[34]

Economic historians have debated the causes of what is now understood to be an exceptional period of growth, stability and general prosperity in Europe for the two decades after 1950. On the supply side, the Western European economies benefited from the abundance of cheap labour, capital and energy. The significance of energy was demonstrated in the wake of the first OPEC oil shock in 1973. As for the labour force, despite the low birth rates of the 1930s, the Scandinavian economies were able to benefit from the continued transfer of the population from the primary sector to manufacturing industry (see Table 3). This was aided by the establishment of a Nordic passport union in 1954 that allowed the migration of a large number of people from rural Finland to work in Swedish industry. Some migrant labour was also recruited from southern Europe, especially in Sweden. From the 1960s the Scandinavian labour force expanded due to the large-scale participation of women in the labour market.[35] Capital inputs were stimulated by government policies promoting investment and resulting in very high capital to output ratios in Norway and Finland in particular, reflecting the importance of heavy industry in these countries. Despite these favourable conditions, the influence of the supply side on growth should not be overstated: 'no more than permissive' in the words of two Nordic economists.[36]

On the demand side, exports formed the main contribution to economic growth in the small open economies of Scandinavia. Late nineteenth-century industrialization was to a large extent export-led in Scandinavia, as was the relatively swift recovery from the 1930s Depression. The terms of trade favoured the Scandinavian economies after 1945. Exports accounted for between 20 and 25 per cent of GDP in the Nordic countries in the period 1950–70, the main markets being the EEC, the UK and the other Nordic countries.[37] The Danish economy, which relied heavily on the export of processed agricultural products, struggled during the 1950s, though manufacturing's share of exports grew thereafter.[38] But no Scandinavian economy was as dependent on a single commodity as Iceland, where fish and fish products continued to contribute more than half of the country's foreign currency earnings until the 1970s, even though the proportion of the population engaged in fishing declined considerably.[39]

There were clearly, then, some important structural reasons accounting for Scandinavian economic performance during the golden age. Given the position of the Nordic countries as open economies able to benefit from the favourable conditions in the rest of Europe, it might be expected that economic policy would have less impact. However, the significance of economic policy has also been widely debated, especially in the case of Sweden and the so-called Swedish model. It is suggested that even though Swedish economic performance was not in itself unique, the policy arguments and the political circumstances surrounding policy, especially the influence of the Trade Union Federation (LO), were.[40] The following discussion will attempt to assess the significance of policy, as well as exploring the similarities and divergences in economic policy across the Nordic region.

Emboldened by the successes of the 1930s, the social democratic parties of Denmark, Norway and Sweden emerged from the Second World War with new and ambitious ideas about the role of the state in the national economy. To some extent this was a product of the expansion in central regulations and planning during the war, but it was also informed by international influences, such as the English liberals Beveridge and Keynes.[41] The post-war social democratic programmes contained a certain paradox. On the one hand, new party programmes such as the Danish *Fremtidens Danmark* (1945) were imbued with an optimistic faith in the social democratic future.[42] The immediate post-war period was seen in Sweden as *skördetiden* ('harvest time'), when at last the perennial problems of poverty, inequality and economic instability appeared to have been overcome and all could look forward to the socialist future. On the other hand, there was also widespread uncertainty about the likely direction of the post-war economy, and the expectation that the cessation of hostilities would lead to a depression, as it had done after the First World War.[43] The SAP's post-war plans, presented in 1944, were devised in expectation of a post-war recession, and amounted to a radical programme declaring the need for an entire reorganization of economic and social life.[44] There was further uncertainty over whether the post-war mood of cooperation, compromise and a willingness to forget the past, expressed in the joint programme agreed by all the Norwegian political parties in June 1945, could survive the economic uncertainties. The bitter ideological divisions of the inter-war period were still fresh in the memory, after all.

That said, there was a broad political consensus that the main goals of economic policy after 1945 should be full employment and economic growth. Following the successful Swedish experiment with counter-cyclical policy in the 1930s, the idea was taken up by the social democratic parties in Denmark and Norway. Despite the difficulties of reconstruction, by the end of the 1940s it was clear that the expected economic crisis had failed to materialize. The main economic problems were not unemployment but inflation and balance of payments constraints.

This was the background to the economic policy proposal presented by the Swedish LO economists Rudolf Meidner and Gösta Rehn, and endorsed by the LO congress in 1951. The 'Rehn-Meidner' model was to become the cornerstone of Swedish economic policy for the next two decades and even beyond. The model was conceived as a modification of Keynesian demand-management policy, designed to tackle inflation while at the same time maintaining full employment. It was unusual in its comprehensive view of economic policy and its reliance on supply-side measures, as well as demand management.[45] There were four elements: i) stimulation of public savings and directed public investment; ii) solidaristic wage policy; iii) a liberal trade policy and toleration of extensive private ownership; iv) active labour market policy. Of these, it was the policies relating to the labour market that have attracted most attention and were seen as the cornerstones of the Swedish model. What made it possible to adopt these policies was the unusual centralization of the trade union movement, its close links with the ruling Social Democratic Party, and the new atmosphere of compromise and co-operation between labour and capital stemming from the Saltsjöbaden Agreement in 1938.[46] This agreement, negotiated between LO and the Swedish Employers' Federation (Svenska Arbetsgivareföreningen, SAF), established a centralized framework for the resolution of labour market conflicts through collective bargaining. It set up a joint committee to function as a central negotiation and arbitration board, and also agreed a protocol for making workers redundant. In the context of its time it was a major breakthrough achieved against a background of bitterness and conflict. The agreement was concluded in the face of a government threat to introduce legislation on compulsory arbitration. But *Saltsjöbadsandan* (the spirit of Saltsjöbaden) and the 1938 agreement prevailed for several decades after 1945, and the original agreement was followed by several ancillary ones. It helped to create the conditions for post-war growth and the implementation of the active labour market policy, based on an understanding that the government would not intervene in the labour market.[47]

The principal method of implementing the Rehn-Meidner model was restraint, rather than the more conventional 'stop–go' Keynesian demand management that was practised in other parts of Europe. Tax became an increasingly important policy tool, used as a means to encourage saving in public funds and stimulate investment. But the cornerstone of the counter-cyclical policy was the active labour market policy, implemented by Arbetsmarknadsstyrelsen (Labour Market Board, AMS), which became a powerful public body with a budget to match. The AMS acted as an employment agency, and was associated above all with assisting the mobility of workers from declining regions to those where new dynamic industries – and thus employment – were located. For this reason it acquired the nickname *Alla Måste Söderut* ('everyone must go south'), which had some truth in it given the extent to which it presided over the depopulation of the rural districts in the north.[48] This regional restructuring was assisted by massive public investment in the construction of private housing, culminating in the 'million homes' programme in 1965. The policy also reflected the continued faith in the ability of experts to undertake social engineering for the good of society. Solidaristic wage policy, which was implemented through the cooperation of LO and the SAF, was designed to reduce wage differentials and thus answer the socialist desire for greater equality, while at the same time improving international competitiveness by forcing low-wage firms to cease business or to increase productivity. How did this policy differ to that pursued in the other Scandinavian countries?

The country showing the greatest similarities with Sweden was Norway, where the social democratic Labour Party enjoyed a similar position of political dominance for two decades after 1945, and where the government pursued the full employment objective perhaps more rigorously than in any of the other Scandinavian countries. Inflation was treated as a secondary concern, to be tackled mostly through incomes policy.[49] As in Sweden, Norwegian industrial relations were also highly centralized following the Hovedavtal ('main agreement') between LO and the NAF in 1935. This meant that it was possible to pursue solidaristic wage policy as in Sweden, with some effectiveness especially during the 1950s.[50] Unlike Sweden, however, where active labour market policy helped to promote the depopulation of rural regions in the north of the country, Norwegian priorities were the opposite. There was a perennial concern, shared by all political parties, to preserve traditional economic activities in the peripheral regions. There were strong cultural reasons for this, given the importance of northern and coastal Norway in the self-image of what was still a relatively young nation, and also the political strength of the relevant interest groups. None of these was stronger than the fishing industry, which had shrunk to a position where it accounted for only 0.9 per cent of full-time employment in 1975, but nonetheless remained politically influential, especially in the coastal communities of northern Norway.[51] For this reason, significant amounts of public resources were directed in subsidies and investments to these districts through the Nord-Norge plan, established in 1952 and replaced in 1961 by a regional development fund (Distriktenes Utbyggningsfond). On top of subsidies and cheap loans, fishermen were eventually also guaranteed a weekly minimum income by the state. Agricultural producers in the same regions were protected by import restrictions.[52]

The Danish Social Democratic Party never reached the same position of political dominance as its Norwegian and Swedish counterparts after 1945. In any case, the post-war Danish governments, whether formed as a coalition of the bourgeois parties or as Social Democratic minority governments, found their position severely constrained by the difficulties of the Danish export sector and the recurrent balance of payments deficits. Terms of trade had worsened substantially in 1949-51 and throughout the 1950s governments found themselves constantly having to apply the brakes to economic growth when the foreign deficit threatened to get out of hand.[53] From the end of the 1950s these restraints were removed by an improvement in the terms of trade and the opening of international capital markets, which made it possible to finance a balance of payments deficit, and the Danish economy grew much more rapidly in the 1960s. Manufacturing expanded to become the main export sector, while agriculture declined.

In contrast to the remarkably peaceful state of labour market relations in Norway and Sweden, Denmark experienced several waves of industrial unrest during this period, with serious outbreaks of strikes in 1946-7, 1956, 1960 and 1973.[54] The Danish trade union movement was much less centralized than its Scandinavian counterparts, reflecting its earlier and more piecemeal development in the late nineteenth century, and the dominance of craft unionism.[55] The Danish labour market lacked a central agreement equivalent to the Saltsjöbaden Agreement, but an arrangement negotiated between the trade union federation (Landsorganisationen i Danmark or LO) and the employers' federation (Dansk Arbejdsgiverforening or DAF) in 1936 provided for three levels of negotiation in wage bargaining: direct negotiation between the trade union federation and the industry, followed by central negotiations between LO and DAF with a provision for the intervention of the state mediator if agreement could not be reached. In practice, no agreement was reached without mediation during the years 1952–79.[56] The relative strength of the communists immediately after the war also contributed to heightened militancy on the shop floor. In 1956 there were several days of political unrest when 200,000 people demonstrated outside the Parliament building in Copenhagen, and more than one million working days were lost to strike action.[57] This meant that although LO was committed to a solidaristic wage policy similar to that pursued in Sweden and Norway, it lacked the central control it needed to be able to carry this through, and skilled workers were able to exploit their sectional power to negotiate wage rises through decentralized bargaining. Thus, the wage pattern in Denmark remained largely unchanged, even though there were substantial gains in real wages during the 1960s for all groups except the farmers.[58]

Industrial conflict was also more of a problem for the Finnish government after 1945. Here, employers had resisted nation-wide collective agreements before the 1940s, despite the formation of central labour market organizations during the early twentieth century as in the other Nordic countries.[59] The so-called January engagement of 1940, by which employers and unions agreed to try to improve industrial relations through negotiation, had some symbolic significance, but employers continued to refuse to accept collective agreements.[60] The Cold War helped to promote a climate of cooperation between social democratic trade unions and employers, but there was also a strong communist presence within the labour movement, and during the 1940s this sought on several occasions to use strike action for political means. The most serious incident occurred in the summer of 1949, when a communist demonstration against the use of strike-breakers to clear a log jam on the river Kemi provoked the police to open fire, and two people were killed.[61]

The central trade union federation (Suomen Ammattiyhdistysten Keskusliitto or SAK) expelled the forestry workers' unions associated with the strike, but militancy within the labour movement continued during the 1950s. When the wage and price controls introduced under the post-war Emergency Powers Act expired in 1955, SAK formed a united front with the employers' association (Suomen Työnantajain Keskusliitto or STK) to try to negotiate a new index, but their proposals were opposed by the agrarian producers' organization MTK (Maa- ja metsätaloustuottajain Keskusliitto). On 1 March 1956 SAK began a three-week general strike demanding an overall increase in wages; on the same day MTK halted deliveries of agricultural produce. The strike involved half a million workers and resulted in the loss of nearly seven million workers. SAK achieved a victory of sorts, but it was a Pyrrhic one: in the long run, real wages continued to fall as prices rose, and the strike also deepened the schisms within the labour movement. In 1968 the government was finally able to negotiate a new central agreement, necessitated by the inflationary pressures of a major currency devaluation the previous year. This led to the reunification of the trade union federation (under the new name Suomen Ammattiliittojen Keskusjärjestö), and began a new period of centralized tripartite wage negotiations that more closely mirrored the arrangements in the other Nordic countries.[62]

Another exceptional feature of Finnish economic development was the importance of the agricultural question, and the much larger role played by agrarian interest organizations alongside the representatives of industry and labour. Finland was the only OEEC country where the number of farms actually increased during the years after 1945, at a time when the trend for the rest of Europe was towards fewer and larger farms. Many of these new farms were created to resettle the Karelian refugees and were intended to defuse social tension by providing work in the difficult years immediately after the war. But the farms created were generally too small to be viable, and from the 1950s many of their occupants left the land to seek industrial work. This meant that unemployment rates were consistently higher than in the other Nordic countries, despite the high rates of economic growth. It used to be assumed that Finnish industrialization was stimulated above all by the reparations requirements, a quarter of which were to be made in traditional exports such as wood and paper, but the rest in the products of new heavy industries: ships, machinery, equipment and cable. Recent research has cast doubt on this assumption. The process of Finnish industrialization had begun much earlier, and in 1945 the economy possessed a high level of industrial capacity, infrastructure and expert knowledge; what it lacked were the raw materials.[63] The Finnish economy was thus able to develop rapidly after 1945. The last reparations payment to the USSR was made in 1952 and the same year Helsinki hosted the Olympic Games (postponed from 1940), giving a further boost to national self-confidence.[64]

Notwithstanding the important differences discussed here, it is nonetheless possible to distinguish some common patterns in Scandinavian economic policy in the period 1950–70. First, full employment remained the main policy goal throughout the region, even though it was pursued in different ways and with varying degrees of success. Secondly, in all five countries the period was marked by the expansion of the public sector, and substantial increases in the tax burden in order to finance it (see Table 4). Although the social democrats took the lead, there was a general political consensus about the desirability of expanding the welfare state, and the healthcare and social security sectors grew rapidly. In all countries substantial public funds were also directed towards the construction of domestic housing.[65] With this came the major re-planning and reconstruction of many Scandinavian towns and cities, and the development of public transport infrastructures to support them.[66] Thirdly, despite the growth of the public sector, the Scandinavian economies remained largely mixed. There were no attempts to promote large-scale nationalization, and private industry remained influential, even to the extent that it might have been said to act as a constraint on social democratic power.[67]

Fourthly, and perhaps most importantly, one of the most distinctive features of the Nordic economies was the organization of economic interests. In the international industrial relations literature, the Nordic countries have often been described as exemplifying a 'corporatist' system in which collective bargaining was institutionalized and highly centralized.[68] One reason for this centralization was the unusually high density of union membership, which placed the Nordic countries at the top of most international comparisons (see Table 5). But the strength of the central trade union confederations were mirrored by that of the national employers' confederations, which were equally striking in an international context, and were equally influential in the development of centralized collective bargaining agreements.[69]

Some scholars have traced the roots of this model to the foundation of central confederations for trade unions and employers before the First World War, and central collective bargaining agreements were established in Sweden and Norway during the 1930s.[70] It was not, however, until the late 1960s that it became possible to speak of a truly *Nordic* model of labour relations, when a central bargaining agreement was adopted in Finland too. Paradoxically, the emergence of a truly pan-Nordic model seemed to coincide with the very moment, in the early 1970s, when the model began to show signs of decline, although the scholarly consensus indicates the continuing endurance of the corporatist arrangements in Scandinavia for the time being at least.[71] The same could be said of the Nordic welfare model (see chapter Four). Above all, this cautions against a perception of the 'Nordic model' in static terms, as a fixed historical entity belonging to the years c. 1950–70. There was no blueprint for the implementation of economic policy after 1945; instead, the elements of what retrospectively came to be known as the 'Nordic model' emerged gradually, usually as the result of short-term and pragmatic decisions. The nearest thing to a coherent plan was the Rehn-Meidner model in Sweden, although it should be noted that the proposals originally presented to the LO congress in 1951 were never implemented as fully as their authors intended.[72] Nonetheless, the Rehn-Meidner model could be considered as an original and distinctive contribution to European economic policy in the years after 1945, whereas it is debatable how many other aspects of Nordic development in this period were in fact distinctive, rather than typical of wider patterns in contemporary Western Europe.

3. The Nordic economies since 1970

With hindsight, economic historians generally agreed that the period 1950–70 was exceptional. The fourfold rise in the price of oil triggered by the action of the OPEC countries in 1973 was seen as a watershed for the post-war European economies that brought to an abrupt end the period of high and stable economic growth that had relied heavily on the supply of cheap and abundant energy. However, there were also some important continuities. In the Nordic countries, the immediate effects of the oil shock partly concealed some more general underlying economic problems that had begun to emerge from the late 1960s. Inflation was already above the OECD average by the end of the decade, and there were signs of serious financial disequilibrium in Sweden and Denmark in particular.[73]

Inflation was a particular problem in Iceland during the 1970s. The 1960s were a turning point for the Icelandic economy, which saw the abandonment of traditional protectionist policies and the liberalization of trade, culminating in the decision to join the EFTA in 1971. The main driver of economic growth during the 1960s was the herring fishery. Technological advances in the fishing fleet increased the catch sizes, but also promoted unsustainable exploitation of the fish stocks, and they collapsed suddenly in 1967–8, triggering an economic recession. In the light of these problems, the government began to take steps to diversify the Icelandic economy, and in particular to exploit its abundant energy supply, especially following the oil crisis. The economy was opened up to foreign investment, and this allowed the development of aluminium smelting in particular, using hydro-electric power. But fishing remained very important. The fisheries limits were extended, to 50 miles in 1972 and 200 miles in 1975, and the fish-processing industry was modernized. Once again, this promoted the over-exploitation of a fragile natural resource, and quotas and restrictions had to be imposed on cod and herring fisheries from the late 1970s. The expansion of the industry helped to drive a period of economic growth in the 1970s, accompanied, however, by hyper-inflation (see Figure 1).

Given its dependence on the fishing industry for its exports, and the historic legacy of extreme protectionism, the Icelandic economy is rather unusual. The difficulties faced by the other Scandinavian economies during the 1970s were more similar to those experienced in the rest of Western Europe. This was especially the case for Denmark. A spell of rapid growth at the start of the 1970s brought the traditional Danish balance of payments difficulties to the fore again, and meant that the government was in no position to try to resist the recession following the oil shock with a counter-cyclical policy. Instead, it was forced to adopt restrictive measures, which led inevitably to falling output and rising unemployment.[74] This meant that Denmark, alone among the Nordic countries, experienced the 'stagflation' that was characteristic of the 1970s in many other parts of Western Europe: low rates of growth and investment, high inflation, high unemployment and a deterioration in the balance of payments. Unemployment peaked at 11.1 per cent in 1975 but remained not far below this level for much of this decade, much worse than the other Nordic countries though not than other OECD countries.[75] The government initially tried to sit out the effects of what was widely assumed to be a temporary recession more or less passively, intervening only to try to ameliorate the worst effects of unemployment. Government attempts to stimulate demand only worsened the already severe balance of payments deficit, which had to be tackled by a drastic devaluation of the currency in the years 1979–81.

The governments of Finland, Sweden and Norway attempted to respond to the problems of the early 1970s as if to a 'normal' cyclical downturn. To some degree this was successful. Expansionary policies in Sweden contributed to some inflationary pressure, though inflation remained near the OECD average, and unemployment remained low.[76] The Norwegian government also adopted a traditional counter-cyclical policy, made possible partly by the anticipation of future North Sea oil revenues, which were just beginning to appear as if they might be commercially viable around this time. Fiscal support for struggling industries was combined with an incomes policy intended to remove the pressure for inflationary wage settlements, by providing government support for extra benefits. These appeared to be reasonably successful: unemployment was controlled and the OECD cited the actions of Norway as a good example of a successful crisis policy.[77]

By the end of the decade, however, it was becoming clear that the economic problems were the symptoms not of a temporary cyclical downturn, but of a much more serious structural crisis. In retrospect, economic historians would adopt the term 'third industrial revolution' to convey the significance of this transformation from an industrial economy to a post-industrial one, where the majority of the population would come to be employed in the service sector.[78] With hindsight it was easy to identify the beginnings of a terminal decline in the traditional industrial sector in Scandinavia (and elsewhere): the textiles and clothing industries from the 1970s, and mining, steel and shipbuilding from the 1980s.[79] But the Scandinavian societies were largely shielded from the worst social effects of the loss of employment in manufacturing by a huge expansion in the public sector, that is, the welfare state and the public bureaucracy required to service it. The welfare state also employed the growing numbers of women who entered the labour market in all the Nordic countries from the early 1970s.[80]

These structural changes were matched by equally far-reaching changes in social and political attitudes that were to have a profound effect on the ideology and policy of the Scandinavian social democratic parties above all. In the first place, the emerging environmental movement presented a challenge to the traditional social democratic faith in the industrial economy as providing the foundations for material prosperity. Secondly, the general wave of radicalization in the late 1960s gave rise to new movements, and new factions within existing ones, that sought to challenge traditional sources of authority and campaigned for greater equality. In Norway and Denmark, the foundation of new socialist parties had already begun to present a significant electoral challenge to social democracy, but they were mirrored by an increase in industrial unrest, especially in Denmark. Particularly shocking for the Swedish Social Democratic government was the wildcat strike held by the employers of a state-owned mining company in Kiruna in northern Sweden in 1969. The strike was a protest not only against the traditional adversary, the employer, but also against the leadership of the trade union movement. The response of the social democratic parties was to attempt to radicalize their policies, through measures such as the effective socialization of the banking sector in

Norway from 1978 (later reversed by a right-wing government), and the proposals for industrial democracy and wage-earners' funds in Sweden and Norway.[81]

Some economic historians have suggested that the Rehn-Meidner model contained the policy tools required to deal with the structural crisis faced by the Swedish government during the 1970s.[82] The problem, it is suggested, was not that a policy model developed for an earlier age was unsuitable for new problems, but that the government departed from the main tenets of the model, and pursued instead a straightforward counter-cyclical policy that concealed the underlying problems and prevented the necessary restructuring of the Swedish economy from taking place. Companies were able to make easy profits through the award of generous state subsidies, which cut the Rehn-Meidner model's inbuilt emphasis on industrial dynamism. Even more importantly, the government departed from the tradition of wage restraint that had characterized Swedish economic policy since 1945. Motivated by aggressive demands for equality from a radicalized grassroots element in the party and the trade union movement, the Rehn-Meidner principle of equal pay for equal work was abandoned in favour of a more general aspiration to equality.[83] The Swedish economy thus avoided the mass unemployment seen in Denmark, but at the cost of huge growth in public sector borrowing and a growing tax burden to pay for it, so that marginal tax rates had reached over 80 per cent by the early 1980s. Even following the election of a bourgeois government in 1976, the basic tenets of economic policy remained the same, thus preventing what in hindsight became clear was a necessary fundamental restructuring of the Swedish economy.[84]

Nonetheless, the Swedish social democrats were re-elected in 1982, and, together with the Norwegian Labour Party, achieved some success in adapting their ideologies and policies to the changed conditions of the 1980s. The party leaders – Olof Palme and Gro Harlem Brundtland respectively – were in many respects similar politicians. Unlike many of their predecessors, they lacked a traditional base of support within the trade union movement and were thus associated with the modernizing wing of their parties, but they sought to maintain their left-wing credentials in other ways, especially through the championing of international solidarity (and gender equality in the case of Brundt-land). Under Palme, the Swedish Social Democrats eventually introduced their controversial proposals for wage-earner funds, albeit in a much-diluted form compared to the original proposal. Under the rubric of the 'third way', presented as a social democratic alternative to neo-liberal-ism, they also embarked on a programme of financial deregulation that was intended to stabilize the economy and promote exports, invest-ment and profitability.[85]

The expansionary policy pursued by the Norwegian government had run into difficulties by 1977, when it became clear that the econ-omy was overheating. Acknowledging the depth of the structural difficulties that it was now facing, the Labour Party adopted instead a policy of austerity, and some measures intended to improve interna-tional competitiveness, including a devaluation of the krona. A cut in the marginal rate of tax in 1981 amounted to a fundamental change of principle for the Labour Party, since it meant implementing for the first time a tax reform that benefited those with the highest incomes.[86] From the early 1980s, however, Norway began to reap the rewards of the commercial exploitation of North Sea oil, which was to transform the economy over the next two decades and place Norway at the top of many international measurements of prosperity and living standards. By 1982 oil income amounted to 18 per cent of government revenue and 32 per cent of Norwegian exports, even though the sector still only accounted for 3 per cent of total employment.[87] The Labour govern-ment initially declared a policy of 'going for growth' on the basis of the oil bonanza, and the public sector underwent a massive expansion, but this was checked in 1986 when international oil prices suddenly declined from $30 to $8 a barrel, and Norway's external deficit rose dramatically. The subsequent recovery of oil prices meant that public debate on economic policy was generally focused on the handling of the public oil revenues, and the ways to safeguard the economy against the day when oil reserves would inevitably decline.

The neo-liberal economic thinking of the 1980s thus had some influ-ence in Sweden and Norway, under the guise of reformed social democracy, but it was to have a much greater impact elsewhere in Scandinavia. In Iceland, the main political issue of the 1980s had become the need to control hyper-inflation. In 1983 the indexation of wages was abolished to that end, and this was followed by a programme of deregulation and liberalism. By the end of the decade this appeared to have had the desired effect as far as inflation was concerned, but at the expense of a recession and a period of high unemployment. Meanwhile in Denmark, the Social Democrats recovered from the setback of the 1973 'earthquake' election, but were eventually replaced in 1982 by a Conservative government led by Poul Schlüter. The success of the populist Progress Party in the early 1970s was also influential in promoting a political critique of the high taxes associated with the social democratic welfare model.[88] The result of this was to expose the Danish economy to neo-liberalism to a much greater degree than the other Scandinavian countries. The Schlüter government made concerted efforts to reduce public spending, including making cuts in social benefits for families and the unemployed, for example.

In summary, then, the Scandinavian economies seemed to diverge in the period after the 1970s. Denmark was worst affected by the international economic problems of the 1970s, but as a consequence had undergone more restructuring that seemed to leave it in a stronger position during the 1990s. Unlike the other Nordic countries, Denmark was also faced with the need to adapt to membership of the European Community after 1973, which affected its agricultural policy in particular. The Icelandic economy had undergone a drastic liberalization of its foreign trade, but faced severe inflationary problems during the period 1970–90, and its exports remained dominated by fish. Meanwhile, Sweden, Norway and Finland seemed to have avoided the worst consequences of the oil shocks, and had maintained, indeed expanded, their comprehensive welfare systems. Indeed, as far as Finland was concerned, there were signs of convergence with the other Nordic economies, both in terms of industrial output and welfare spending.[89]

For Sweden and Finland, however, this success came to an abrupt end during the international recession of the early 1990s. Both countries experienced negative growth in 1991; private investment and consumption fell, and unemployment rose sharply (see Table 6). The crisis was partly caused by external events, including an international recession and the rise in interest rates as a result of German unification. For

Finland, the sudden collapse of the Soviet Union was also important: Finnish exports to the USSR fell by 70 per cent in 1991.[90] However, most economic historians agreed that although these external shocks exacerbated the situation, they were not the primary cause. The severity of the recession could instead be explained in two ways: as a structural crisis, for which earlier government policies shielding the economy from necessary structural change in the 1970s and '80s were partly to blame; and as a financial crisis.[91] The governments of both countries had embarked on a major programme of financial deregulation during the 1980s, abolishing restrictions on domestic bank lending rates and on private borrowing, which triggered a speculative boom based on property and foreign loans.[92] Private consumption and investment rose drastically, but this was not countered by a restrictive fiscal policy, with the result that growth accelerated and both economies were seriously overheating by the late 1980s. The boom came to an end in a spectacular crash in 1989–90. Both countries experienced a deep financial crisis, where the banking sector was saved only thanks to government intervention. Over-valued currencies were initially linked to the European Currency Unit (ECU), but were eventually allowed to float in the autumn of 1992 and suffered drastic devaluations. Unemployment rose dramatically, to over 9 per cent in Sweden by 1993, and to over 16 per cent in Finland. Both countries experienced several years of negative growth and were ranked bottom of OECD countries.

The crisis had a profound and long-lasting psychological impact on the populations of both countries. For Sweden, the crisis marked a major social, political and cultural watershed, when many aspects of the Swedish model and Swedish identity itself seemed suddenly to unravel. The Social Democratic government's announcement of its intention to seek membership of the European Community in 1990 was seen by many of its critics as a partial admission of defeat and an acknowledgement that the traditional tenets of the Swedish model had failed. This seemed to be confirmed by SAF's unilateral withdrawal from the collectivized central bargaining arrangements established by the Saltsjöbaden agreement in 1938.[93] In May 1991 the government finally abandoned its commitment to counter-cyclical policies intended to stimulate full employment.[94] Finally, in the autumn of

1991 the Social Democrats were defeated for only the second time in nearly sixty years, and the new Conservative government that was elected announced its intentions to undertake sweeping reforms and retrenchment in the public sector through direct cuts in public transfers and taxes.[95] The next few years were marked by some intense public debates about many aspects of twentieth-century Swedish history that had previously been taken for granted: examples included the publication of Maria-Pia Boëthius's book on Sweden during the Second World War, and state inquiries into forced sterilizations and Cold War neutrality policy.[96]

The acute crisis was even worse in Finland. Measured by most economic indicators, the recession was more severe than the Great Depression of the 1930s, and comparable even to the famine years of the 1860s in terms of its traumatic impact on the population.[97] Most damagingly, the crisis had a profound social impact, first through consumer debt and the loss of consumer confidence, and secondly through the very high rates of unemployment, which hit the traditional industries hardest. Indeed, the unemployment rate for men was well over 20 per cent in Finland during the winter of 1993–4, and older workers were particularly badly affected.[98] In the longer term, however, the overall effects of the changes were perhaps experienced less negatively in Finland than they were in Sweden. First, the decision to join the European Union in 1994 marked the end of Finland's Cold War isolation, and the embrace of a new, urban, cosmopolitan identity, at least for the populations of the south and west coasts.[99] Secondly, the profound structural transformation that came about in the wake of the recession quite quickly gave Finland a new status and identity as one of the world's leading nations in the information and communications technology (ICT) sector. The export share of high-technology industries grew rapidly, from 8.8 per cent in 1990 to 22.1 per cent in 2002.[100] A similar expansion took place in Sweden (corresponding figures were 16 per cent in 1990 and 21.9 per cent in 2002), and companies such as Nokia and Ericsson had by the turn of the twenty-first century gained an international status as brands that matched companies in the traditional sectors such as Volvo and Saab.[101]

The roots of the spectacular growth in Nordic ICT can be traced in part to the early deregulation of the Nordic telecommunications market and the adoption of a common standard for mobile telephony in the 1980s.[102] In any case, the telecommunications sector was historically well established, especially in Sweden, which had had one of the highest frequency of telephones per capita in Europe since the late nineteenth century.[103] Ericsson had existed as a telephone manufacturer since the early twentieth century, and Nokia was also a well-established company, concentrating, however, on forestry products, rubber and cables. Moreover, as Darius Ornston has suggested, although the extent of corporatist organization in Finland 'should' have inhibited such a radical transformation according to conventional economic wisdom (ICT was supposed to thrive in liberal, deregulated Anglo-Saxon economies), in fact there were many elements to this economic structure that actually favoured the development of the new sector. On the one hand, the central organization of the labour movement allowed the government to achieve national incomes agreements in 1995 and 1997 covering 98 per cent of the workforce, which helped to improve cost competitiveness, while on the other hand business leaders cooperated with the government in order to accelerate restructuring and promote research and development (R&D).[104] At the turn of the century, Finland and Sweden led the OECD in the percentage of GDP spent on R&D, and in the number of researchers employed as a proportion of the total workforce.[105] Finland's emergence as a high-tech economy was thus no accident, but 'reflected a fundamentally political bargain between collectively organized economic actors, framed by inherited traditions and shaped by the preferences of these social partners'.[106] Finnish self-perceptions were altered radically: instead of a relatively backward, raw material-exporting nation on the fringes of the Nordic model, some researchers at home and abroad now began to speak of a distinctively 'Finnish' model.[107]

CONCLUSION

The myth of the Nordic transformation from poverty to affluence is very persistent: it appeared again in at least two books published in

2005 and 2006.[108] In some ways, the very concept of the Nordic model rests on the myth, for it purports to explain how these cold, sparsely populated, small northern countries reached such a position of affluence. In fact, economic historians have qualified the myth by demonstrating that the Nordic countries were not necessarily backward or isolated before the twentieth century: on the contrary, they have been well integrated into the European and North Atlantic economies as trading nations since the early modern period. Nonetheless, the myth of Nordic economic distinctiveness continues to be a powerful trope. For those on the left it has served for many years as comforting evidence that economic prosperity in a capitalist system can indeed be combined with high levels of welfare spending and economic equality. Meanwhile, for those on the right the severe economic crises in Sweden and Finland in the early 1990s provided further evidence of the misguidedness of high levels of government intervention.

As this chapter has explored, there were indeed some important similarities in the economic development of the Nordic countries since 1945, in terms of both structure and policy. Against this, it should be noted that there were also some important differences. Sweden was undoubtedly the strongest Nordic economy for most of the post-war period, and the one with the most developed industrial sector. Agrarian interests (including fishing) remained relatively more important in the other Nordic countries, especially Finland, though the nature of the Finnish transformation was very different from that of Denmark, which already had a well-developed agricultural export industry. In social terms, this meant that in Norway, Iceland and Finland in particular, much of the population retained personal connections with the countryside relatively late in comparison to other parts of Europe, though by the last quarter of the twentieth century this had been translated into the ownership of rural second homes for leisure purposes. Given the relative tardiness of the industrial transformation in Finland, it is only really from the 1970s that it is possible to identify a strong convergence within Nordic economic development and economic policy. At the same time, there were other trends promoting divergence, such as the exploitation of North Sea oil.

At a discursive level, and at a time when the phenomenon of 'globalization' seems to be challenging the possibilities for nation states to pursue an autonomous economic policy, it seems to have become noticeably more prevalent to speak not of one Nordic model but of several: a Danish model based on the concept of 'flexicurity'; a Finnish model emphasizing research and investment in ICT; and Göran Persson's famous bumblebee metaphor, coined to denote the paradox of the supposedly over-regulated yet economically effective Swedish model. It is important to note that the notion of the model does, however, conceal some problems, not least the persistently high rates of long-term unemployment in Sweden and Finland, although some might prefer to identify this as a wider European malaise.[109] In 2007 three things seem to stand out as particular features of the Nordic economies. First, the high-technology sector is strong across the whole region, including not only ICT but also other industries such as pharmaceuticals. Secondly, despite the decline in corporatism, economic interests in the Scandinavian economies remain highly organized. Thirdly, for the present at least, the public sector remains large, and high levels of national income remain devoted to maintaining the famous Nordic welfare system.

Chapter 3

The Nordic Model of Welfare

Despite the political influence of the social democratic left, post-war Nordic economic policy remained, as we saw in the previous chapter, tolerant of capitalist enterprise. The Nordic governments made few attempts to take control of the commanding heights of the economy through nationalization. Instead, their primary concern was with the distribution of the fruits of capitalist prosperity and the development of state welfare systems that have generally been recognized as some of the most comprehensive, far-reaching and ambitious in Western Europe. The welfare state is central to any discussion of the Nordic countries after 1945. The so-called Nordic welfare model has attracted the attention of countless scholars and policy makers, and at the beginning of the twenty-first century remains one of the most enduring stereotypes about the Nordic countries.

Scholarly discussions of the Nordic welfare model have often concentrated on social insurance schemes established to take care of those citizens who for different reasons were unable to support themselves through paid employment. It is generally agreed that the Nordic social insurance systems were more comprehensive than those of many other welfare states, and that they also shared certain features, such as universalism, that meant that they went further than many other countries' systems in reordering social relations and promoting high levels of social equality. The distinguishing characteristics of the Nordic social security systems, and the possible historical causes for their development, are thus discussed in some detail in this chapter.

The Nordic welfare states were more than social insurance systems, however. In fact, in all the Western European welfare states during the post-war period the welfare state was seen as an integral part of managing the capitalist economy: a force for promoting economic efficiency, ordering social relations and securing the reproduction of society. Where the Nordic governments seemed to stand out was in the breadth and ambition of their vision for the welfare state, and their faith in their own ability to create the good society. No other democratic societies seemed to be quite so affected by extensive state intervention into all areas of human life as the Nordic countries. As the historian Henrik Stenius has put it, 'All the doors are open – to the living room, the kitchen, the larder, the nursery, not to mention the bedroom – and they are not just open: society marches in and intervenes, sometimes brusquely.'[1] Remarkably (from an Anglo-Saxon point of view), this intervention has generally been tolerated by the citizens of the Nordic countries, though some aspects have, of course, provoked debate, such as the issue of reproductive rights and eugenic sterilization discussed later in this chapter. Moreover, despite the rise of neo-liberalism from the 1970s, there is still strong political support for the welfare state, and everything seems to suggest in fact that the concept of the welfare state is now more than ever an integral part of national identity in the Nordic countries.

WELFARE MODELLING: TYPOLOGIES OF THE WELFARE STATE

Although most modern capitalist societies have developed some form of state welfare, there are major differences in the way in which these provisions are organized. By comparing the distinguishing features of different welfare states, social scientists have attempted to group different types of welfare state and to develop a typology of welfare regimes. The most basic division is a dual one, between 'residual' welfare states that provided only a basic safety net for the poorest citizens, and 'institutional' (or sometimes 'universal') welfare states with much greater social ambitions and comprehensive provision of benefits.[2] Perhaps the most influential typology was Gøsta Esping-Andersen's three-part classification of welfare regimes: the 'three worlds of welfare capitalism'. According to Esping-Andersen, welfare states were not only mechanisms for providing benefits for the needy, but should also be recognized as systems of social stratification: active forces in ordering social relations. For example, the poor relief schemes found in most European countries until the late nineteenth century reinforced existing social hierarchies by allocating welfare according to notions of the 'deserving' and 'undeserving' poor. The social insurance model of welfare developed in Bismarck's Germany was designed to favour the special status of certain social groups, especially public servants. The main yardstick for classifying welfare states was therefore the extent to which welfare regimes 'decommodified' social relations; in other words, the extent to which different groups of citizens were freed from dependence on the market for the provision of welfare.[3]

The 'three worlds of welfare capitalism' were categorized as follows. The first group, the liberal welfare regimes found in the USA, Canada and Australia, provided a means-tested, basic safety net for the poorest citizens only, with minimal or non-existent redistributive aims. Entitlement to benefits was based on strict rules and recipients were stigmatized, so that there was a basic divide between the majority of citizens who relied on the market for their welfare needs and the minority who were too poor to do this. In the second group, the corporatist or conservative welfare regimes of central Europe, rights to welfare benefits were attached to the status of individuals within the labour market, meaning that the welfare system tended to consolidate the existing social structure. These regimes were typically found in those countries of western and central Europe that were influenced by the Catholic Church, which meant that the welfare state was also designed to reinforce traditional patterns of family relationships. Finally, the social democratic welfare regimes of the Scandinavian countries promoted social equality through the provision of universal benefits. In these regimes social rights were highly decommodified, with even middle-class citizens benefiting from the welfare state and thus prepared to give it their electoral support.

Esping-Andersen's typology has become the standard reference for comparative studies of the welfare state published in the 1990s and after. There have been attempts to modify the three-part model. Evelyne Huber and John D. Stephens suggested a 'fourth world', encompassing the wage-earner welfare states of Australia and New Zealand, while the Swedish sociologists Walter Korpi and Joakim Palme proposed five types based on differences in entitlement (whether universal or targeted to the neediest) and the determination of benefit levels (whether flat-rate or earnings-related)[4] Nonetheless, most welfare state typologies seem to agree that the Nordic countries share certain features and can be clustered together: that there is a 'Nordic model' of welfare in other words.[5]

The distinctive features of the Nordic welfare model can be summarized as follows. First, the Scandinavian welfare regimes were also welfare states.[6] Welfare benefits were provided mostly by the public sector, leaving little room for the private sector, for philanthropic or voluntary provision, or for the family. Secondly, provision of welfare benefits was comprehensive and universal, which meant that the Scandinavian welfare states were also redistributive, and produced societies characterized by a relatively high degree of social equality. Universal in this context meant that, 'social programs – old-age pensions, health care, child-care, education, child allowances and health insurance – are not targeted at the poor, but instead cover the entire population with no consideration given to their ability to pay'.[7] Thirdly, the Scandinavian welfare states were financed principally out of general taxation, rather than through contributions related to employment, for example. Taxation accounted for over 50 per cent of GDP in Denmark, Norway and Sweden in 1980; only the Netherlands had a similar tax burden.[8] Fourthly, the Scandinavian welfare state was never seen merely as a safety net for less fortunate citizens, like the more residual welfare systems of countries such as the USA, Canada and Australia. Instead, it was regarded as an integral part of post-war economic policy, firmly linked with the maintenance of high levels of economic growth, low unemployment and a high standard of living.[9] Full employment was to be achieved above all through active labour market policies such as education and training to mobilize the workforce. Fifthly, Scandinavian welfare policies helped to promote a dual breadwinner family model, where women's entitlement to benefits was based on their status as independent citizens rather than as the wives or mothers of male breadwinners.[10]

It is important to note that the 'three worlds' of welfare capitalism must be considered ideal types: no single welfare state has ever conformed exactly to any one of the three models.[11] Indeed, some scholars have questioned the wisdom of creating welfare state typologies, arguing that to do so may obscure important differences within welfare state clusters.[12] Examined in more detail, all the features assumed to be typical of the Nordic welfare states require some qualification. Esping-Andersen's identification of the Scandinavian social democratic welfare regime seems to fit Sweden more neatly than it does the other Nordic countries. Moreover, the classification is based on a snapshot of a particular historical moment during the 1980s, which works much less well in a longer historical perspective. The road to the Nordic welfare model was long and varying, and its trademarks did not appear in some parts of the region until they had already started to wane in others.[13] As the welfare state came under pressure during the 1990s, scholars became more interested in its historical development, and this in turn has helped to present a more detailed and nuanced picture of the similarities and differences between welfare policy in the Nordic countries.[14]

THE HISTORICAL DEVELOPMENT OF THE WELFARE STATE

The 'social democratic welfare state' may be understood in two ways. First, it describes welfare systems that, in their de-commodification of social relations and their emphasis on universalism and redistribution, embodied the social democratic ideological commitment to social equality and solidarity. Secondly, it suggests that the welfare state was the realization of the ideological programme of the social democratic parties that dominated Scandinavian politics during the second half of the twentieth century. As such, the Nordic welfare state should be acknowledged as the major political achievement of the organized working class. It was not, however, the sole achievement of the working class acting on its own, but was instead a testament to the ability of the Scandinavian labour movements to form cross-class alliances with other social groups, most notably with the farmers.[15] The welfare state was thus constructed following the negotiation of 'Red–Green' coalitions in the 1930s, which allowed the social democrats to form majority governments and introduce comprehensive social reform legislation.[16]

The main problem with this explanation of the roots of the Nordic welfare model is that it is anachronistic. As Peter Baldwin has pointed out, it ignores the important welfare reforms that were agreed in the Nordic countries in the late nineteenth and early twentieth centuries, *before* the emergence of social democracy as a major political force. In Denmark, the pension law of 1891, which established the principle of a universal, tax-financed pension system, was the result of a political compromise agreed between Højre (the Right) and Venstre (the Agrarian Liberal Party) in the context of contemporary debates over constitutional reform.[17] The same applied to Sweden, where the 1913 pension scheme was legislated for by bourgeois parties and politicians. Unemployment insurance was introduced in Norway and Denmark by bourgeois liberal governments (in Denmark acting with the support of the Social Democrats), following major democratic reforms in Norway in 1884 and in Denmark in 1901. The main supporters of the voluntary, publicly funded insurance schemes were non-socialists: indeed, the Norwegian trade unions were initially indifferent or even hostile to the new funds.[18] Thus the beginnings of the welfare state were linked not to the political compromises of the 1930s, but to the emergence of a predominantly agrarian liberal middle class in the late nineteenth century.[19]

In turn, this means that the ideological influences on the Nordic welfare states were far more heterogeneous than the social democratic designation implies. Bismarck's social insurance reforms sparked widespread interest in the Nordic countries, not merely among conservatives.[20] As examples, the Labour Commission, established in 1885 by the Norwegian state, was typical in studying schemes in both Germany and Britain as potential models for reform, and the ideas of German social reformers such as Adolph Wagner (1835–1917) were widely read and debated by liberals, conservatives and social democrats alike in late nineteenth-century Sweden.[21] But of the social insurance laws subsequently passed around the turn of the century, very few directly resembled the German ones. For example, the Danish pension reform of 1891 explicitly rejected the Bismarckian model in that it was tax-based, financed not through insurance contributions but through state and local taxes.[22] What made this possible was the specifically Danish (and by extension Scandinavian) state tradition, which generated widespread expectations of state involvement in this field. This stemmed in turn from the unusually close relationship between the reformed Lutheran church and the state in Scandinavia, and the crown's assumption of the church's traditional welfare responsibilities at the local or parish level after the Reformation.[23] For this reason, like similar schemes in Norway, the Danish reformers also showed a preference for local administration over the central bureaucracy.[24]

Lutheranism was also influential in directing the moral imperatives of early welfare legislation. Alongside the willingness to embrace the strong state lay an equally strong current of support for the principle of self-help. All the early social insurance schemes in Scandinavia were predicated on the expectation that individual independence and self-reliance through work were the desired goals of social policy. Willingness to work was invariably a condition for receiving benefits.[25] Social reform would help to integrate the working classes and prevent social unrest, but this was to be achieved primarily through creating the means for individuals to support themselves. In Sweden, these ideas found expression in the *egnahem* or 'own-your-own-home' movement of the 1890s and after. The proposal to promote self-owned smallholdings in the countryside came first from conservatives, as a means to counter the contemporary threats of socialism and emigration, but the idea was also taken up by radical liberal groups seeking to liberate the rural population from social and economic dependency and to promote self-reliance.[26]

It should be noted that the Scandinavian social welfare reforms of the early twentieth century were generally limited in their scope, and as in most other European countries provided only the most basic assistance to citizens, attached to some stringent conditions. The point is, however, that the legislation from this period established the framework and basic principles for the subsequent expansion of the welfare state under the political influence of the social democrats. The strongest example of this 'path dependency' was in Denmark, where the means-tested tax-funded pension introduced in 1891 was not reformed until the 1980s.[27] The Swedish pension system proved much more open to reform, but scholars have considered the 1913 law to be significant for introducing the principle of universalism. This was indeed the case, though universalism was of symbolic rather than practical importance, because the basic level of benefits was very low and the scheme also included a means-tested supplementary pension.[28] In Norway, the introduction of sickness insurance in 1909 has also been seen as an important milestone because it was obligatory, but like the 1894 accident insurance this was targeted at certain groups of citizens only, and thus was not strictly universal.[29]

The second wave of Nordic welfare legislation came following the social democrats' achievement of parliamentary majorities during the 1930s. As in many other parts of Europe, these reforms were partly motivated by the need to tackle the social deprivation created by the economic crises of the inter-war period. The social democratic parties were undoubtedly the driving force behind these changes, but it is important to acknowledge the limits to their influence, and the piecemeal and contested nature of welfare reform.

This is best illustrated by a closer examination of the question of universalism, assumed to be one of the cornerstones of the Nordic or social democratic welfare state. It has been suggested that the adoption of universalism as a guiding principle pre-dated the social democratic influence on the welfare state, for example in the Swedish pension introduced in 1913, although its extent was very limited as we have seen.[30] The expanded pension schemes adopted during the inter-war period all included some means-testing intended to exclude better-off citizens and thus divert scarce resources to where they were most needed.[31] Of all the Nordic countries, Norway came closest (in 1937) to adopting a pensions system based on citizens' rights, which guaranteed a standard minimum income in old age to all regardless of previous wage labour or contributions to insurance schemes. But even here, two groups were excluded: those who had lived abroad and those who had been convicted of vagrancy, drunkenness or begging.[32] The guiding principle that 'self-reliance through work' should be the main basis for the benefits system meant that social insurance schemes were designed to benefit 'respectable workers' (*skötsamma arbetare*) first and foremost.[33]

This meant that the pre-1950 Nordic social insurance schemes must be considered as corresponding more closely to a wage-earner model than a universal one based on citizens' rights. Moreover, Norway was exceptional among the Nordic countries in adopting a compulsory unemployment insurance scheme in 1938; elsewhere the so-called Ghent model, where insurance funds were administered through trade union funds run and supported by the state, was preferred.[34] This meant that the funds themselves – and by extension the trade union movement – assumed responsibility for distinguishing between the 'real' unemployed who confirmed to the required values of diligence and sobriety and those whose behaviour excluded them from entitlement. It also gave the trade unions a powerful means of control over their members, which they later fought hard to defend.[35] But it also meant that the funds were never universal in their coverage: even as late as the 1960s, 1.4 million wage-earners (about half the workforce) in Sweden were not covered by an unemployment insurance scheme.[36] The wage-earner model also excluded many groups of workers that were difficult to categorize as wage-earners or whose working conditions meant that their requirements were hard to monitor: small business owners, home workers, seasonal workers, small farmers and fishermen, and the employees of family farms. Members of these categories were gradually accommodated by a series of piecemeal reforms, but exclusions remained, some of them affecting groups that were particularly vulnerable, such as young people, women, low-skilled workers and immigrants.[37]

The identification of the social democratic labour movement with wage-earners, and the trade unions' administration of the insurance funds, meant that the wage-earner principle persisted during the phase of welfare state expansion after the Second World War. For this reason, it makes more sense to describe the Nordic welfare states as mixed universal/wage-earner systems, where benefits remained linked to the status of individuals as wage earners rather than being understood solely as an entitlement of citizenship. In other words, if universalism is defined as a welfare system where '[a]ccess to, and rights to, social security benefits are ... a consequence of being a citizen of the country one is living in', then the Nordic welfare states could be described as only partly universal.[38] This is not perhaps very surprising, given that most welfare states exhibit mixed features, rather than corresponding exactly to the ideal types of welfare models. The point is instead that the universal elements of the Nordic welfare states were more important than they were in other systems. In most areas of Nordic social insurance, the common pattern during the post-war period was the adoption of a universal scheme guaranteeing a basic minimum, supplemented, however, by some form of income-related benefits generally tied to wage-earner contributions.[39] That said, it should be pointed out that the welfare states encompassed more than social insurance systems, of course, and that the provision of services in kind such as healthcare and education was generally governed by the principle of universalism in all the Nordic countries.

What is more problematic is the assumption that universalism was the guiding principle of the social democratic programmes for welfare reform, as least as far as social insurance was concerned.[40] As the Swedish historian Klas Åmark has shown, in his detailed comparison of the development of social insurance in Sweden and Norway, it was hard to distinguish a clear ideological position for or against universalism among post-war social democrats.[41] Instead, the Swedish labour movement was divided, with the Social Minister Gustav Möller supporting universal insurance based on flat-rate benefits, and the trade unions favouring income-related benefits. The trade union-administered unemployment funds were able to mount a powerful defence of the wage-earner principle and contribute to the defeat of an opposition motion for compulsory insurance in 1966.[42] These funds were less powerful in Norway, where compulsory unemployment insurance had been introduced in 1938, but here too universalism was never the labour movement's main goal: its ambition was to create social insurance schemes for wage-earners rather than a system based on social rights for all citizens.[43] The complex income-related benefits system, which divided benefit-recipients into categories according to income, was a means for the labour movement to maintain and legitimize wage differentials within the labour market, and also to exert internal control over its membership.[44] The Scandinavian welfare state, as it developed after 1945, was thus not the result of a coherent strategy so much as a piecemeal development resulting from a complex process of negotiation and compromise, where the different influences of political parties, expert opinion, interest groups, committees of inquiry, administrative capacity and the institutional legacy all had to be taken into account. In Åmark's words, social policy reform was 'a constant search for possibilities – the art of the possible'.[45]

The thesis of the universal welfare state as the child of a strong social democratic labour movement is also challenged by the cases of Finland and Iceland, where social democracy did not achieve the same political dominance. Whereas Finnish politics was characterized by broad-based coalitions during the post-war period (and a strong Communist Party), Icelandic politics was dominated by the centre-right Independence Party, which was able to stamp its individualist, pro-market ideological outlook on Icelandic welfare policies.[46] Public expenditure as a percentage of GDP remained low in comparison to the other Nordic countries, and social expenditure was moreover always vulnerable to economic recession. In Iceland it was not until after the Second World War that the state assumed a role as the main provider of welfare. Moreover, despite rapid expansion in the 1940s, the Icelandic welfare state was not as generous as its Nordic counterparts, and it was also influenced more by principles reminiscent of American self-help and individualism than by Nordic collectivism.[47] Meanwhile in Finland, the workers' accident insurance scheme remained the only national social insurance provision until the 1960s. For the two decades after the Second World War social policy remained subordinate to economic goals, and the dominance of the agrarian sector meant that agrarian subsidies played a major role in income redistribution in a way that had no parallel elsewhere in Scandinavia.[48]

For these reasons, the welfare states of Finland and Iceland have often been described as backward in comparison to Denmark, Norway and Sweden, a backwardness that has in turn been related to the tardiness of their development from being relatively poor agrarian societies to modernized, prosperous industrial ones. In Finland, this 'backwardness' gave way to a 'breakthrough' for the welfare state from the 1960s, when an ambitious programme of social legislation took social expenditure as a proportion of GDP from 7 per cent in 1960 to 22–3 per cent in the mid-1980s. The Finnish welfare system began to assume many of the characteristics found in the other Nordic countries. For this reason, some scholars have argued that it is not really possible to identify a truly Nordic welfare state until the 1980s, when Finland and Iceland had begun to catch up and converge with the 'core' of the model.[49] Against this, Pauli Kettunen has cautioned against the reductionism of an approach that sees the Finnish and Icelandic cases as 'exceptional' when measured against a Nordic standard, pointing instead to the contingency of the political decisions concerning welfare reforms. As an example, he cites the case of the Finnish social insurance act, which was passed in 1963 and is thus taken as an example of Finnish backwardness. However, the social insurance question had been debated in Finland since the late nineteenth century, and legislation was in fact almost passed by the Eduskunta in the 1920s, only to fall at the last minute on the opposition of the Communists. Moreover, even though social democracy was not as politically dominant as it was elsewhere in Scandinavia, Finland had introduced strong labour protection laws before the other Scandinavian countries, partly as a result of demands from the trade union movement.[50] In Iceland, the labour movement found itself in a position of strength during the period of post-war economic growth, and was able to use its strong position in labour-market bargaining to extract welfare reforms, even if it lacked the parliamentary influence of its counterparts in the other Scandinavian countries.[51]

To summarize, there was no set path for the development of a Nordic welfare model, and no blueprint for how it should be constructed. Possibilities for reform were at times limited by the administrative capacity of the state to introduce complex social insurance schemes, and by the legacy of institutional traditions from legislation that was established in the late nineteenth century and even earlier. Moreover, although the politically strong social democratic parties in Denmark, Norway and Sweden undoubtedly were driving forces in initiating welfare reforms after the 1930s, there was not necessarily unity in the labour movement on the best way to achieve these reforms, and the different possibilities could sometimes provoke heated debates. The question of pensions dominated Swedish politics for most of the 1950s, but the disagreements over how to organize income-related supplementary pensions cut across traditional party lines. Radical social democratic reformers such as Gustav Möller found themselves allied with the political right in their opposition to compulsory supplementary pensions, though for different ideological reasons. Eventually, the pension reform was passed by a majority of only one in the Riksdag. By contrast, a proposal for a very similar system in Norway secured a broad consensus in the Storting and was adopted without controversy.[52]

A NORDIC WELFARE MODEL?

Much comparative welfare state research in the social sciences has focused on the details of social insurance schemes in particular. A close analysis of the historical development of social insurance helps to reveal the complexity of these arrangements, and the ways in which they differed across national contexts. But if the Nordic welfare model is understood in broader terms, as a discourse that was influential in helping – in some cases retrospectively – policy makers to legitimize their attempts at reform, then it seems possible to distinguish some common characteristics that seem to apply across the Nordic region.

Broadly, of course, the historical trajectory of the Nordic welfare states corresponds to that of the rest of Europe, with welfare policy influenced by periods of economic growth and crisis.[53] There were three main periods of expansion in the European welfare states: first, the introduction of basic social insurance schemes by bourgeois governments in the late nineteenth and early twentieth centuries, intended to mitigate the effects of industrialization and urbanization and integrate the growing working class. The second phase came during the inter-war period, when welfare policies were expanded in an attempt to respond to the mass unemployment and social deprivation in the wake of the Great Depression. The major expansion of the welfare states occurred during the period of high economic growth and full employment in the two decades after the Second World War. Finally, since the oil crises and recession of the early 1970s many governments have attempted to pursue retrenchment in welfare spending.

Some scholars have argued that the roots of Nordic distinctiveness in welfare policy pre-date the beginnings of welfare legislation in the late nineteenth century. The early development of a comprehensive elementary school system (Denmark was the first country in the world to introduce compulsory elementary education in 1814, followed by Norway in 1827 and Sweden in 1842), and the unusually well-developed capacity of the state for local action through the Lutheran parish network, have been cited as examples of this distinctiveness.[54] Only from the inter-war period, however, following the relatively successful Scandinavian response to the Great Depression, did the Nordic countries begin to attract international attention as examples of success in social policy. During the 1920s it was

Denmark that was perceived as the epitome of a progressive modern state, following the publication of the social democrat K. K. Steincke's plan for social reform *Fremtidens forsørgelsevæsen* in 1920. The Danish Social Democrats' reform bill presented to the Folketing in 1933 amounted to the most comprehensive proposal for social legislation in any European country at that time.[55] Policy ideas were shared across the Nordic region, however, transmitted through regular meetings of the Nordic social ministers after 1919 and a network of informal contacts between civil servants.[56] These contacts were particularly important for Finland, where the idea of a 'Nordic' model (derived in particular from Sweden) was seen as a blueprint for the future of a recently independent nation. As Klaus Petersen has shown, however, the term 'Nordic' also came to be an important discursive tool to legitimize national reforms across the region, especially after 1945.[57]

What were the common features of the thinking behind the Nordic welfare states? Above all, the Nordic welfare states seem to be distinguished in the ambitiousness of their aims. Early social legislation in the late nineteenth century was intended to help individuals alleviate social risk, but during the inter-war period this rather modest ambition was superseded by a much greater one. Social policy was intended to be prophylactic; it provided the state with the means to create the good society.[58] From the beginnings of the twentieth century, therefore, Nordic social policy was closely connected to ideas of national economic efficiency.

These ideas formed the backbone of much social democratic thinking, of course, but some scholars have understood them as part of more deep-rooted Nordic values and cultural traditions. First, the labour movement shared with both the free and the state Lutheran churches an emphasis on the individual's own responsibility for social welfare through sobriety, education and respectability, and the role of paternalism and tutelage in creating good citizens.[59] This current could be found especially in welfare state attitudes to personal transgressions such as alcohol or drugs abuse where treatment could be administered compulsorily, but also in an emphasis on the desirability of prophylactic policy in healthcare. All the Nordic countries experimented with some form of state control of alcohol consumption during the early twentieth century, under the influence of strong temperance movements.[60]

Secondly, many scholars have noted the early development of the centralized state in Scandinavia, and the state's role in promoting top-down reform – most famously through the great agrarian reforms of the eighteenth century, for example – which meant that it was generally regarded as a benign force and its presence in citizens' lives was largely tolerated.[61] From the early twentieth century this was coupled with a strong faith in the ability of technology, rational planning and social engineering to transform society for the better and to promote economic efficiency and prosperity.

The best-known example of this enthusiasm for social engineering could be found in the population debates of the 1930s. Early twentieth-century Scandinavia was affected by a profound pessimism about the ability of the national populations to reproduce themselves, in the wake of declining birth rates and mass emigration to the New World. As in many other parts of Europe, this meant that family life was thus placed at the centre of many early social reforms. However, the policies that were proposed differed in important ways from the pro-natalist ideas found in many (Catholic) parts of Europe, such as France and Germany. The most influential contribution to the debate was Alva and Gunnar Myrdal's *Kris i befolkningsfrågan* (1934), but this was mirrored by similar texts elsewhere in the Nordic countries, such as the Norwegian Margarete Bonnevie's *Familiekrisen og botemidler mot den* (1935).[62] The Myrdals made radical proposals for the collectivization of the public sphere and of family life, to be realized in practical terms through the provision of practical help, both in cash and in kind, for families and collective childcare in order to allow mothers to participate in the labour market.[63] These policies were to be combined with improved education about and access to birth control; having children was to be a rational, planned activity. The full impact of these ideas, and the Myrdals' radical challenge to the prevailing 'housewives' contract' (*husmorskontrakt*), were not fully realized until the 1960s or after, but the Scandinavian countries did stand out in comparison to the rest of inter-war Europe for their provision of economic assistance to working-class families, and their tolerance of married women's employment and of contraception and abortion.[64]

A further example of Nordic exceptionalism in this respect may be found in the eugenicist laws passed in all four mainland Nordic countries in 1934. Supporters of eugenics could be found across Europe and North America in the early twentieth century, but only in a handful of countries, including Switzerland, Nazi Germany and the Nordic countries, did this result in legislation. Denmark was the first European state to introduce a legal provision for eugenic sterilization in 1929.[65] The 1934 laws permitted the use of involuntary sterilization on eugenic grounds where individuals were deemed legally incompetent to give their consent, usually on grounds of mental incapacity. The intention of the laws was to prevent the transmission of mental disabilities or illness thought to be hereditary, though sterilization was also indicated for medical reasons, for example to prevent further pregnancies in women exhausted by repeated childbearing.

Between 1935 and the 1975 many thousands of sterilizations were carried out under this legislation, nearly 63,000 in Sweden alone.[66] The eugenic indication was used extensively in the early years of the legislation: 82 per cent of sterilizations carried out in Sweden in 1942 were performed for eugenic reasons, nearly all of them affecting individuals deemed to be mentally retarded.[67] The question of how many of these were compulsory, that is, carried out without the patient's consent, is more difficult to answer. Unlike Nazi eugenicists, the Scandinavian medical authorities preferred persuasion rather than force, but the line between the two was sometimes blurred. Sterilization was frequently made a condition of discharge from an institution, such as an asylum or special school, or before marriage where one or both partners was thought to be suffering from a hereditary condition (it should also be noted that Sweden prohibited the marriage of epileptics until 1968).[68] For many women, sterilization was often granted in connection with abortion, and although some women may have accepted it gratefully as an effective means of contraception, there is also evidence of young and vulnerable patients giving their consent to a procedure they did not really understand, and which they came to regret in later life.[69]

It should be noted that eugenics in Scandinavia never became associated with the pseudo-scientific racial ideas that it accrued in Nazi Germany. The reasoning behind eugenic sterilization was economic efficiency and productive capacity, not race: if the low birth rate was to be overcome, then it was essential to create a healthy, efficient and productive population.[70] Nonetheless, it cannot be denied that certain social groups were clearly over-represented in the figures for sterilization, among them the working classes, women and the *tattare* or traveller population. Although the presence of the last group was undoubtedly accounted for in part by the racist assumptions prevailing in most European societies in the inter-war period, what it indicates above all is that the laws affected the poorest and most marginal groups disproportionately. It would be hard to disagree with the assessment of the Swedish scholars Gunnar Broberg and Mattias Tydén that, in Sweden at least, 'in practice the implementation of the sterilization laws came to focus on persons perceived as different'.[71] The diagnosis of mental incapacity was frequently applied, by the standards of the time, to those who challenged social norms rather than those who were genuinely suffering from mental illness, and in practice the laws were also used as a means to control female sexuality in particular.[72]

Although eugenicist sterilization generated some controversy in the 1990s, there was little of this at the time.[73] The laws attracted broad support across the political spectrum, and were opposed only by a small group of Catholics and political conservatives.[74] For the social democrats who supported compulsory sterilization, including Steincke, the Myrdals and Gustav Möller, eugenicist policies were motivated only when combined with social reform that would make family life more decent and humane.[75] Few saw a contradiction between the liberal concern with individual freedom and their aspirations to harness the new possibilities for state planning and intervention in order to create the good society. Steincke stated his vision of a welfare system that was 'humane but not soft, democratic but not demagogic, a blend of radical and conservative so far as is necessary if we are not to end in reaction or Bolshevism. It would distinguish itself both from the bleeding-heart sentimentalism that is so nauseating and from the ice-cold rationality that is so chilling.[76] The welfare state came during the inter-war period to stand above all for modernity; for societies that were organized in new ways characterized by efficiency, rationality and hygiene. This aspiration came to acquire its own aesthetic in the contemporary functionalist movement for architecture and design, epitomized above all in the Stockholm Exhibition of 1930. Leading functionalist architects, such as Uno Åhren, Gunnar Asplund and Sven Markelius, were co-opted by the state to help construct the new *folkhem* or People's Home, and to provide bright, comfortable and rationally designed new housing.[77]

The assumption of a link between social policy and economic efficiency remained central to the expansion of the Scandinavian welfare state after 1945. As Jenny Andersson has shown, social democratic policy in Sweden in the 1950s was marked by a remarkable confidence in the ability of the state to shape the good society, and the recognition of the close relationship between the welfare state and the successful management of the capitalist economy. High and stable rates of economic growth (*tillväxt*) were a prerequisite for high levels of welfare (*trygghet*), but the opposite was also true: a stable economy required a comprehensive welfare state.[78] The metaphor of the 'strong society' (*det starka samhället*) came to be regarded as the guiding light for the adaptation of a new generation of social democrats to the era of mass affluence.[79] Perhaps the best example of this type of thinking was the active labour market policy pursued through the Swedish Labour Market Board (Arbetsmarknadsstyrelsen or AMS), which now became the principal policy tool for tackling unemployment.[80] The Swedish welfare state was thus not just a fortunate by-product of the so-called record years (*rekordåren*), but a crucial influence in shaping the Scandinavian transition from poverty to affluence.

As such, it came to be closely identified not only with social democracy as a political project, but with the idea of Nordic nationhood more generally. This was most famously expressed in the Swedish concept of the welfare state as the 'people's home' (*folkhem*). The term was first used in the early twentieth century as part of a conservative polemic against the internationalism of the labour movement, but it was adopted by Per Albin Hansson during the mid-1920s, and described in a famous and much-quoted speech to the Riksdag in 1928:[81]

> The foundation of the home is community and solidarity. The good home knows no privilege or neglect, no favourites and no stepchildren. There, no one looks down on another, no one strives to gain advantage at the expense of others, the strong do not repress and rob the weak. In the good home equality, thoughtfulness, co-operation and helpfulness prevail. Applied to the great people's and citizens' home this would mean the breakdown of all social and economic barriers that now divide citizens into privileged and deprived, into the rulers and the ruled, into rich and poor, the propertied and the destitute, the robbers and the robbed. Swedish society is not yet the good citizens' home . . . If [it] is to become [so] class differences must be banished, social care must be developed, there must be an economic levelling out, the workers must be accorded a share on economic administration, democracy must be introduced and applied to social and economic life.[82]

Although the *folkhem* expression did not translate directly into the other Nordic countries, the links between the welfare state and national identity were no less strong than they were in Sweden. Inevitably, this meant that the challenges to the welfare state from the late twentieth century came to be perceived to some extent as direct challenges to the very idea of Nordic nationhood, as will be examined in the final part of the chapter.

CHALLENGE AND REFORM: THE NORDIC WELFARE STATE SINCE THE 1960S

The first major ideological challenge to the post-war welfare states came not from the political right but from the left. According to the

critique of the so-called new left, by the late 1960s the social democratic parties were presiding over a paradox: why did inequality
persist after two decades of more or less undisturbed economic
growth and the construction of a comprehensive welfare system?
Rather than being regarded as the necessary condition for the expansion of welfare, economic growth was instead seen as the source of
new social problems that were articulated with a new vocabulary:
alienation, social exclusion, environmental degradation.[83] The
redesigned town centres and new functionalist housing blocks
constructed through the Swedish 'million homes' programme came
to stand not for the rational, efficient and cosy people's home, but as
a concrete and brutal symbol of social alienation. Perhaps one of the
best-known and enduring symbols of this discontent came to be the
Danish community and self-proclaimed 'free town' of Christiania,
established on the site of an old barracks in Copenhagen in 1971.[84]

The social democrats were forced to respond to these criticisms by
the electoral defeats of the 1970s. Under a new generation of youthful and radical leaders, the parties stated their commitment to tackle
inequality.[85] Nowhere was this more marked than in a new emphasis on gender equality, and the adoption of new social policies, in
particular state-run childcare and generous maternity benefits,
designed to enable women to combine the care of young children
with paid employment.[86] This happened in Sweden from the 1960s,
in Denmark from the 1970s and in Norway from the 1980s,
promoted by Gro Harlem Brundtland's Labour government elected in
1986. Many of the women affected found employment in the expanding public sector. By the 1990s the Nordic labour markets
demonstrated some of the highest female labour force participation
rates in the world, a characteristic that was described by many scholars as a further distinctive feature of the Nordic welfare model.[87]
Indeed, it has been suggested that the Scandinavian welfare state has
helped to undermine the status of the family, given that the state has
assumed responsibility in areas previously regarded as belonging to
the sphere of the family, such as caring for very young and very old
citizens. In doing so, the welfare state helped not to undermine individual autonomy, as some critics have suggested, but to strengthen it

by freeing citizens from their family obligations as well as from the constraints of the market.[88]

The impact of the new family and childcare policies should not be over emphasized, however, for there is also evidence to suggest that women's participation in paid employment pre-dated the expansion of the welfare state in the 1960s and after.[89] Nordic women had in fact already made progress towards economic citizenship during the early twentieth century with the enactment of marriage laws that were advanced by European standards in their recognition of women's rights.[90] Tolerance of the dual breadwinner model was born out of necessity in countries where low birth rates and high levels of emigration created an acute labour shortage around the turn of the century.[91] In agrarian societies men and women had traditionally shared the heavy farming work between them, and thus the dual breadwinner model had become institutionalized long *before* the expansion of the welfare state, especially in Finland and Iceland.[92] Norway was exceptional here, because the ideology of sexual difference seemed to be stronger and more enduring than in the other Nordic countries, and married women were barred from paid employment by legislation in the 1930s.[93] The adoption of wage-earner social insurance systems further helped to institutionalize Nordic gender patterns because it meant that married women were entitled to benefits on the basis of citizenship rather than as wives and mothers.

It remains a matter for debate whether the combination of structural circumstances, the wage-earner benefit system and extensive family policies has actually helped to challenge traditional patterns of gender relations and promote gender equality.[94] Despite high rates of female participation, the Nordic labour markets remained highly segregated, with women and men continuing to enter particular types of occupations, and this has been reflected in persistent inequalities in pay between men and women.[95] The adoption of an income security-based benefits system made no difference in principle between men and women, but reproduced in practice the pay differences already existing in the labour market.[96] In Iceland, the high number of women in paid employment was associated above all with the expansion of part-time work.[97] Moreover, although family policies permitted women to re-organize their lives around the double burden of childcare and employment, they did not challenge traditional gender relations.[98] Only during the 1990s and after were caring and family responsibilities debated more thoroughly in terms of men's roles, but even here there seemed to be more rhetoric than concrete action.[99] At the beginning of the twenty-first century all the Nordic countries had instituted some provision for paid paternity leave, and even required fathers to take a limited amount of this (e.g., a month), but only Sweden had gone as far as debating proposals for a compulsory and equal division of the full period of leave between both parents.

The left-wing critique of the welfare state ultimately had a relatively modest impact, for it was easily absorbed. More significant therefore was the political challenge presented from the right. This took two forms: on the one hand it amounted to a moral critique of the welfare state, and the 'sinful' behaviour and permissive values that it was thought to promote, which resulted in the foundation of Christian-based parties in the Scandinavian countries between 1958 and 1970.[100] Secondly and more importantly, the right was critical of the extent to which the comprehensive welfare state appeared to compromise individual freedom. There was nothing new in this, of course; these concerns formed part of the bourgeois response to the social democratic concept of the 'strong society' during the 1950s, which partly motivated the bourgeois parties' opposition to the proposed supplementary pension reforms in Sweden.[101] But from the early 1970s these ideas found political expression in the emergence of new right-wing parties. The Progress Parties of Denmark and Norway made their electoral breakthroughs in the early 1970s campaigning on a platform of tax reform and anti-bureaucracy. Their critique of the Scandinavian welfare systems as overpowering monoliths forcing their citizens into drab conformity was mirrored in the international literature with the publication of the journalist Roland Huntford's polemic, *The New Totalitarians*, in 1971.[102]

Their case was given further weight, especially in Denmark, by the contemporary economic difficulties caused by the rise in the price of oil.[103] As Jenny Andersson has shown, the main result of this was to undermine the link between growth and welfare in political discourse.[104] While Social Democrats had successfully argued in the 1950s and '60s that welfare and the 'strong society' were the prerequisites for economic growth and efficiency, now they stood accused of hindering economic effectiveness. It was not merely that the welfare state had become an unaffordable luxury in times of economic hardship, but that it was an actual hindrance to economic growth. According to the neo-liberal economics gathering steam especially in the English-speaking world, the large public sectors and generous benefit systems associated with the Nordic welfare states acted as a brake on economic productivity, efficiency and flexibility.

As discussed in chapter Three, however, the impact of the economic difficulties of the 1970s was relatively limited in the Scandinavian countries in the longer term. The most severely affected was Denmark, and here neo-liberalism did indeed make some impact during the ten years of bourgeois government from 1982 to 1992. Perhaps most significantly, the Danish government was forced to abandon the goal of full employment as early as 1973–4. In Sweden and Finland, economic reform (in Sweden under the auspices of the Social Democratic Party's 'third way') took the form of financial deregulation during the 1980s. But there was no Thatcherite attempt to dismantle the welfare state. On the contrary, welfare spending actually expanded during the 1970s, much of it as a result of the new policies on parental leave and collective childcare discussed above.[105]

For this reason, the various stock-taking assessments of the Nordic welfare model that appeared during the 1990s and after demonstrated a striking degree of consensus in their conclusions that the model remained intact. Even more remarkable, most of these analyses came after the very severe economic crises of the early 1990s in Finland and Sweden, when it did indeed seem for a while that the welfare state was about to be fundamentally reformed, perhaps even dismantled. Most scholars seem to conclude that this did not happen. There was some minor tinkering with the details of policy but the basic tenets of the Scandinavian welfare model remained intact.[106]

There was some evidence for a decrease in generosity: benefit levels were reduced and the periods over which they could be claimed were shortened; eligibility requirements were tightened; and more emphasis was placed on rehabilitation and training. But these cuts were generally part of a pragmatic, short-term response to economic difficulties, rather than a comprehensive programme for reform. State benefits remained relatively generous in comparison with other countries, though 'the balance between universal, earnings-related and means-tested components of social reform' was altered.[107] There was no substantial increase in inequality or deterioration of living standards.[108]

That said, the welfare state continues to be the source of much debate, within political and policy-making circles and within academic ones: indeed, the field of welfare state studies seems to have become a veritable industry in the Nordic countries during the 1990s and afterwards. During the early part of the decade, much of this academic discourse was highly critical, especially in Sweden. The apparent demise of the social democratic project in the midst of economic crisis produced a sense of disillusionment with the welfare state as the epitome of twentieth-century social democracy. Drawing on the work of Michel Foucault (who had developed some of his ideas on the operation of power while a young and apparently unhappy student at Uppsala University during the 1950s), several influential studies criticized the welfare state as an institution of social control, and emphasized its role in creating normative categories such as normality and abnormality.[109] Matters came to a head with the highly public debate on eugenic sterilization, and the award of government compensation to some of those affected by the policy.[110]

The storm of controversy raised by the sterilization debate died away remarkably swiftly. By 2007 what distinguished the political discourse seemed to be instead the *absence* of any challenge to the legitimacy of the welfare state. There were in the early twenty-first century no political parties in Scandinavia opposing the welfare state. On the contrary, most of them positioned themselves as its defender, against the appearance of new internal and external threats. These can be summarized briefly. First, in common with the rest of Europe, one of the most serious problems is the ageing of the population and the consequent increase in dependency ratios. With the continued escalation of costs for providing healthcare in particular, it seems that Nordic governments will inevitably be forced to contemplate some means of rationing and the introduction of more non-state provision of welfare services. Secondly, long-term unemployment, much of it existing in the form of high rates of long-term sickness or disability, appears to be a problem for many of the Nordic countries, and for some economists the only viable cure would be to trim the generous benefit systems and incorporate greater elements of rehabilitation and training. Indeed, this formed part of the electoral programme of the new bourgeois government elected in Sweden in September 2006. Thirdly, the thesis of globalization suggests reduced autonomy for the nation state, and that generous welfare systems may become a luxury in an international economy favouring flexibility above all. The effects of this are probably overstated; indeed, the survival of the Nordic welfare states is interpreted by some as providing evidence that ideology and government policy still matter in a globalized world.[111] The Scandinavian economies were historically small, open and dependent on exports.[112] Governments have moreover claimed to have adapted their social policy to the new conditions, for example in the Danish government's attempt to brand its combination of active labour market policy with generous social rights as 'flexicurity'.[113]

Fourthly, and most controversially, some would see the Nordic welfare states as vulnerable to the related external pressures of European integration and immigration. The debates on Nordic EU membership during the mid-1990s reflected these fears: would European integration dilute the Nordic model? More recently, the focus of 'welfare nationalism' as a political phenomenon has shifted to the question of immigration and multiculturalism, with right-wing parties such as the Danish People's Party and the Norwegian Progress Party most outspoken in their portrayal of mass immigration as an unaffordable burden on the welfare state.[114] Perhaps rather surprisingly, there are signs that this trend seems to have been mirrored within the academic discourse, where the recent 'historical turn' (or alternatively 'cultural turn') in welfare state research has tended to paint the welfare state in terms of its roots in national historical specificity: state formation, Lutheranism, pre-modern social structure and cultural values. The clearest example of this trend was Henrik Berggren and Lars Trägårdh's provocative title *Är svensken människa?* (2006), which suggested that the Swedish welfare state rested on a peculiarly Swedish 'theory of love' defined by its emphasis on equality and respect for individual self-reliance (*oberoende*).[115]

CONCLUSION

Any attempt to create typologies of welfare models is inevitably concerned with ideal types. No matter what method of classification is used, no welfare state will exhibit all the features identified as belonging to that type: most welfare states are instead mixed systems. The creation of typologies can even lead to deterministic thinking that tends to homogenize cases and ignore the important differences between them.[116] Nonetheless, and despite these caveats, there is a broad consensus that the similarities between the Nordic welfare states were more important than the differences, and that it is possible, therefore, to talk of a Nordic welfare model, even though it may be preferable to speak of 'one model with five exceptions'.[117] Perhaps the most important difference is that the Nordic welfare regimes were indeed welfare states, where for most of the twentieth century the state had indisputably the largest role as the provider of welfare, and other institutions such as the family, voluntary organizations and private philanthropy were correspondingly small.

Moreover, there were also important similarities in the historical development of the Nordic welfare model. As elsewhere, the waxing and waning of the welfare state in the Nordic countries has been linked to periods of economic growth and crisis. The growth of welfare states has also been influenced by international political events, though the experience of the Second World War had less impact on welfare policies in Scandinavia than it did in the UK, for example. That said, it should be acknowledged that the welfare state was also part of the ideological weaponry of the Cold War, and that despite important differences in their foreign policies all five Nordic countries promoted the idea of the Nordic model as a 'middle way' between communism and free market capitalism.[118] This suggests, as I have attempted to do throughout this book, that the term 'Nordic model' needs to be understood on two levels. Although it has some heuristic value as a category of analysis for comparative social scientists, most of its power was derived from its role as a discourse: a means of imagining and describing this part of the world. For some foreign observers Sweden in particular continues to allure as the model of social policy par excellence, though now as previously this role seems to be based on utopic visions rather than a truly informed view. Further, where the Nordic welfare model was once seen as resting on universal values and thus available for export, recently it has been discussed in increasingly ethnic terms. Even if not all would seek to discriminate between groups of citizens' entitlement to welfare benefits as some politicians have argued for, especially in Denmark, there has been considerable debate over how or whether the welfare state should promote assimilation, integration or multi-culturalism. This might prove to be the most important challenge for the Nordic welfare states in the future.

Even so, many would agree that the view of the Nordic model as utopia is justified.[119] The criticism of the welfare state as an instrument of social control is valid, but should not be overstated. Against the more negative side must stand the very impressive achievements of the Scandinavian welfare systems: the Nordic countries consistently top international surveys and comparisons based on measurements of indicators such as health, education, life expectancy and social equality. The question now is whether this achievement is sustainable. Increasingly, the welfare state, and the ideas and ideology that underpinned it, is beginning to look like a project of modernity above all, and one that might have a questionable relevance in a post-modern, globalized world. Perhaps the most significant shift of all is the apparent loss of confidence in the welfare state as a force for good, and a disappearance of the ambition to use innovative welfare policy in order to create the good society. Although few would challenge the legitimacy of the welfare state, equally few – if any – seem confident enough to articulate a vision for its future: instead, the welfare-supporting parties of Scandinavia seem to base their statements on a defensive nostalgia for the 'good old days' of a mythical past. For the moment, however, the welfare state is still regarded as an integral part of the meaning of Scandinavia.

Chapter 4

Between East and West? The Nordic Countries in International Relations

The existence of the Nordic region as a geo-political entity was taken for granted in international relations for most of the twentieth century. From the inter-war period the governments of Denmark, Norway and Sweden had made some efforts to present a united front to the outside world and, in turn, outsiders had begun to perceive them as a bloc. This tendency was reinforced by Scandinavian participation in international institutions such as the League of Nations, where seats on the Council and the League's other committees were rotated between the four Nordic countries in turn.[1]

During the period 1949–91, the status of Scandinavia as a distinct region gained a further dimension within the bipolar configurations of the Cold War, so that it now came to be seen as occupying a special position between east and west. Scandinavia's reputation for innovative social policy was mirrored by its status as a 'security community', distinguished by its common institutions, its mutual sense of identity and above all its peacefulness. War between the different Nordic countries had become unthinkable. Indeed, according to one recent survey, 'the Nordic area has been perhaps *the* area in Europe where there has been least expectation of conflict throughout much of the nineteenth century and the twentieth century'.[2] In 1957 the political scientist Karl Deutsch suggested that Scandinavia could serve as the model for building such a security community on a grander scale in the Atlantic region.[3] The governments of the Nordic states promoted this idea through their continued engagement in international organizations such as the United Nations and their apparent willingness to use their status as small states to work towards reducing superpower tensions and fostering peace in international relations. This aspiration was personified in prominent Nordic politicians such as Olof Palme and Gro Harlem Brundtland. It was also strengthened by the ideological polarity of the Cold War, and the representation of Scandinavia as an ideological 'middle way' between the extremes of capitalism and communism.

Since the end of the Cold War in 1989–91, however, the idea of the Nordic security community has been questioned. What seemed to be striking about the Scandinavian countries during the period 1949–91 was in fact the *failure* of efforts to promote Nordic cooperation and unification, at least at the level of 'high' politics and economics. Two ventures in particular, the proposals for a Scandinavian Defence Alliance in the late 1940s, and several attempts to form a Scandinavian customs union, both foundered. The foreign policies of the Scandinavian countries seemed instead to have been driven by narrow nationalist interests throughout the period. According to Petri Joenniemi, the Nordic peace was thus not a successful model for emulation by other parts of the world so much as an unintended peace, which came about accidentally.[4] In this way, the geo-political idea of 'Norden' differed fundamentally from the 'Europe' of the European Union.[5]

This chapter will consider the reasons for the apparent failure of formal Nordic cooperation, but it is also concerned with a wider question: how significant was 'Norden' in geo-political terms? What did the Nordic countries share with each other in terms of international relations? Nordic history seemed to point towards division rather than unity; indeed, one Nordic historian has described the inter-war period as an 'ice-age' in intra-Nordic relations.[6] There had been peace in the region since 1814, but during the first half of the twentieth century, at least, there was always the possibility that differences between the Scandinavian countries would lead to war, as the various crises in intra-Scandinavian relations attest: the break up of the Swedish-Norwegian union in 1905; the Finnish–Swedish dispute over the Åland islands in the 1920s and the Danish–Norwegian Arctic conflict in the 1930s. During the inter-war period the Scandinavian states developed closer relations united by their vulnerability as small neutral states, but ultimately national differences proved irreconcilable and prevented the establishment of a closer Nordic union. Danish governments were dominated by fears of German expansion; in Finland the main fear was the Soviet Union, as it was in Sweden, although this was partly mitigated by the presence of Finnish territory to shield the Swedish border. For Norwegian politicians, meanwhile, Swedish dominance remained a constant threat for many years after 1905, and produced a reorientation of Norwegian international and trading relations towards Britain and the north Atlantic.

THE LEGACY OF THE SECOND WORLD WAR IN SCANDINAVIA

The aspirations of the nineteenth-century pan-Scandinavianists to unite Denmark, Norway and Sweden into one state had faded by the beginning of the twentieth century, and with their demise came the end of any residual ambition to achieve great power status in Europe. Instead, the main challenge for the Scandinavian states during the inter-war period was to adapt to their vulnerability as small states within an unstable international system. The rather frosty intra-Nordic relations of the first decades of the twentieth century had by the 1930s given way to attempts to promote greater cooperation between the Scandinavian states. Indeed, Scandinavia became something of a pioneer region in the use of cross-national institutions to settle regional conflicts.[7] From before the First World War, representatives of the Scandinavian governments met regularly to discuss their common interests, and even to negotiate common guiding principles on their neutral status.[8] The deteriorating international situation during the 1930s gave an even greater impetus to their talks, to the extent that the possibility of a Nordic defence pact was discussed, though never realized.[9] Following independence in 1917, Finland too was increasingly drawn into this Nordic fold.[10]

There were, however, limitations to these aspirations to Nordic unity. In a speech that was delivered in 1934, yet foreshadows the nature of post-war Nordic cooperation, the Swedish prime minister Per Albin Hansson stated:

> [w]e have never been subject to any illusions about a fusion [among the Scandinavian states] which eliminates all reasons for friction; we have not dreamed of new unions which would make Scandinavia into a Great Power in the usual sense; we do not speculate about defence pacts and such things. What we strove for and are striving for, is nothing other that a trusting and practical co-operation without any encroachment on the various countries' independence.[11]

Moreover, even these limited aspirations to Nordic unity were to be severely tested by the events of 1939–40. All four Scandinavian states were determined to uphold their neutrality on the outbreak of war in Europe, but the position of Norway and Iceland in the strategically sensitive north Atlantic, and the importance of resources such as Swedish iron ore to the German war economy, meant that they were unlikely to avoid being drawn into the conflict.[12] The Soviet Union's invasion of Finland in November 1939 divided the Swedish government, with the foreign minister Rickard Sandler advocating a defensive alliance to assist Finland, but others, including the prime minister Per Albin Hansson, upholding non-intervention as the only strategy to keep Sweden out of the war.[13] Nonetheless, Finland's so-called Winter War provoked widespread sympathy among the Swedish population. The Swedish government donated humanitarian aid; Swedish families received many thousands of Finnish child evacuees; and approximately 8,000 Swedish volunteers went to fight in Finland, motivated by the sentiment expressed in the slogan 'Finland's cause is our cause'. This response to the war in Finland was in contrast to Swedish passivity following the Nazi invasion of Norway and Denmark in April 1940.

The Second World War thus did little to consolidate the fragile sense of Nordic unity that had begun to emerge during the 1930s. If anything, the experiences of the years 1939–45 had the opposite effect, promoting a strong sense of national unity and loyalty to wartime policies in each country. The Swedish failure to intervene in the fight for Norway in 1940 was regarded with great bitterness by many Norwegians, and this was compounded by what were seen as Swedish concessions to the Germans, notably regarding the passage of German troops and military equipment through Sweden to Norway. Over three years, approximately two million German soldiers entered and left Norwegian territory via this route: the so-called *permitteringstrafik*.[14] As Francis Sejersted has pointed out, the Second World War must therefore be seen as one of the major crises in twentieth-century Swedish–Norwegian relations, following the breakup of the union in 1905.[15] For occupied Denmark and Norway, the war came to be seen mainly as a moral struggle against the Nazis. The small numbers of active resistance fighters in each country were acclaimed as heroes, but, as in many other parts of occupied Europe, 'resistance' was broadly defined to include all forms of civilian non-cooperation and disobedience, both active and passive. Resistance thus became a category with which the majority of the population could identify. This was especially the case in Norway, where the efforts of Quisling and his Nasjonal Samling (National Unity) party to 'nazify' Norwegian society meant that the conflict was seen in ideological terms to a greater extent than in Denmark.[16]

Despite these differences, however, the response to war in its immediate aftermath was similar in Denmark, Norway and Sweden. First, despite the experience of occupation in Denmark and Norway, there was relatively little long-term disruption to either the constitutional machinery or to everyday life. In the words of one Danish historian, 'significant remnants of the forms and regulated patterns of behaviour which we call civilisation were able to survive'.[17] For this reason, in retrospect the war came to be seen not so much as a domestic watershed, but instead as an unwanted interruption to the great social democratic project begun during the 1930s. Secondly, the wartime experience generated in each case a strong feeling of consensus and national unity: in Norway and Denmark the heroism of the resistance; in Sweden the pragmatism of neutrality. This sense of unity allowed the social democratic parties of Norway and Sweden, under a new generation of relatively youthful leaders, to consolidate their position and expand the ambitious programme of social reform begun during the 1930s.[18] In Norway, the leaders of the Labour Party, many of whom had spent the war in exile, entered government in 1945 determined to put the war behind them and proceed with the task of building a social democratic society.[19] But it was in non-combatant Sweden, above all, that the war years were seen as a distraction from the main course of history, when normal political life had been disrupted by the anomalies of the party truce and the need for unity behind the government's crisis policy (kristidspolitik).[20] As Åsa Linderborg has pointed out, the Swedish Social Democratic Party was unique in that it was the anti-fascists, not the collaborators, that were threatened with expulsion after the war. Individuals such as Ture Nerman, editor of the wartime opposition journal Trots Allt!, were isolated within the party for their criticism of the government's pragmatism.[21]

For Finland and Iceland the war years came to represent more of a watershed. In Finland, the two wars fought against the Soviet Union between 1939 and 1944 resulted in defeat, territorial losses and the imposition of an obligation to pay economic reparations to the Soviet Union. The war was influential in three ways: first, it created a sense of national unity that helped to heal the animosities stemming from the 1918 civil war; and secondly, the Winter War in particular raised international awareness of Finland. Thirdly, and most importantly, the experience of war forced the Finnish political elite to acknowledge the need to accommodate the strength and proximity of the Soviet Union if Finnish independence were to be preserved.[22] For Iceland, the Second World War also meant occupation, when the government agreed to accept the presence of first British and then American troops to guarantee its security.

Although the occupation was thus voluntary rather than forcible, the presence of foreign troops nonetheless provoked fears about the contamination of Icelandic culture.[23] Meanwhile, the Nazi invasion of Denmark in 1940 meant *de facto* independence for Iceland, and an Icelandic Republic was formally proclaimed on 17 June 1944. Independence was acclaimed by the political elite as the culmination of 700 years of struggle, and 60,000 people assembled at Þingvellir, the site of the medieval Alþingi, to celebrate this achievement.[24]

SCANDINAVIA DURING THE COLD WAR

The divergent experiences of the Nordic countries during the Second World War contributed to shattering the fragile sense of Nordic unity achieved during the inter-war period. Events during the immediate post-war years did little to soothe these tensions. In Sweden, neutrality seemed to have been vindicated by the experiences of the Second World War, and the government now came forward as the self-appointed leader of the Nordic bloc. This did not attract enthusiasm in Norway, where the Swedish position was seen, in the words of Halvard Lange, as an attempt 'to demonstrate control, so to speak, of the unruly child Norway, which had begun to go its own way'.[25] In May 1948, against the background of the Berlin airlift and mounting international tension, the Swedish prime minister Tage Erlander put forward a proposal for a Scandinavian Defence Alliance as a means to prevent divergence between the Nordic countries and to protect the credibility of the Swedish government's own neutrality policy. Negotiations over the pact took place over the winter of 1948–9, but collapsed following a meeting in Oslo in January 1949.[26]

The failure of the attempt to establish a Scandinavian Defence Alliance reflected the different experiences of the war in the Scandinavian countries. Neutrality might have been vindicated as an unqualified success in Sweden, but this was not the case in Denmark and Norway. Rather, the Second World War had 'conclusively demonstrated their small power status to the Nordic countries, the end of the possibility of isolationism, and their subjection to the international system'.[27] In Denmark, the effect of the war had been to revive the 'fear of going under' (undergangsångst) that had been a driving force behind foreign policy ever since the defeat by Prussia in 1864.[28] Invasion and occupation had demonstrated that isolation and neutrality were no longer possible. Bevin's speech on the development of the North Atlantic Alliance in January 1948 was positively received in Norway, and by the end of the year it was clear that both states would be invited to join the new NATO.[29] According to Barbara Haskel, however, the main reason for the ultimate failure of the Scandinavian Defence Alliance was not so much the divergent experiences of the war or Norway's reorientation towards the United Kingdom as the failure to resolve fundamental differences between the three national leaders on several key questions. The Swedish government emphasized the deterrent effect of a potential pact, while the Norwegians put more faith in the Americans. Moreover, the domestic political environments in all three countries were different, with the Swedish government able to draw on solid popular support for neutrality, while the ruling Danish and Norwegian social democratic parties faced internal dissent over the direction of their foreign policy.[30] The Oslo meeting agreed to abandon the attempt to set up a SDA, and in March 1949 Denmark and Norway signed the NATO treaty.

The stabilization of international relations after the end of the Korean War thus revealed Scandinavia to be a divided region. The division was a three-way one. Denmark, Norway and Iceland became founding members of NATO in 1949, but membership of the alliance remained politically controversial and all three countries joined on minimum conditions that prohibited the stationing of foreign troops within their territories. The Norwegian Labour Party was seriously divided over the issue, with clear majorities within its central committee and the influential Oslo branch in favour of joining, but many Storting members and grassroots activists opposed. The communists were also staunchly opposed to NATO, both in Norway and Denmark. Yet such was the moral authority commanded by the Labour Party leader and prime minister, Einar Gerhardsen, that once he had publicly decided in favour of the NATO option, he was able to take most of the party with him and get the policy unanimously agreed at the party's congress in February 1949.[31] Opposition to the treaty did not simply disappear, however, and was to surface again in the formation of a new Socialist People's Party (Sosialistisk Folkeparti) in 1961. In post-war Denmark, the Social Democratic Party largely ignored the question of foreign policy, preferring to maintain its pre-war stance of neutrality. No mention of foreign policy was made in the party's 1945 programme, 'The Future of Denmark'. Its main concern was to regain the confidence of the working class and to reduce communist influence in the trade union movement. However, the Social Democratic government's acceptance of the Marshall Plan in June 1947, as a necessary remedy for the severe balance of payments difficulties in the Danish economy, helped to change these attitudes and may be seen as the first step away from neutrality.[32]

In Iceland, NATO membership proved to be of less direct relevance in determining foreign and security policy than the bilateral defence treaty signed with the USA in 1951. Under the conditions of the treaty, the USA undertook formally to defend Iceland, while the Icelandic government was to facilitate the stationing of American troops in the strategically sensitive north Atlantic by maintaining the Keflavík air base. Decisions about the presence of these troops in Iceland were to be taken bilaterally. The treaty thus overrode the clause in Iceland's NATO accession agreement prohibiting the presence of foreign troops on Icelandic territory during peacetime.[33] Mirroring the internal opposition to NATO membership in Denmark and Norway, Iceland's formal alignment with the USA produced some political controversy.[34] The centre-right Independence Party remained consistently in favour of both NATO membership and the US presence, while the far left was equally consistently opposed and the centrist Progressive Party was divided. Following the period of détente after Stalin's death in 1953, opposition to the American base gained support. The pro-American Independence Party became isolated, and in 1956 a broad coalition government, including representatives of the Communist Party, took office with a commitment to undertake a thorough re-evaluation of Iceland security policy. The pendulum swung quickly back again following the Soviet Union's intervention in Hungary during the autumn of 1956, and the challenge to the base faded.[35] The special relationship with the USA was also cemented economically. US troops made a significant contribution to the economy, and Iceland received a large amount of Marshall aid, which continued well into the 1950s.

NATO membership was clearly never an option for Finland, given its close proximity to and relationship with the USSR. The years 1944–8 have been described as 'years of danger' for Finland. Internally, there were real fears that the country was vulnerable to a communist *coup d'état* similar to the one that took place in Czechoslovakia in 1948, though in fact there is no evidence that such an action was ever seriously contemplated in the spring of 1948, either by the radical left or the right.[36] The chaos and social instability of post-war Finland was probably no worse than that prevailing in most other parts of Europe at the same time. The external threat came from the expectation that Finland would be occupied following its defeat by the USSR in 1944, as Germany's other defeated allies were. Although the terms of the armistice were hard, with regard both to territorial losses and economic reparations, Finland was not occupied and survived with its pre-war institutions and constitutional machinery intact. It was the only post-1918 successor state to do so.

The cornerstone of Finnish foreign policy during the post-war era was the Treaty of Friendship, Mutual Co-operation and Assistance or YYA treaty (in Finnish *Sopimus ystävyydestä, yhteis-toiminnasta ja keskinäisestä avunannosta*), signed with the Soviet Union in April 1948.[37] This was not a military pact, although it did provide for Soviet military assistance to Finland if the country were to be attacked by Germany or its allies, and it also stipulated that Finland was to aid the USSR if the latter were attacked through Finnish territory. Under these terms, post-war Finnish foreign policy could be interpreted as a struggle for neutrality or at least to gain international acceptance of its nominal neutral status and the country's desire to remain outside 'antagonistic great power interests', as it was stated in the preamble to the treaty. Indeed, the insertion of this line constituted a major difference between the Finnish YYA treaty and the similar pacts between the USSR and other East European countries. An important milestone in this respect was the USSR's decision to return the leased Porkkala military base to Finland in 1955, which enhanced the status of Finnish neutrality in the eyes of the west.[38] The central tenet of Finnish foreign policy became the so-called Paasikivi-Kekkonen line, named after the two influential presidents who saw the maintenance of good relations with the Soviet Union as the principal guarantee of Finnish security. In this respect they departed from the more ambitious outlook of their predecessors during the inter-war period, though the roots of Paasikivi's pragmatism could be traced back to his support for an accommodation with imperial Russia during the last days of the grand duchy.[39]

President Kekkonen continued with this policy of accommodation, developing a strong personal relationship with his Soviet counterpart Khrushchev. During the 1960s Kekkonen's 'preventative diplomacy' attracted hostile criticism from some western observers, who suggested that the autonomy of the Finnish government had in fact become seriously constrained, and that Finland had been drawn into the Soviet sphere of influence to a degree that was incompatible with the sovereignty of an independent state. The pejorative term 'finlandization' was coined as a description of this state of affairs, and came to be used rhetorically in the domestic debates on foreign policy in other European countries, for example by the critics of Willy Brandt's Ostpolitik in West Germany.[40] In response, Finnish politicians maintained that western observers simply did not understand the precarious nature of the Finnish–Soviet relationship, and failed to recognize therefore that Finnish acquiescence to Soviet demands was largely voluntary, motivated by pragmatism.[41]

The extent to which Finnish independence was compromised has been widely debated in Finland since the end of the Cold War, even to the extent that the term 'finlandization' has been adopted into the Finnish language (*suomettuminen*; in Swedish *finlandisering*).[42] Where Kekkonen differed from his predecessor Paasikivi was in his recognition that Finnish foreign policy was unavoidably intertwined with domestic politics, and his critics have suggested that he skilfully manipulated his foreign policy concerns to suit his own domestic political interests. An example of this was the so-called Note Crisis of 1961–2 when the intervention of the Soviet Union apparently prevented a successful electoral challenge to Kekkonen's presidency.[43] Others have pointed to the apparent compliance of the Finnish political elite with Soviet wishes in security matters and the lack of a truly independent and critical media. By the 1970s self-censorship was practised widely throughout the mass media, and in some cases it went beyond pragmatic caution to include flattery, embellishment and distortion of the truth.[44] Against this, it could be pointed out that although the Finnish political and media elite were deferential, the rest of Finnish society was not 'finlandized'. Finland was never behind the Iron Curtain; it retained an uncensored cultural and intellectual life; and despite its long history as a grand duchy, Russian and Soviet culture had little impact. Indeed, American popular culture and patterns of consumption were as influential in Finland as elsewhere in the Nordic countries.[45]

On the face of it, Sweden's continued adherence to the traditional Scandinavian policy of non-alignment in peace, neutrality in war, seemed uncontroversial. Indeed, such was the popular consensus in support of the policy that neutrality became much more than an official doctrine. It was seen as a crucial part of Swedish identity, to which was attributed over a hundred years of peace and stability and the avoidance of two world wars, and to question it was tantamount to treason.[46] This continuity was a myth, of course. As recent studies have demonstrated, Swedish neutrality was a flexible policy that was adapted and readapted to the international situation.[47] Two points should be made about post-war Swedish neutrality: first it was not backed by any legal guarantees, as was the case in Switzerland, for example; and it was an armed neutrality, which was founded on the belief that national defence needed to be independent and capable of defending Sweden from attack. This stance was opposed outright by the communists, but many social democrats also found it necessary to compromise their strong moral support for disarmament. The defence industry became an important part of the economy, so that by the mid-1970s Swedish expenditure on defence as a proportion of GDP was second only to France among Western European states.[48]

As in Finland, the end of the Cold War sparked a major reappraisal of Swedish security policy, and the extent of Swedish non-alignment was questioned.[49] Swedish neutrality was predicated on the tacit assumption that any attack would come from the east, and that the USA and NATO would come to the rescue in the event of such an attack. This was confirmed in 1994 when an official inquiry revealed that the military and diplomatic elites had maintained extensive secret contacts between Sweden and NATO countries, including not only neighbouring Denmark and Norway but also the UK and the USA.[50] Moreover, although media scrutiny of foreign policy was probably more robust than it was in Finland, like many other western countries Sweden fought its own Cold War against the internal enemy of communism, and communists were routinely marginalized and kept under surveillance.[51]

The security configuration described here – Denmark, Norway and Iceland as members of NATO, Sweden and Finland neutral but tacitly semi-aligned – came to be known as the 'Nordic Balance'. This did not imply a balance of power in the nineteenth-century sense, but the term was more than merely descriptive of the security arrangements in the Nordic region. It was prescriptive, in that maintaining the Nordic Balance was understood to reflect the best interests of the Nordic states, and it also offered an explanation as to why Nordic security arrangements were as they were, with the Finnish–Soviet YYA treaty acting as a counter-balance to the NATO states. For some international observers, the Nordic Balance also came to be seen as an extension of the Nordic model. Scandinavia was cited as an example of a 'security community', defined as a region where international relations were characterized by little or no expectation of war, and where intra-regional tension had been replaced by a sense of mutual interdependence and 'we-feeling'.[52]

The Nordic governments have also helped to promote this view of the region, acting either collaboratively or unilaterally to establish the idea of the Scandinavian countries as the world's peacemakers and conscience.[53] The foreign policy of all the Nordic countries during the Cold War era was informed by the belief that small states should play an active role in international affairs.[54] This aim was partly pursued through the United Nations, where the Scandinavian nations received extra prominence through the appointment of the Norwegian Trygve Lie (1946–52) and then the Swede Dag Hammarskjöld (1953–61) as secretaries-general. With the exception of Iceland, which was simply too small to be able to spare the necessary resources, the Nordic governments also established a reputation for generosity in their support of overseas aid programmes.[55] The political scientist Christine Ingebritsen has suggested that the Nordic countries have acted as 'norm entrepreneurs', using their status as small states to try to achieve a moral influence over international policy in three important areas: environmental policy, international security and global welfare. This she sees as the logical extension of the Scandinavian commitment to social solidarity at home, while at the same time the historic legacy of non-engagement in international conflict made such a strategy possible.[56]

It is true that Scandinavian foreign policy owes something to the legacy of Socialist internationalism and idealism informing the foreign policy outlook of the ruling social democratic parties, especially in Sweden.[57] But it was also the case that foreign policy was often motivated by considerations of *Realpolitik*, even in the 'active neutrality' policy associated with the Swedish social democratic prime minister Olof Palme. Palme's political and ideological interventions on the side of the Soviet Union, such as his outspoken criticism of American policy in Vietnam, acted as a counterweight to Sweden's cultural, economic and military liaisons with the west, as well as helping to appease radical left-wing critics within his own party. Swedish neutrality did not follow a straight course, but should instead be seen as 'a skilful management of contradictions, some would say exceedingly skilful'.[58] In Finland, Kekkonen's attempt to mediate between the superpowers by initiating the talks that led to the Conference on Security and Co-operation in Europe was an important means to answer the critics of 'finlandization' and to secure unprecedented international recognition for Finland as a neutral state.[59]

The revisionist reappraisals of Nordic foreign policy since the end of the Cold War have also cast some doubt on the extent to which Scandinavia could be understood to constitute a security community in the Deutschian sense. The idea of the Nordic Balance was an *ex post facto* rationalization of the existing security arrangements rather than a blueprint for achieving a security community.[60] Unlike the nascent European communities, the Scandinavian security community was not born of the aspiration to overcome a shared history of conflict – though such a history did indeed exist in the Scandinavian region – but evolved from an 'absence of war so self-evident that there was no point in bringing up the issue'.[61] The Nordic peace was an 'unintended peace' therefore, which was premised on the marginalization of security concerns in intra-Nordic relations and the maintenance of national autonomy in the conduct of security policy.[62] After the failure of the Scandinavian Defence Alliance negotiations in 1948–9 there were no further attempts to initiate intra-Nordic security cooperation during the Cold War period.

NORDIC COOPERATION

In international relations the term 'security community' implies not only the absence of conflict, but also a sense of integration based on the acknowledgement of mutual values and togetherness or 'we-feeling'. This would include cooperation and integration not only in security and defence, but in other areas of policy as well. As we have seen, there had been some attempts to promote cooperation between the Scandinavian countries during the inter-war period. Following the collapse of the Scandinavian Defence Alliance negotiations, the Danish social democrat Hans Hedtoft proposed the establishment of a forum for more general cooperation, and the Nordic Council, consisting initially of Denmark, Sweden and Norway, was founded in 1952.

Most commentators have emphasized the limited aims of the Nordic Council. Its remit was to promote cultural, juridical and social connections, and to seek to harmonize policies and regulations in these fields, but it had no supranational ambitions. It was a strictly advisory body with no power to make binding decisions that placed formal limitations on the sovereignty of its members.[63] The foundation of the Nordic Council of Ministers in 1971, consisting of one representative of each Nordic government with special responsibility for Nordic cooperation, did little to extend the limits of Nordic cooperation. For this reason it seems reasonable to describe the Scandinavian countries as 'reluctant Nordics'.[64] However, although this was partly attributable to the existence of some residual tensions, between Norway and Sweden for example, the main reason for the limited nature of Nordic cooperation had more to do with the politics of the Cold War. The USSR was from the outset very suspicious of Nordic cooperation as a means to draw Finland into the western sphere, and blocked Finnish membership of the Nordic Council until 1955. During the 'first détente' after 1953, this attitude softened, and the Soviet leadership began instead to see the Nordic Council as a means of influencing Nordic affairs. Finnish membership was thus a guarantee that the Nordic Council would refrain from developing any foreign policy interests, which indeed it did.[65]

In the longer term, the politics of the Cold War also served as a brake on the development of Nordic cooperation in the economic sphere. To protect its economic interests as a capitalist economy trading largely with Western Europe, Finland negotiated associate membership with the EFTA in 1961 and joined the OECD in 1969. The USSR acceded to the EFTA agreement on condition that it would retain its most favoured nation status in Finland's external trade. Finland also participated in the negotiations to establish a Nordic

Customs Union known as Nordek, based on a Danish proposal first made in 1968. But by the time the agreement was ready to be signed, it had become clear that Nordek would be seen as more than a forum for intra-Nordic economic cooperation in its own right, and instead the first step towards Nordic membership of the EEC.[66] This amounted to a direct provocation to the Soviet Union, forcing the Finnish government to withdraw suddenly from the negotiations in the spring of 1970, with the result that the whole plan collapsed.[67] Although the Finnish government attracted criticism for its actions, both at home and from the other Nordic governments, the negative consequences were to some extent outweighed by the significance of Finland's full participation in the Nordek negotiations, which confirmed once and for all its status as a Nordic country.[68]

Apart from the constraints of security policy, a further hindrance was the lack of a strong economic incentive for closer integration. The Nordic market was too small to make it worthwhile to take steps to develop intra-Nordic trade, and for the highly open economies of Scandinavia the larger markets of Western Europe were therefore always more important. Further, although the legacy of intra-Scandinavian rivalry and imperialism may have helped to prevent closer cooperation, at the same time it lacked enough importance to provide an incentive for closer union as a means to overcome old hostilities, as it did in Western Europe.[69] As in the European Community, Nordic cooperation has thus always served partly as a means of protecting national interests rather than pooling them. It was noticeable that it was the two former dominant regional powers, Sweden and Denmark, that consistently showed the most support for closer Nordic cooperation; Norway was consistently more reluctant. Meanwhile, for Iceland and for the small autonomous regions of Scandinavia, Nordic cooperation came to provide a forum for national self-assertion, with Åland and Faroe sending their own delegates to the Nordic Council from 1970, and Greenland from 1984.

Despite these limitations, Nordic cooperation did flourish after 1945 in several different ways. First, the Scandinavian countries formed a consensus on the need to preserve the appearance of regional unity to the outside world.[70] This can be described as the operation of a 'Nordic filter' where each government appraised the effects of its actions on the other Scandinavian countries before responding to a particular situation.[71] This was most clearly demonstrated in the operation of an unofficial Nordic caucus in international organizations such as the UN, and although there was never a formal obligation to consult, the convention of doing so almost came to take on the sanctity of an ethical principle. To take an example of this, in 1965 the Danish foreign minister Per Hækkerup attracted criticism from his Scandinavian counterparts for failing to consult them before proposing that the UN adopt a tougher line on South African apartheid.[72]

Second, the Nordic Council helped to promote integration across the region by establishing structures to help develop intra-Nordic contacts and networks. The most significant of these have been the initiatives to foster the free movement of Nordic citizens throughout the region: the Nordic labour market established in 1954 (Iceland joined in 1983), which meant that the citizens of one Nordic country no longer required work permits to seek employment in another; the social security union in 1955, which entitled citizens to draw social benefits throughout the region; and the Nordic passport union in 1957. The most visible impact of these changes was the migration of several hundred thousand Finnish workers to Sweden in the 1960s. Other successes have included the establishment of a joint Scandinavian airline (SAS) in 1951, the Nordic investment bank set up in 1976, and an agreement to coordinate laws on environmental protection, also in 1976. Harmonization of legislation has been one of the principal areas of Nordic Council activity, mostly affecting law in non-controversial fields such as the family, business, copyright and transport.

Third, there was some success in efforts to promote informal Nordic cooperation at a cultural level. This partly took the form of government-sponsored cultural and educational exchanges, such as the 'Nordplus' scheme for the mobility of university students, and the establishment of institutions such as the Nordic Prizes for literature, music and film. Integration in these fields was assisted by the mutual intelligibility of the Danish, Norwegian and Swedish languages, although there is some evidence for linguistic divergence since 1945.[73] Equally important was the impact of voluntary organizations in promoting a common Nordic identity, including the Nordic Associations founded in the different countries during the early twentieth century and the tradition of 'worker Scandinavianism' (*arbetarskandinavism*) in the social democratic labour movements, which found expression in the foundation of a common trade union organization, Nordens Fackliga Samorganisation, in 1972.[74]

THE NORDIC REGION AFTER THE COLD WAR: TOWARDS EUROPEAN INTEGRATION

The coming of the Cold War in the 1940s had thus marked an important turning point in the security arrangements for the Nordic countries. For Denmark, Norway and newly independent Iceland, it brought to an end the neutrality and non-alignment of the previous one and a half centuries. The differences between the countries should not be stressed too much. As we have seen, Denmark and Norway were members of NATO only on minimal terms, while the Swedish government, despite its declared neutrality, actually operated under the tacit assumption that Sweden would be defended by NATO in the event of an attack by the USSR. Meanwhile, the networks of intra-Nordic cooperation first established during the inter-war period continued to develop, though there was never the ambition to pursue supranational integration along the lines of the European communities.

The years 1989–91 are generally acknowledged to be a major turning point in European history. The fall of the Berlin Wall and the revolutions against the communist regimes of Eastern Europe during the autumn of 1989 were followed by the reunification of Germany, the collapse of the USSR and the end of the Cold War.[75] In Finland and Sweden, these changes, with all their profound implications for neutrality and security policy, also coincided with a very severe economic recession during the early 1990s.[76] For Sweden in particular, the first half of the 1990s was a period of rapid and traumatic change when many of the previously held certainties about politics, society and national identity were profoundly shaken. In Finland, too, the 1990s also witnessed a period of intense scrutiny and public debate over Cold War foreign policy, partly triggered by the release of new archives following the collapse of the Soviet Union. But for all the Nordic countries, as indeed the rest of Europe, the events of 1989–91 marked a watershed in perceptions of the recent past, when Europe finally emerged from the long 'post-war' period. As one historian commented on the 1990s, 'What we are witnessing . . . is a sort of interregnum, a moment between myths when the old versions of the past are either redundant or unacceptable, and new ones have yet to surface.'[77]

We should be wary of making too much of the impact of these years as a caesura, especially when it is still too soon to distinguish with confidence any real trends in the period since 1991. Moreover, there is also a danger of imposing a static homogeneity onto what we now know as the 'Cold War, 1949–91' that does not accurately convey the constantly evolving nature of the security situation in these years, an interpretation that is perhaps born out of a nostalgia for what seems in retrospect to be a more predictable age. This was far from the truth, of course. Nordic foreign policy responded dynamically to shifting international relations throughout the Cold War period. The 'first détente' following Stalin's death in 1953 encouraged the Scandinavian governments to adopt a more optimistic and sympathetic attitude towards the Soviet Union, though these hopes were swiftly dashed following the Soviet oppression of the Hungarian uprising in the autumn of 1956. Likewise, the *Ostpolitik* of the German chancellor Willy Brandt helped to promote another partial thaw in the early 1970s, culminating in the Helsinki Agreement on the CSCE in 1975, but this gave way to the so-called Second Cold War of renewed tension in the time of Brezhnev and Reagan. For Sweden, the discovery of two Soviet submarines violating Swedish territorial waters in 1981 and 1982 – one in the archipelago of the main Swedish naval base at Karlskrona – caused serious embarrassment and raised new security concerns.

Nonetheless, the collapse of the Soviet Union and the end of the Cold War in the 1990s had a profound impact on all the Scandinavian countries. The end of the east–west conflict necessitated some reconsideration of policy for the two neutral states, but it also changed the security environment in other ways, provoking fears about new and perhaps less predictable security challenges. These included, among other things: environmental issues and the management of scarce resources such as the north Atlantic fish stocks (though of course these problems had emerged long before the end of the Cold War);[78] the safe disposal of the vast Soviet arsenal, much of which was located near the Scandinavian region; trans-national criminal activity resulting from the social instability within the former Soviet Union; and the immigration of refugees displaced by conflict, above all from the former Yugoslavia.[79] From the turn of the twenty-first century, these concerns were augmented by two others as potential sources of conflict: energy, especially in relation to the deposits of oil and gas in the North and Barents Seas, and international terrorism. The controversy over the cartoons of the prophet Mohammed published in a Danish newspaper, which led to serious rioting and attacks on Danish interests in the Middle East in January 2006, served as an uncomfortable reminder to many Scandinavians that they could not afford to consider themselves isolated from conflicts in the wider world.

Finally, there was also the question of European integration. None of the Nordic countries had been signatories to the Treaty of Rome, though Denmark and Norway had debated the question of membership since the early 1960s, and Denmark had indeed joined in 1973. For Finland, membership of an organization so closely associated with the west was unthinkable, and the question was never even discussed. Sweden, too, was constrained by neutrality, though here the growing importance of the EEC markets for Swedish exports during the 1960s provoked a debate on whether Sweden could join the EEC without formally acceding to the obligations of political integration. The matter was clarified in 1971 when the

Swedish government formally declared that it would not be seeking membership.[80] But the raising of the Iron Curtain changed the context of European integration, and that, in turn, had profound implications for the identity of the Nordic region. The very idea of the Nordic model no longer seemed relevant as something 'better than' the rest of Europe when the ideological division on which it rested had vanished. With the signing of the Single European Act in 1986 and the Treaty of Maastricht in 1991 the European Community had embarked on a new and dynamic phase of integration. Whereas Scandinavia and Sweden in particular had once been defined as the epitome of modernity, suddenly, at least for a brief moment during the early 1990s, it was Europe itself – and the political freedom, rights, free market reforms and integration that 'Europe' stood for – that assumed this role.[81]

For this reason, the announcement by the Swedish government in the autumn of 1990 of its intention to seek membership came as a major shock. The decision, which was presented as part of an economic crisis policy, amounted to a practical admission of defeat for the Social Democratic prime minister Ingvar Carlsson, who had previously maintained the traditional line that EU membership was incompatible with neutrality. The application was taken up enthusiastically by the incoming Conservative government after the Social Democrats lost the 1991 election.[82] In Finland, meanwhile, the decision to seek EU membership was announced in March 1992, shortly after the YYA treaty had been declared null and void. Membership was put to a referendum in both countries and both formally acceded to the EU, together with neutral Austria, on 1 January 1995.

The changed situation, and the Swedish and Finnish applications, prompted the two non-EU members, Norway and Iceland, to re-examine their positions as well. As members of NATO, these states were not constrained by foreign policy from contemplating membership of the EEC during the 1960s. For Denmark and Norway, the most important consideration was economic: the close trading links that both states had with Britain. Accordingly, both countries were, with Sweden, founder members of EFTA, but, unlike Sweden,

Denmark in particular viewed membership of the new trading organization as a step towards eventual accession to the EEC itself. In 1961–2 Norway and Denmark followed Britain and Ireland in making an application for membership, but this and a subsequent application in 1967 was vetoed by the French president Charles de Gaulle. The third application was accepted in 1972 and the decision was put to a referendum in both countries. This produced a 64 per cent majority (on a 90 per cent turnout) in Denmark but in Norway membership was rejected by 53.5 per cent. The Norwegian referendum was purely advisory, unlike the Danish one, which was a constitutional requirement, but nonetheless the government decided it had no choice but to withdraw its application.

The 1972 referendum polarized Norwegian opinion across the traditional party divisions, and meant that there was a general preference for avoiding debating the issue altogether for the following twenty years. Even in 1990, opinion was still divided to the extent that the Conservative coalition government was forced to resign in October 1990 when the Centre Party contested the negotiations taking place over the EEA. The changed security environment and the possibility of the emergence of a Nordic bloc within an enlarged EU persuaded the advocates of membership to try again; a new accession treaty was negotiated but once again it was rejected in a referendum. For Iceland, meanwhile, full membership of the EU had never really been seriously considered, but the very fact that the matter was debated in the 1990s was seen as a significant change, and following a close vote in the Alþingi, the country became, like Norway, a member of the European Economic Area (EEA) in 1992. This provided some benefits. With the extension of the single market to cover all of the members of the EEA, Norway and Iceland were able to gain the economic benefits of European integration without having to compromise their sovereignty, which in the case of Iceland meant avoiding the imposition of strict quotas and territorial limits for fishing. The objection to this was that by remaining outside the EU they simply agreed to forego the right to participate in decision-making on matters that increasingly affected their sovereignty. The adoption of the Schengen Agreement covering border controls, which applied in both Norway and Iceland, was a case in point.[83]

The EU enlargement in 1995 thus left a divided Nordic region. Of the three Scandinavian countries that were now full members of the EU, two continued to exhibit strong 'euro-sceptic' tendencies. Denmark was unable to ratify the 1991 Maastricht Treaty on social and political union after the 'no' side gained a narrow majority in a referendum in 1992, and was forced to renegotiate exemptions from some of the treaty's clauses. A further referendum in 2000 produced a majority against joining the single currency. Danish euro-scepticism has partly flourished due to constitutional requirements, which have meant that Denmark has held the highest number of referenda on EU matters (six up to 2007) in Europe.[84] In Sweden, the narrow majority in favour of accession in the 1994 referendum served as a constant reminder of the divisions in the country over membership, and a 2003 referendum also produced a majority against the single currency. Only in Finland did it seem that European integration had been embraced with any degree of enthusiasm.

The results of these referenda suggest that there is some justification for applying the epithet 'reluctant Europeans' to the Nordic countries. As the divergence of the Scandinavian responses to European integration indicates, however, it is difficult to find a common Nordic explanation for Nordic euro-scepticism. Moreover, the Nordic populations are themselves divided: referenda have generally produced relatively small majorities either for or against and the arguments have been heated on both sides of the debate.

Nonetheless, some common points can be made. During the first phase of European integration, before the first enlargement in 1973, economic and political considerations pulled in opposite directions. For small open economies, the need to maintain advantageous terms of trade with the larger European states provided a powerful incentive to join, but this was tempered by the political demands of neutrality in the case of Sweden and Finland, and domestic fears about national sovereignty in the case of Iceland, Norway and Denmark. Only in Denmark were the trading benefits strong enough to outweigh objections to membership on political grounds, a function largely of the nature of the Danish economy and its shift from an export sector based mainly on agriculture to one based on manufacturing industry.[85]

The removal of the neutrality constraint changed the debate in Finland and Sweden, but by this time the European Union had become a very different institution. The most powerful argument in favour of EU membership for the Nordic countries has remained the economic one. Like the United Kingdom, the Scandinavian countries have generally acknowledged the economic benefits of membership over the supra-national ambitions towards political union, and have therefore supported a more limited functionalist approach to European integration. Only in Finland was there perhaps some support for German-style supra-nationalist federalism.[86] This functionalist position could be interpreted as an extension of the general Nordic predilection as small states for participation in international (as opposed to supra-national) organizations such as the UN. The strongest support for EU membership in the Nordic countries came from groups representing business, especially those branches producing mainly for the export market. In Sweden, the right-wing government elected in 1991 promoted EU membership as a means of introducing what it saw as necessary neo-liberal reforms to revive an over-regulated and over-taxed economy. The campaign for EU membership by the Swedish Employers' Federation (SAF) should be seen in the context of its general attack on many aspects of the Social Democratic Swedish model, which came to a head during the economic crisis of the early 1990s.[87] But their argument for the economic benefits of EU membership was also supported by the leadership of both the Social Democratic Party and the trade union federation (LO), for whom the EU was seen as the best means of achieving the prosperity needed to maintain the Swedish welfare model. Their view was not necessarily shared by the rank and file of the labour movement, however, and the eventual majority of the 'yes' side in the accession referendum was probably attributable to Ingvar Carlsson's success in winning over members of his own party.[88] He did this by seeking to re-define the

EU question as an economic one, thus avoiding the still awkward question of neutrality. A similar sense of economic crisis had accompanied Denmark's entry to the EEC in 1973. By contrast, the two 'no' votes in the referenda on the single currency in 2000 and 2003 came against the background of a much stronger economic performance in both countries.

Some scholars have suggested that the divergence of the Nordic countries can be explained with reference to the relative strength of different economic interest groups in the Scandinavian countries.[89] In Finland and Sweden, the main pressure to join the EU came from the organized representatives of business groups, as we have seen, but there was no equivalent lobby in Norway. This was partly because of the much stronger performance of the oil-exporting Norwegian economy during the 1990s. But the Norwegian 'no' vote was also a result of the successful mobilization of an anti-EU move-ment drawn mainly from the traditional rural sectors of the economy – fishing and farming – allied with public sector workers. This source of opposition existed in Sweden and Finland as well, but the Norwegian movement was much better organized, and able to mobilize as an extra-parliamentary protest movement that attracted high publicity.[90]

Indeed, in all the Nordic countries there seemed to be a major divide between the inhabitants of the metropolitan areas around Helsinki, Stockholm and Oslo, who supported European integra-tion, and those dwelling in the rural peripheries, especially the north, who did not.[91] Although nearly all the major political parties, with the exception of the Icelandic ones, were in favour of EU membership, many experienced internal divisions over the matter, with the grassroots members generally more sceptical than the leadership. This was particularly true for the social democratic parties of Norway and Sweden. In Iceland, however, these divisions seemed to be partly reversed, with more support for EU member-ship among the general population than among the political elites.[92] This, according to Baldur Thorhallsson, was partly a func-tion of the Icelandic parliamentary system, which over-represented the rural districts at the expense of Reykjavík and meant that the

Alþingi representatives and the government retained their main power base in the countryside. The fishing industry continued to wield an enormous political influence out of all proportion to its size in terms of numbers employed (the same argument could also be made for Norway). But Icelandic euro-scepticism also stemmed from a realist view of foreign policy among the political and bureaucratic elite, who realized that Iceland simply lacked the resources to undertake major international engagements, and, unlike their Nordic counterparts, had little previous experience of participating in these.[93]

An alternative view of euro-scepticism is that it should be seen less as a question of economic and political interests, and instead as one of cultural and national identity. Europe was generally conceived as the 'other' in Nordic nationalist discourse, and national identity in the Nordic countries – and indeed also Nordic identity – was historically represented in terms of opposition to Europe.[94] Writing in 1950, the Norwegian ambassador to the OEEC, Arne Skaug, expressed his scepticism towards 'continental' efforts to promote integration:

> The British-Scandinavian view is to a large extent the opposite of the continental-European one. The wish to maintain full employment and consideration of social justice comes first, and other goals are subordinated to these. The primacy of these goals creates state responsibilities that are often alien to the continental philosophy.[95]

The Nordic countries were Protestant, as opposed to the Catholic Christian Democrats, who were the main drivers of integration. The six foreign ministers who signed the Treaty of Paris in 1951 were all Christian Democrats, a fact that was not lost on the then Swedish prime minister Tage Erlander.[96] As the failed attempts at deeper Nordic cooperation had shown, they also had a shared suspicion of supra-national federalism, as states that were historically remarkable for the degree to which they were centralized. Moreover, the Scandinavian countries lacked the impulse towards integration that was provided by the Second World War. Unlike France and Germany, there was in Scandinavia no shared history of enmity to be overcome through a conscious process of integration, or rather there was a shared history but it had been sufficiently suppressed and forgotten by the post-war period to make no difference.[97] Finally, since the 1930s Scandinavia had been associated with a welfare model that was distinguished from Western European capitalism in its pursuit of egalitarianism and solidarity: 'a specific egalitarian social democratic community of destiny'.[98] This 'welfare state nationalism' cut right across the political spectrum: it was articulated, for example, by both the Swedish Left Party and the right-wing Danish People's Party.[99]

Against this, the Nordic supporters of EU membership, and especially the Swedish social democrats, argued that entry to the EU would help to shape the European institutions in a social democratic, Nordic way. This rather self-aggrandizing desire encapsulated a more general fear in the region at the end of the Cold War: that of marginalization in the new Europe.[100] As relatively small states within an expanding European Union, what possibilities were there to maintain the influence of Norden as a distinctive region? In the early 1990s the Scandinavian states suddenly rediscovered the Baltic Sea as the focus for a larger and potentially more influential region. The Council of Baltic Sea States was founded in 1992, and there was a sudden flurry of interest in pursuing new contacts with the Baltic states.[101] The Swedish prime minister Carl Bildt made a speech in 1993 expressing remorse for certain episodes in Swedish/Baltic relations, such as the extradition of Baltic refugees at the end of the Second World War. Despite these attempts at atonement, there was, however, an unmistakeably missionary element to Swedish interests in the Baltic.[102] Self-interest was certainly a motive since the newly independent Baltic states also offered rich investment opportunities for Nordic businesses. Above all, the interest was rather one-sided. For Latvia, Lithuania and Estonia, the goal was not to be incorporated into Norden, but to seek the much greater prize of membership of the European Union, achieved when these states became full members in 2004. Perhaps for that reason, Nordic interest in the Baltic as a source of regional identity seemed to wane somewhat from the late 1990s, to be replaced by a new focus on 'the North'. This was introduced with the Finnish prime minister's announcement of a 'Northern Dimension' for the EU in April 1997, preceded by the Norwegian government's foundation of the Barents Euro-Arctic Region (BEAR) in 1994.[103]

The significance of alternative regional identities will be discussed further in the conclusion to this book. It is perhaps too soon after the post-Cold War upheavals to assess these trends, never mind to predict new ones. But in many ways, the division between EU and non-EU members in the Nordic region does not seem to present any greater obstacle to Nordic unity than the division between NATO and non-NATO members during the Cold War. Indeed, the end of the Cold War has introduced the possibility of security cooperation within the region in a way that was simply unthinkable earlier, to the extent that in 2000 the Nordic countries (with the exception of Iceland) agreed to establish a joint Nordic brigade called NORDCAPS, to be placed at the disposal of international organizations such as the EU, NATO and the UN. Meanwhile, closer integration within the EU has become a reality for all the Nordic countries. Even Norway and Iceland have, as members of the EEA, found themselves obliged to adapt their legislation to the EU in many fields, so that by 2005 Norway had followed more EU directives than Sweden. As Lee Miles has suggested, the Swedish bureaucratic and political elites have gradually become Europeanized, leading to an unconscious 'fusion' between Swedish and EU policy, where, despite the persistence of anti-EU rhetoric, the EU acts to some extent as a practical tool for the Swedish government to achieve their own national policy goals.[104]

CONCLUSION

This chapter has examined the bases for Nordic distinctiveness in international relations since 1945. As we have seen, following rather different experiences in the Second World War, the

Scandinavian countries pursued different security arrangements during the Cold War. Denmark, Norway and Iceland joined NATO, while Sweden and Finland remained neutral. Although this arrangement divided the region, it was generally conceptualized as the Nordic Balance, where the open (NATO members) and tacit (Sweden) support for the Atlantic alliance was counter balanced by Finland's close relationship with the USSR. This arrangement endured more or less unchallenged until 1991, and helped to keep the peace in a strategically sensitive area on the front line of the Cold War. Some commentators went further, citing Scandinavia as an example of a security community, where common institutions and a mutual sense of 'we-ness' had promoted peace and could even be taken as a model for peace-building efforts in other regions. Most would agree, though, that the Nordic peace was an 'accidental peace', though perhaps it was no less remarkable for this, given that there was a shared history of conflict in the region, and that the extent of formal Nordic cooperation remained very limited and mostly confined to the cultural sphere.

Yet there were strong similarities between the Scandinavian countries in government, politics and policy, as this book has attempted to show, and it would be reasonable to ask therefore whether it would be possible to identify a Scandinavian model in foreign policy. There is some justification for the view that the Scandinavian states have acted as 'norm entrepreneurs' in Christine Ingebritsen's term: that they have sought to use their position as small states to mediate between larger ones and promote peace. They have not always done this for purely altruistic reasons. Scandinavian interventions have served both the national interests of the states concerned and the personal interests of certain politicians. Examples of hypocrisy can be identified, such as the refusal of the Norwegian and Icelandic governments to contemplate a ban on whaling, and Sweden's position as a major arms exporter. But even despite these blemishes this is a role that does not seem to have diminished since the end of the Cold War. Norwegian diplomats played a major role in brokering an agreement between Israel and Palestine in 1993 and have also intervened in the Sri Lankan/Tamil conflict; Marti Ahtesaari and Carl Bildt both acted as mediators in the Balkan conflict, and Scandinavian nationals have continued to hold prominent roles in UN organizations.[105] As Peter Lawler has suggested, the Danish government has even attempted to present its controversial participation in the US-led invasion of Iraq in terms of its traditional commitments to internationalism and solidarity.[106]

Three reasons can be suggested why the Scandinavian states have chosen to pursue this role, and have done this with some success. First, unlike most other European countries, the Scandinavian states lack a history of colonialism and violence in the Third World. This is not to say that the Scandinavian states were entirely untainted by colonialism. Scandinavians participated in the European imperial expansion as missionaries, for example, and they shared the European self-image of superiority in relation to the colonial 'other'. But with the exception of Denmark's colonies in the north Atlantic and briefly in the Caribbean, Africa and India, the Scandinavian countries have not had colonies of their own, and they thus avoided the traumatic experiences that shaped the foreign policies of several declining colonial powers during this period, such as France and the UK.

Secondly, Scandinavian foreign policy was often (though not exclusively) formed by social democratic politicians with a background in socialist internationalism. At the turn of the twentieth century Scandinavian social democrats had made common cause and established Scandinavian labour organizations to campaign against the threat of conflict over the breakup of the Swedish–Norwegian union. For many, the idealism of social democratic foreign policy in Sweden was irrevocably tainted by the compromises of the Second World War, but it cannot be denied that Olof Palme in particular was held in high esteem overseas for what many regarded as his principled and idealist approach to foreign policy.

Finally, the idea of the Scandinavian model of social justice and solidarity endured in the eyes of the world even into the twenty-first century, and thus undoubtedly gave Scandinavian politicians some moral leverage. The greatest threat to the idealist vision of

Scandinavian foreign policy is likely to come not from revelations about foreign policy transgressions in the past, but from the rise of social tensions in response to mass immigration at home, and the challenge that this presents to the Scandinavian self-conception as the home of tolerance and social justice.

Chapter 5

Scandinavian Society: Equality, Ethnicity and Multiculturalism

The supposed ethnic, linguistic and cultural homogeneity of the Nordic countries underlies many of the assumptions about Scandinavia as a *Geschichtsregion*. In the imaginations of many, Scandinavia has always been populated by blond-haired, blue-eyed people speaking mutually comprehensible languages, and this ethnic stereotype has profoundly shaped perceptions about who the Scandinavians are, both outside and inside the region. If the nineteenth-century Nordic peasant was the principal embodiment of democracy and freedom, as Sørensen and Stråth suggest, then he was also viewed as a symbol of a language and culture that could be traced back to the Vikings, and thus the bearer of an ethno-cultural tradition.[1] The idea of a post-Enlightenment *Sonderweg* in Scandinavia, based on the reconciliation of the tensions between freedom and equality, came to be indelibly linked to the notion of ethnic distinctiveness and homogeneity.

Historically, of course, the homogeneity of the region was much exaggerated. The two Scandinavian monarchies that emerged during the early modern period were multi-ethnic states where linguistic and cultural pluralism was generally tolerated. It was only with the emergence of nationalism and nation-building during the nineteenth century that Scandinavia began to be defined in terms of ethnicity. The Norwegian constitution of 1814 contained a clause explicitly excluding Jews from Norwegian citizenship.[2] The nineteenth-century pan-Scandinavian movement was in part a liberal movement for reform, but it was also influenced by the philological, ethnological and literary research of the period, which emphasized the common bonds between the three Scandinavian countries, and the ethnic and linguistic roots of these bonds. The three Scandinavian states became officially monolingual and monocultural, and appeared to lack the ethnic, religious and linguistic cleavages that beset so many other European nation states. Where there were ethnic minorities, such as the Sami population of northern Norway, Sweden and Finland, assimilationist policies were pursued, driven by contemporary ideas about social Darwinism and 'race hygiene'. The Scandinavian countries before 1940 have been described as the most ethnically homogeneous in Europe.[3]

As the geographer Allan Pred has shown, the pervasiveness of this myth of ethnic homogeneity was demonstrated in Sweden following the economic crisis of the early 1990s.[4] Recession and high unemployment, the decision to seek membership of the European Union, the end of the Cold War and the shake-up in the political system all served to challenge a number of long-held assumptions about Swedish politics and society during the post-war period. The sense of dislocation and loss engendered by these changes was fuelled by the growing presence of non-Europeans within Swedish society, as a result mainly of the very rapid immigration that had taken place during the 1980s and '90s. This provoked in turn the emergence of racist responses to the presence of these 'others', and scholars have noted that cultural racism in particular has been very prominent in Scandinavia.[5] The existence of racism itself has only contributed further to the identity crisis, since it runs counter to the Scandinavian self-image of solidarity and social justice.

This chapter examines the radical shift from relative ethnic homogeneity in Scandinavia in the 1940s to ethnic pluralism. The extent to which the Scandinavian countries were ever ethnically homogeneous is examined briefly, and particular attention is given to the Sami, the indigenous people of the north of the region, and their changing relationship with the state. Then attention is turned to post-war immigration to Scandinavia, and the broad patterns of immigration are described. The shift in policy, from assimilation towards integration and multiculturalism, is discussed, and finally the existence of ethnic tension, intolerance and racism. Of course, this is hardly a

Scandinavian phenomenon, but has to be seen in the context of similar issues across Europe.

HISTORICAL ETHNIC MINORITIES IN SCANDINAVIA

The early modern Danish and Swedish states were multi-lingual and multi-ethnic. The sixteenth-century Danish kingdom included among its territories present-day Norway, with its varied dialects and sub-cultures; several north German provinces; the North Atlantic islands of Faroe, Iceland and Greenland; the provinces of Blekinge, Halland and Skåne and the island of Gotland in present-day southern Sweden; as well as Jutland and the Baltic islands. Meanwhile, the Swedish empire at its height in the seventeenth century was equally extensive and diverse, encompassing all of present-day Finland as well as extensive territories in the lands bordering the south of the Baltic Sea. The struc-ture of local society and the arrangements for its government varied widely throughout the kingdoms. The independent peasant farmer remained far more important in Norway, where there was no rural aristocracy, than in Jutland and the Danish islands, where there was. On the other hand, there was never any formal provision for multi-culturalism in the constitutional foundations of either state, and, on the contrary, in both states there was a strong tendency towards centralization and assimilation, pursued in tandem with the state Lutheran church. An example of this is the Swedish state's remarkably swift, comprehensive and enduring success in incorporating the former Danish provinces of Skåne, Halland and Blekinge into the state after the peace of Roskilde in 1658. The completeness of the Scandinavian Reformation, and the strength of Lutheranism, meant that the Scandinavian countries lacked the potentially divisive reli-gious cleavages found elsewhere in Europe. Nor, with the exception of Denmark's sparsely populated north Atlantic possessions, did they experience directly the presence of other racial and ethnic groups in the colonial periphery, though it would probably be more accurate to see the Scandinavians as participants in a wider European colonial project.[6]

Nonetheless, there were a number of historic ethnic minorities throughout the Nordic states, including a small and largely assimilated Jewish population, and unknown numbers of Rom or Gypsies, whose itinerant way of life fell foul of the Swedish state's prohibitions on vagrancy in the early modern period, and who were frequently treated with the same hostility and discrimination that this unfortunate group encountered throughout Europe.[7] It is worth pointing out that nine-teenth-century Finland was part of an exceptionally large and diverse empire, and that this heterogeneity was partly reflected in the ethnic make up of the grand duchy. As one of the main western outposts of that empire, nineteenth-century Helsinki was perhaps the most cosmopoli-tan and linguistically diverse of the Nordic cities. Twelve per cent of the permanent population spoke Russian as their first language in 1870, and large numbers of Russian troops and civil servants were temporarily present, depending on the fluctuations of war and peace.[8] The presence of a small Tatar minority from central Asia, who had come to the Baltic as traders in furs and textiles, meant that Helsinki had an Islamic associa-tion as early as the 1830s, and a permanent Muslim congregation from 1924.[9] Most importantly, of course, the close historical ties with the Swedish kingdom had left a substantial Swedish speaking minority in Finland, which necessitated the adoption of an official bilingual policy after independence in 1917. Despite numerical decline in the number of Swedish speakers (the nearly 290,000 Swedish speakers made up 5.5 per cent of the population in 2006), Finland remained a bilingual country, as confirmed by its new constitution in 2000. There was also a degree of linguistic pluralism in Norway, with the dialect and sub-culture of *nynorsk* afforded a special status alongside the majority *bokmål*. The centralization tendency was in any case never quite so strong in Norway as in the other Scandinavian states.

Perhaps the most distinctive minority of all, however, was the indigenous Sami population of northern Norway, Sweden and Finland. Numerically, the Sami population was insignificant. In the late 1990s there were about 40,000 Sami people living in Norway, 17,000 in Sweden and 5,500 in Finland, together with about 2,000 on the Kola peninsula of north-western Russia.[10] Although the Sami territory or Sapmi extends as far south as the mountains of Härjedalen and

Jämtland in Sweden, there are only a few districts of the far north of Scandinavia where the Sami population is a majority. Despite this, the relations between the Sami and the Scandinavian states and majority populations serve, when considered in historical perspective, as a useful indicator about wider questions of Scandinavian policy towards ethnic minorities, and deserve to be discussed in some detail.

Although it is tempting to imagine the Sami homelands in the Arctic north of Scandinavia as remote, inhospitable and thus of little interest to other populations, this is far from the truth. The area known as North Calotte (Nordkalotten) had been economically and strategically important since at least the Middle Ages, and the Sami population lived alongside Norwegian fishing communities and the Finnish-speaking *kven* farmers. The Swedish and Danish-Norwegian states claimed sovereignty over the region during the early modern period, but made little attempt to assimilate the Sami population before the nineteenth century. On the contrary, there was some protection for traditional Sami rights within the multi-ethnic Danish-Norwegian state, supported by the Romantic sympathy for indigenous culture.[11] From the mid-nineteenth century official state attitudes towards the Sami began to change, however, when a new emphasis on Scandinavian nation-building coincided with economic and demographic expansion. The Arctic north took on the status of a frontier territory, ripe for exploration and exploitation.[12] The indigenous people who lived there came to be regarded as backward, primitive types who needed to be assimilated into the mainstream culture and society, a Nordic version of the white man's burden.

The key word here was assimilation, especially as far as language and religion were concerned. Sami people were to be incorporated into the Norwegian state and society, *as Norwegians*, speaking Norwegian, baptized as Lutheran Christians, adopting Norwegian values and customs. Even as late as the 1950s there were cases of some Sami children being taken from their parents without consent and placed in foster homes in southern Norway, to be assimilated better into Norwegian society.[13] When the Sami question was debated by the Storting in the 1960s, many Norwegian politicians expressed deep regret for the state's activities in this respect. But the assimilation policy should not be seen merely as an example of state racism and assumptions about Sami inferiority. It was also closely related to the construction of welfare states that were based on equal rights and universalism for all citizens, regardless of their cultural or ethnic backgrounds, within which the notion of separate rights for minorities was anathema. This disjuncture presented a paradox that was to occur constantly in discussions of Nordic policies towards ethnic minorities.

Indeed, there was some resistance from the Sami themselves towards the attempts to delineate them as a separate group after 1945. Some Sami continued to identify themselves as 'Sami-speaking Norwegians', who sought equality with other Norwegian citizens within the welfare state rather than any special recognition of their rights as an ethnic minority or indigenous population.[14] This viewpoint partly steered the outlook of the Norwegian Labour Party, hegemonic in Finnmark where many Sami lived, which tended to view Sami problems as matters for regional development policy rather an ethnic question, to be treated in the same way as economic problems in other Norwegian regions. However, by the 1970s the momentum was unmistakably in the opposite direction, away from assimilation towards policies promoting cultural pluralism and ethnic self-determination. The Norwegian state commission on the Sami, which reported in 1959, defined Sami identity more subjectively than hitherto: '[the category] Sami includes all those who have Sami as their mother tongue or who consider themselves to be Sami'.[15] Particular emphasis was placed on the Sami language – recognized by the government in 1962–3 as having equal status with Norwegian – and of the state's responsibility to create the conditions for Sami language and culture to flourish, for example, through support for Sami education, radio broadcasts and newspapers.

The defining event in the development of a Sami movement was the Alta dam affair in the late 1970s. The Norwegian Labour government insisted that its plans to dam the Alta-Kautokeino river were essential in order to secure adequate electricity supplies for Finnmark and thus contribute to the economic development of the region. Sami opposed to the development made common cause with the environmental movement and its critique of large-scale, state-driven technology, and also with other movements for indigenous rights outside the Nordic countries. The Alta affair thus marked the 'aboriginalization' of Sami politics. An ethnic Indian member of the Bolivian parliament took part in the demonstrations against the dam, and contrasts were drawn between the willingness of the Scandinavian governments to promote indigenous rights overseas while ignoring them at home.[16] Above all, the Alta affair forced the acknowledgement that Sami interests were not necessarily accounted for in the normal democratic processes of the Norwegian state: 'Sami policy was no longer a problem for welfare or peripheries [policy] but concerned the question of how two different ethnic groups with a different culture and traditions and different economic interests could live together in one state.'[17]

In the wake of the Alta affair, the governments of Finland, Norway and Sweden made further efforts to support Sami linguistic and cultural self-determination. Language acts in all three countries in 1992 entitled the citizens of some municipalities in the north to use the Sami language in their dealings with the authorities, and the status of the language was also strengthened within the schools. The Sami College at Kautokeino was very important in these developments. Elective assemblies were also established in Finland in 1975, in Norway in 1989 and in Sweden in 1993. Although by 2007 these still had neither the power nor the resources to make policy affecting the Sami people, they did have a growing degree of de facto authority in questions concerning the Sami, and were regularly consulted on relevant policy matters. In 2000 the Sami assemblies in Finland and Norway formed the cross-national Sami Parliamentary Assembly. This was joined by Sweden in 2002, and also included representatives of Russian Sami from the Kola peninsula as observers. An illustration of how much had changed was provided by King Harald of Norway, who, when opening the Sami parliament in 1997, spoke of a Norwegian state consisting of the territories of two peoples: Norwegians and Sami.[18]

The old paradox remained unresolved, however: how to reconcile the now recognized Sami right to self-determination with state sovereignty and the demands of a universal welfare state and equal rights for all, regardless of ethnicity. Although there have clearly been very significant changes in policy concerning culture and language, the more difficult issues of rights to land, water and traditional sources of livelihood remain unresolved. In this respect there are some important differences between the Nordic states. There has been more resistance in Sweden to recognizing indigenous land rights and the idea of an independent Sami region than in Norway.[19] In Norway, of course, the centralization impulse was always weaker. The state directed its resources towards the economic development of the regions, and the two-language policy (*bokmål* and *nynorsk*) and its recognition of the importance of a traditional regional counter-culture perhaps allowed more space for cultural pluralism than it did in Sweden. The paradox thus seems to have been more keenly experienced in Sweden than it was in Norway. But the difference may also be connected to the greater economic pressure on the land and resources of the far north in Sweden, where the territory in question is much larger, and those competing for its use – mining companies, forestry, farming, tourism – more numerous. Part of the problem seems to be the tendency to understand the Sami land question as a matter of reindeer husbandry alone, avoiding the wider question of general rights to water, fishing and hunting. This rather narrow understanding of Sami issues is mirrored in the cultural sphere as well. Paradoxically, the effect of policies designed to recognize cultural and linguistic *difference* within the nation state has also helped to impose uniformity on Sami cultures historically marked by their great diversity, especially in language.[20]

POST-WAR IMMIGRATION TO SCANDINAVIA

The situation of the Sami raises important questions to do with language, culture and identity, and illustrates the changing focus of minority policy between assimilation, integration and multicultural-ism. It is no accident that the governments of Norway and Sweden began to adopt a more inclusive attitude to Sami language and culture at more or less the same time as they began to face similar challenges from other ethnic groups within the state. In other words, the Sami people 'arrived' in the Scandinavian consciousness at the same time as other ethnic minority groups literally arrived within the state in significant numbers.

Until the 1930s, the Nordic countries were for the most part countries of net emigration. Motivated by poverty and the promise of a new life, thousands of mainly peasant farmers left Scandinavia for the New World. Indeed, after Ireland, the Scandinavian countries exhibited the highest per capita rates of emigration in Europe for much of the second half of the nineteenth century. The only significant immigration to the Nordic region before 1945 took place in Finland, where proximity to the Soviet Union caused two major waves of refugees: first during the early 1920s, when more than 30,000 people sought temporary or permanent asylum in Finland after the Bolshevik Revolution; and in 1944 following the Finnish territorial losses to the Soviet Union, which necessitated the resettlement of 400,000 refugees from eastern Karelia.[21] As a proportion of the total population (about 12 per cent), this last movement of population was probably one of the most significant of its time in Europe.

Since 1945 this trend was reversed, and, with the exception of Finland and Iceland until relatively recently, the Nordic countries became societies of net immigration. Patterns of migration differed markedly across the region, as Table 7 illustrates. Denmark, Norway and Sweden all pursued what were, in effect, policies of open immigration from 1945 until the early 1970s, although the effects of this were much more significant in Sweden than in Norway and Denmark. Sweden was a country of net emigration until 1930, but thereafter experienced net immigration every year except for 1972 and 1973.[22] There were two reasons for this. First, as a neutral country during the Second World War, Sweden was inevitably attractive to war refugees, including about 70,000 children evacuated from Finland. Many of these returned home after the cessation of hostilities, while others remained and became more or less assimilated into Swedish society. Secondly, the economic 'record years' (rekordåren) after 1945 created conditions of full employment and, indeed, labour shortages, forcing many Swedish firms actively to recruit additions to their labour forces abroad. In contrast to other European countries such as West Germany, these labour migrants were not treated as temporary 'guest workers' but instead offered the full benefits of citizenship. Generally, however, immigration to Sweden fits the post-war European pattern of migration from the poorer, agrarian south to the industrialized, wealthier north, with many labour migrants coming from Italy, Yugoslavia, Greece and Turkey.

Unlike Britain or France, Sweden could not draw on a pool of immigrant labour from former colonies outside Europe, but the Swedish economy did rely strongly on intra-Nordic migration. One of the first successes of the newly established Nordic Council was the creation, in 1954, of a Nordic labour market, which abolished the requirement for Nordic citizens to seek work permits in connection with employment in another Nordic country, and also harmonized entitlement to social security benefits across the region. This allowed the most significant migration to Sweden during the period: the arrival of many thousands of Finnish citizens – over 100,000 in the years 1968–70 – to take jobs in Swedish industry. Their movement was stimulated by the unevenness of economic development within the Nordic region, and contributed to a general depopulation of the rural districts within Finland at this time. It also set the pattern for the reception and treatment of immigrant groups within Sweden, with an emphasis on language tuition and assimilation.[23] That said, the Finnish workers continued to constitute an 'other' in Swedish public discourse in many respects, often associated in the popular imagination with a 'rough' culture characterized by heavy drinking.[24]

Mass immigration came rather later to Denmark and Norway than to Sweden, largely because of the favourable position of Swedish industry after 1945.[25] Until the late 1950s Denmark experienced relatively high levels of unemployment, which accounted for the continued emigration of Danish citizens, especially to Australia and Canada.[26] With the expansion of Danish industry from the late 1950s, however, Denmark became a full employment economy that, like Sweden, began to recruit labour from southern Europe. Until the late 1960s immigration was unrestricted for workers that were able to provide for themselves, though unlike Sweden the status of these workers was more akin to the temporary 'guest workers' in contemporary West Germany. Norway too was in effect an open immigration country from

1957, but experienced much lower levels of labour immigration than Sweden or Denmark, at least until the late 1960s.[27] On the other hand, labour immigration to Norway continued into the 1970s after most other European countries had imposed restrictions.[28]

Finland and Iceland, meanwhile, remained countries of net emigration during the years of labour migration before the first oil crisis in the 1970s. Finnish emigration peaked in 1969 when over 54,000 Finnish citizens left the country, mostly to work in Sweden. As a result of this, the total Finnish population actually declined overall during the years 1969 and 1970. The higher levels of immigration experienced during the early 1970s were mostly accounted for by the return of these earlier migrants. Icelandic migration flows were relatively small, reflecting the much smaller population, and show moreover large fluctuations. But measured as a proportion of population, Icelandic emigration has remained high right up to the present, with average yearly emigration running at just under 1 per cent in the entire period 1961–2005 (compared to 1.17 per cent in the peak year of Finnish emigration in 1969).[29]

The era of unrestricted labour migration came to an end across Europe following the oil crisis in the early 1970s. Economic depression and rising unemployment provoked the adoption of much more restrictive immigration policies in the Nordic countries as elsewhere, and Sweden, Denmark and Norway effectively abandoned their free immigration policies in 1972, 1973 and 1975 respectively.[30] For the first time since the inter-war period, Sweden became once again a country of net emigration in 1972 and 1973 as its labour migrants returned home to Finland and elsewhere.

In the longer term, however, the period marked not so much the end of an era of immigration, but a substantial change in its character, as labour migrants were replaced by growing numbers of refugees and asylum seekers. During the 1970s the Scandinavian governments pursued a 'dual policy' towards immigration, combining highly restrictive policies on labour migration with efforts to fulfil their humanitarian obligations to refugees.[31] As a neutral country, Sweden had a long-standing reputation as a safe haven for refugees, which had been strengthened during the 1950s and '60s with the arrival of individuals fleeing political conflicts in Eastern Europe, such as the Soviet repression of the Hungarian uprising in 1956 and the 'Prague Spring' in Czechoslovakia in 1968. From the 1970s, however, the majority of these refugees were to come from outside Europe, including a small group of political exiles from the Pinochet regime in Chile, and during the 1980s refugees from conflicts in South-East Asia, Sri Lanka, Ethiopia and Eritrea, and the Iran–Iraq war.

Two general points may be noted about this phase of immigration during the 1970s and '80s. The first is that Sweden, Denmark and Norway all continued to pursue relatively liberal refugee policies, despite the introduction of ever tighter restrictions on labour migration. A typical example is the Danish government's adoption, in 1983, of the concept of 'de facto' refugees, meaning that asylum could be granted to people merely by virtue of their belonging to a group – by citizenship, for example – that was known to be repressed. The second point is that, with the possible exception of Sweden, the numbers of refugee immigrants entering the Nordic countries remained relatively low. Net immigration was very low for all three of these countries during the early 1980s, even to the extent that it was negative in Denmark. Moreover, much of the immigration during this period was accounted for not so much by refugees, but by family unification, as earlier labour migrants who were now permanently settled were joined by their dependents.

The immigration of asylum seekers and political refugees grew steadily through the 1980s, but rose very sharply from the early 1990s. This growth was driven partly by the emergence of new and bloody conflicts in the former Yugoslavia, Iraq and the Persian Gulf, Somalia and the Horn of Africa, Turkish Kurdistan and the former Soviet Union, but the movement of people was also facilitated by improved transport networks, which made the Nordic countries more accessible to those seeking asylum. As Table 8 suggests, however, the numbers of asylum seekers entering the Nordic countries varied considerably across the region. The numbers of asylum seekers entering the Nordic countries peaked during 1993 at the height of the Bosnian conflict, but thereafter declined in Sweden, Denmark and Norway, though to a greater extent in Norway. Denmark retained its liberal policies, giving asylum to a higher proportion of those seeking it than any other indus-trialized country during the decade 1992–2002.[32] Finland received much smaller numbers of asylum seekers than its Scandinavian neigh-bours, though by the turn of the century there were visible minorites from Somalia and from the former Soviet Union.

The experience of rapid growth in extra-European immigration during the 1990s and after is one that the Nordic countries have shared with the rest of Western Europe. What may be unusual is the suddeness of the changes this immigration brought in its wake. The notion of an ethnically homogeneous Scandinavia was largely a myth, as we have seen, but nonetheless, it cannot be denied that the arrival of large numbers of non-Europeans in Scandinavia during the 1990s was a relatively new phenomenon, and unprecedented in scale. The first-generation immigrant population of Denmark doubled in the decade before 2002.[33] In Sweden, the immigration peak during the early 1990s coincided with a period of severe economic recession and a political and cultural crisis, which was to have some important consequences for popular reactions to the change. It is worth point-ing out that family reunification, not asylum seeking, continued to be one of the most important causes of immigration throughout the period. It was also the case that intra-Nordic migrants continued to account for a very high proportion of the foreign-born citizens of the Scandinavian countries, and not just the Finnish labour migrants in Sweden. However, popular perceptions of the 'immigrant' changed substantially during the 1990s and after: from that of the working-class labour migrant from Finland or southern Europe who was relatively easily integrated but probably only a temporary visitor in any case, to that of the Third World refugee arriving desperate, demoralized and poverty-stricken, culturally distant from the host society with corresponding difficulties in integrating. Since the turn of the century there has been a tendency for immigrant 'others' to be identified above all with Islam in the minds of many. This was to have very important consequences for the ways in which the Scandinavian societies responded to mass immigration and this is discussed in the next section.

There appears to be something paradoxical about historic approaches to integration in Scandinavia. On the one hand, Denmark and Sweden, as two early modern nation states, could be considered as examples of civic nationalism *par excellence*: extensive multi-ethnic monarchies where loyalty to the state overrode local ethnic identities. On the other hand, both states were marked by a strong tradition of centralization and uniformity, which inevitably produced attempts to promote integration and assimiliation. Neither state had a historic tradition that supported multiculturalism.[34] In this respect, the older Scandinavian states contrasted sharply with the newer ones: both Finland and Norway had historic dual-language policies, and were forced to tolerate a degree of cultural diversity and even counter-cultural opposition to the centre that accompanied the presence of linguistic minorities (Swedish and *nynorsk* speakers respectively).

For this reason it is usually assumed that state responses to the first wave of post-war immigration in Scandinavia were strongly assimilationist. In fact, this is probably overstated. It would be more accurate to suggest that the assimilation of recent immigrants was almost entirely taken for granted in Sweden during the 1940s and '50s, and that few, if any, official attempts were made to promote it.[35] Assimilation was also driven by the emphasis on universalism and equality in welfare policies. In common with the rest of Europe, labour migrants were often – officially or unofficially – regarded as temporary residents in any case, and indeed many of them did return home after the economic recession of the early 1970s, as we have seen. Only from the 1960s did Sweden, as the only Nordic country to experience immigration in any significant quantity, make more concerted efforts to integrate its labour migrants, above all through the provision of compulsory state-funded language tuition. Likewise, the Danish government's comprehensive efforts to help family reunification for migrants after labour migration ended in the 1970s should be regarded as forming the first step towards a Danish integration policy.[36]

It was, however, not until the 1980s that integration began to be the subject of serious political debate in Denmark, following the increase in the numbers seeking political asylum. By 1998, when the first legislation on integration was introduced, immigration had increased enormously. The 1998 Integration Law framed integration as an economic question: it was intended to promote the integration of immigrants and their descendants as human capital capable of economic self-sufficiency. This addressed popular and widely expressed fears that immigration was likely to become a burden on the welfare state. The key to integration was thus the labour market, and, to make it easier for immigrants to find employment, the government recognized the need for education, above all, of course, in the Danish language, but also in rather vaguely defined 'basic values' such as tolerance and respect.[37] The government's proposals in its policy document En ny chance til alle ('A new chance for all', 2005) were founded on similar themes. Integration was coupled to the demands of the welfare state and the need for all to contribute through paid employment if it were to be maintained in the long term. Earlier integration policy, it was suggested, had created a passive dependency culture among immigrants, and to tackle this the government turned to a neo-liberal language of individual duties and responsibilities: 'The government's goal is that foreigners should become an active resource in Danish society.'[38]

As these statements suggest, behind the attempts of successive governments to promote the economic integration of immigrants lay a fundamentally assimilationist emphasis. Since 2001, the centre-right government, driven partly by the demands of the right-wing populist Danish People's Party that has supported it in the Folketing, has sought to derive much of its authority and legitimacy from its position as the defender of a homogeneous 'Danishness' based on a shared culture.[39] Rather than seeing cultural pluralism as an end in itself, the government promoted instead a hierarchical view of culture. While it was acknowledged that the majority (i.e., ethnic Danes) should seek to understand minority culture, the main onus was nonetheless on the minority to adapt their cultural behaviour to that of the majority and accept certain fundamental shared values.[40] The problem for the government, of course, was how to define these shared values, and, as the Danish scholar Ulf Hedetoft has pointed out, attempts to do so were frequently contradictory. In seeking to distance themselves from the merely trivial attributes of Danishness – 'Danishness is more than meatballs and gravy' in the words of the Prime Minister Anders Fogh Rasmussen – then politicians were forced to fall back upon very general values – respect for human life, freedom, equality and democracy – that were more readily understood as universal human principles rather than essentially Danish characteristics.[41] In this respect, the debate about Danishness was no different from the contemporary debates about national identity in Britain, France or anywhere else in Europe during these years.

At first glance, this seems to be less true for Sweden, which pursued a very different direction in its integration policy. The new Swedish constitution of 1974 included a clause obliging the state to protect the cultural ambitions of immigrant groups. This was made concrete the following year with the adoption of a new policy that formally proclaimed Sweden to be a multicultural country. The new immigrant and minority policy had three goals: equality (*jämlikhet*), freedom of choice (*valfrihet*) and partnership (*samverkan*). Partnership was understood as 'mutual tolerance and solidarity between immigrants and the native population'. Freedom of choice guaranteed the right of minorities to 'choose the extent to which they are to acquire Swedish cultural identity and the extent to which they are to preserve and develop their original cultural identity'. The main issue here was language, and the adoption of the Home Language Reform of 1977 provided state funding for native language tuition and for minority language press and associations.[42]

The adoption of multiculturalism amounted to a profound break with historical tradition, and marked Sweden as a pioneer within the Nordic countries and indeed more widely. The initial policy shift was driven partly by pragmatism, and in particular by the assumption that many of the labour migrants arriving in the late 1960s and early 1970s would stay only temporarily before returning home. Indeed, many of them did just that, and multi cultural policy was partly influenced by the concerns of the Finnish government that the growth in re-migration back to Finland was likely to present difficulties for a generation of children growing up in Sweden without sufficient knowledge of the

Finnish language.[43] The shift in policy was also influenced by the increased assertiveness of the indigenous Sami population during the 1970s, and the growing recognition of the legitimacy of Sami demands for cultural self-determination. Norwegian minority policy, too, underwent a shift in emphasis from assimilation to state-endorsed pluralism from the early 1970s, with provisions for mother-tongue tuition for children from minority groups, and the adoption of the principle of cultural self-realization as the basis for promoting integration.[44] But in both states, just as in Denmark, minority policy continued to be understood within the framework of the welfare state. Indeed, new immigrants often obtained full social rights long before they received concomitant political rights. Just as in the case of the Sami, this presented a paradox. There was always a tension between the state's promotion of individual freedom of choice and the recognition of special rights – for example to mother-tongue tuition – on the one hand, and on the other, the principles of equality and universalism within the welfare state that insisted that all citizens should be treated the same. According to the Norwegian historian Francis Sejersted, this paradox was partly resolved through the adoption of a broader meaning of the term 'equality' (jämlikhet) to imply equality of opportunity rather than equality of outcomes.[45]

Despite these early attempts to adopt multiculturalism in principle, it was not until the late 1990s that, as in Denmark, the practical questions of integration began to generate serious political debate. As in Denmark, in Sweden this followed a period of unprecedented levels of immigration and a profound change in the ethnic composition of the population. But unlike Denmark, where integration policy continued to be underpinned by assimilationist assumptions, the official point of departure for integration policy in Sweden was ethnic and cultural pluralism. The government's 2002 statement on integration, for example, started from the premise that Sweden was a pluralist society, and that '[t]he cultural inheritance that we call Swedish' had always been exposed to influences from outside.[46] In practical terms, whereas in Denmark the emphasis was on economic self-sufficiency as the basis for integration, and thus the onus to achieve this was left with the immigrants themselves, Swedish policy makers focused instead on tackling structural and institutional discrimination in the labour market and in society more generally.

These differences mean that it would be easy, as many have indeed done, to caricature Sweden and Denmark as polar opposites in their integration policy and more generally their attitudes to immigration and ethnic diversity. The Swedish tolerance of multiculturalism and difference contrasts with the Danish insistence on homogeneity and assimilation; Swedish society is seen as open and tolerant compared to the closed and exclusive nature of Denmark.[47] In this respect, the Danish general election of November 2001, and the 'great northern war of words' (*store nordiske ordkrig*) that followed it, seemed to be a major turning point in relations between the two countries. The election campaign was notable for the absence of significant differences between the parties on matters of traditional political contention such as economic policy, and instead a focus on immigration policy. In part this was driven by the presence of two far-right populist parties, the Danish People's Party and the Progress Party, both of which campaigned on an explicitly xenophobic (and anti-Islamic) platform. But the centre-right Liberal Party (Venstre) also chose to focus its campaigning on the 'immigration crisis', criticizing the outgoing government for failing to control immigration. Venstre also adopted controversial imagery and language, which according to its critics was inflammatory and xenophobic.[48]

The election resulted in an historic defeat for the Social Democrats, and the formation of a coalition between Venstre and the Conservative Party led by the Venstre politician Anders Fogh Rasmussen. The Danish People's Party did not become a formal coalition member, though its strong performance meant that the government was forced to rely on the support of its members in the Folketing. Nonetheless, the election provoked some markedly and hitherto quite unprecedented hostile reactions in the foreign press. Many journalists drew attention to the apparent contrast with the stereotype of Denmark as a liberal and tolerant country: 'this icon of northern European welfare-state progressivism . . . descended into an inflammatory election campaign'.[49] The storm of international criticism increased when the new government announced the introduction of new controls on immigration in May

2002. The new law, of which perhaps the most controversial aspect was the imposition of a minimum age of 24 for those wishing to marry a foreign spouse, was widely interpreted as 'one of Europe's toughest asylum laws', and the government was criticized by the UN's High Commissioner for Refugees, Ruud Lubbers.[50]

The most outspoken criticism of the new Danish government and its immigration policy came from Sweden. The 2001 election campaign was followed with great interest in the Swedish media, with some commentators expressing their dismay in terms that were previously quite unthinkable in their open hostility towards the inhabitants of another Nordic country, as the following example from the tabloid daily *Aftonbladet* illustrates:

> Sit there on your elongated bit of Germany and munch open sandwiches by yourselves. Sit there with your moustaches and drink Tuborg till the cows come home. Sit there, you inbred cavemen. But don't come crawling over the Öresund bridge for sympathy when you get fed up with isolation – because you won't find it here. Danish bastards . . .
>
> By dressing up a racist manifesto as the emperor's new clothes, the openly unpleasant Anders Fogh Rasmussen has succeeded in making Venstre Denmark's largest party.[51]

The Swedish government also formally and publicly criticized the new Danish immigration policy adopted in 2002, through an open letter written by the Social Democratic integration minister Mona Sahlin jointly with her French and Belgian counterparts.[52]

Relations worsened further following the publication of twelve cartoons depicting the Prophet Mohammed in the Danish newspaper *Jyllands-Posten* in September 2005, and the ensuing crisis over the winter of 2005–6.[53] There was a marked contrast between the reactions of the Danish and the Swedish governments. In Denmark, Prime Minister Anders Fogh Rasmussen sought to distance himself personally from the cartoons, but refused to issue a formal apology, stating that it was not appropriate for the government to take responsibility for the actions of the free press. The editor of *Jyllands-Posten* apologized for having caused offence to Muslims, but defended his decision to publish the cartoons, which he had intended to provoke a public debate about religious tolerance, self-censorship and freedom of expression. A legal case was brought against *Jyllands-Posten* invoking the constitutional provisions to protect religious and other groups from scorn and degradation, but the case was rejected by the director of public prosecutions. In Sweden, meanwhile, the government intervened to close down the website of the right-wing party Sweden Democrats once it became known that they had published the cartoons.[54] The hostile portrayal of Denmark in the Swedish press as xenophobic and intolerant was thus mirrored by an equally negative stereotype on the other side: of Sweden as self-censoring and politically correct.[55] The debate flared up again in the autumn of 2006 when the *Dagens Nyheter* journalist Stefan Jonsson accused Danish public opinion of being 'obsessed' with Islam, but where a nuanced debate about its cultural influence was impossible. In response, Danish commentators pointed towards Swedish political correctness (*meningstyranni*).[56]

As with most stereotypes, that of Danish–Swedish differences in immigration policy contains some truth, but the virulence of the debate has inevitably served to obscure the complexities of the situation on both sides. Although Danish caricatures of Sweden as 'political correctness gone mad' were overstated, Swedish multiculturalism was indeed largely an elite phenomenon, supported by a cosmopolitan political class that ignored genuine problems of fragmentation and segregation in the rest of society.[57] According to some critics, the holding of an open and critical debate about problems concerning immigration and ethnic minorities seemed to present some genuine difficulties in Sweden.[58] As the geographer Allan Pred has shown, the presence of racism and intolerance itself was just as much of a challenge to Swedish self-identity as the presence of ethnic minority 'others', and this sometimes made it difficult to acknowledge the existence of social problems. In the minds of many Swedes, especially the elite defenders of multiculturalism, racist attitudes and incidents were attributed to a small minority of extremists, who drew on disaffection among unemployed youth in declining industrial towns for their support. In this account, evidence for racism was thus easily explained, accounted for, and understood as a temporary aberration.[59]

Equally comforting for the Swedish establishment, perhaps, was the presence of the xenophobic Danish People's Party in mainstream Danish politics after 1997, and, more importantly, the absence of an equivalent party in Sweden.[60] Indeed, this seems to have remained one of the main differences between the two countries: why have anti-immigration sentiments found political expression to a much greater extent in Denmark than in Sweden? The Danish People's Party replaced the Progress Party as the main expression of right-wing populism in Danish politics after 1997, and rose rapidly in the opinion polls before the 2001 election, which must be seen as a significant victory for the party.[61] It could be compared with other right-wing populist parties including the Austrian Freedom Party, the French Front National and the Dutch Pim Fortyun's List, though it never sought contacts or alliances with these groups, like them preferring to emphasize its national exclusivity.[62] Unlike similar parties elsewhere in Europe, the xenophobic political right in Denmark seemed to have no links to or roots in neo-Nazism. Indeed, those espousing such views in Denmark (and in Norway) tried to link themselves to the *anti*-Nazism of the wartime resistance movement, positioning themselves as a 'new resistance movement' fighting foreign invaders and the contemporary 'traitors' who would welcome them. This differed from Sweden, where there seemed to be a much closer link between far right xenophobic groups and the European neo-Nazi movement.[63] Indeed, as Allan Pred has suggested, the Swedish elite could for some years comfort itself with the notion that racism 'belonged' to a tiny minority of neo-Nazi extremists, and was not therefore part of 'mainstream' Swedish society.[64]

There was perhaps further comforting evidence of the failure of far-right populism to make a serious impact on Swedish politics in the brief emergence of such a party, New Democracy, in 1991. Reassuringly, New Democracy lost its parliamentary representation in 1994, and its brief presence in the Swedish Riksdag could thus be attributed to the very severe recession and related social upheavals that Sweden experienced in the early 1990s. The re-election of a Social Democratic government in 1994 restored 'business as normal'. The sociologist

Jens Rydgren suggested that there were three main reasons why no right-wing populist party had succeeded in making a permanent breakthrough in Swedish politics before 2002. First, established identities and loyalties were not as severely challenged in Sweden as elsewhere, despite, or perhaps with the temporary exception of, the traumatic experience of the early 1990s. Secondly, the immigration question seemed to be of less importance to Swedish voters than to their counterparts in Denmark. This last point seems to suggest a rather unhelpfully circular argument, however: it could be argued that immigration was not a salient issue in Danish politics before the Danish People's Party made it so. Perhaps more important then is Rydgren's third point, that despite the long years of Social Democratic government, the Swedish Conservative Party remained a viable political alternative, and so there had been much less ideological convergence in Swedish politics.[65] A notable feature of the 2001 Danish election campaign was the lack of ideological difference among the parties on traditional matters of disagreement such as economic policy, following Venstre's decision to abandon its earlier libertarian stance and present itself as the defender of the Danish welfare state.[66] And, after experiencing a serious defeat in the 2002 election, the Swedish Conservatives seemed to follow the same path, abandoning their commitment to neo-liberalism and moving towards the middle ground. In doing so, there were signs, following their victory in the 2006 election, that the vacated territory of the right wing had created the conditions for growth in support for the far-right Sweden Democrats, who had also made concerted efforts to shake off their image as an anti-democratic party on the margins of respectability. That the Sweden Democrats had still not been able to secure parliamentary representation in 2006 was attributable partly to the higher threshold required in the Swedish electoral system to enter the Riksdag: their success would have been enough to secure them representation in Denmark.

Nevertheless, by 2007 Sweden still lacked a right-wing xenophobic party in mainstream politics, and this had perhaps prevented the other parties adopting more restrictive policies towards immigration in the manner of their Danish counterparts. Against this, there was some evidence of greater participation in politics by members of ethnic minorities at grassroots level in Denmark than there was in Sweden.[67] Although the international media in particular concentrated on the success of the Danish People's Party in the 2001 election, the centre-left Social Liberal (Radikale Venstre) Party ran a campaign emphasizing the benefits of a multicultural society.[68] Among the candidates at both parliamentary and municipal level were many with ethnic minority background, more than at any previous election.[69] By contrast, a public inquiry on democracy and political participation in Sweden in 2005 found that citizens from ethnic minorities seeking to participate in Swedish public life faced 'a number of routines, conventions and more or less taken-for-granted ideas that categorise[d] citizens according to their perceived closeness to a Swedish "normality"'. Within institutions that were considered exceptionally important to the smooth functioning of Swedish democracy, including the trade union movement and the workers' educational movement, there was evidence for the operation of exclusionary practices based on assumptions about cultural difference.[70]

Despite their differences, therefore, Sweden and Denmark did seem to show some signs of convergence in the early years of the new millennium. In both countries, the issue of immigration was discussed in terms that bore some hallmarks of cultural racism, that is a tendency to categorize individuals according to their cultural origins and attribute to them fixed and immutable cultural attributes. This was indicated partly in the terminology used to discuss ethnic minorities. In Sweden, the term immigrant (*invandrare*) was widely used as a shorthand for non-whites, even when referring to members of ethnic minorities who had been born and brought up in the country. The effect was often to 'freeze' the identities of individuals as immigrants, in contrast to a native 'Swedish' population regarded as individuals.[71] In Denmark, the official statistics agency introduced in 1991 a formal distinction between immigrants (*indvandrere*) and their descendants (*efterkommere*) – which also contributed to essentializing the difference between these groups and ethnic Danes – but the common term in general usage was 'foreigners' (*de fremmede*), signifying the perceived impermanent nature of their stay. In Denmark, in particular, the category was usually imagined as overlapping with that of Muslim.[72] Since the turn of the century, however, the term 'new Dane' (*nydansker*) was becoming more widely accepted as an alternative.[73]

One area of particular concern in both Denmark and Sweden, and indeed in Norway, was the labour market. Successive studies revealed evidence of discrimination among employers and higher levels of unemployment among members of ethnic minorities compared to the white population. A 1998 study found that only 39 per cent of non-western immigrants were in employment in Denmark, compared to 74 per cent of ethnic Danes. This had improved somewhat (46 per cent: 76 per cent) by 2001, but the problem was clearly severe.[74] There was an equally marked divide in Norway, where only 13.9 per cent of the population groups with Somalian and Bosnian-Hercegovinan background were in paid employment, compared to the national average of 56.9 per cent (and 43.5 per cent for all immigrant groups).[75] Labour market integration was in turn regarded as very important in determining subsequent participation in society, with unemployment contributing to the exclusion of immigrants from the democratic process.[76]

Some academic studies of this problem sought to explain it in relation to changes on the demand side of the economy, namely the shift from industrial production relying heavily on unskilled labour to service sector employment, which required a high degree of flexibility and culturally specific competence. Cultural distance among immigrants could therefore be a hindrance to employment, with correspondingly greater difficulties for non-Europeans to find a job.[77] Other scholars have pointed out the problematic assumptions about culture and cultural difference that underpinned this research, and have drawn attention to the role of academic social science itself in promoting stereotyped and culturally racist ideas about immigrants and their cultural competence.[78] Awareness of this problem was indeed growing from the turn of the century, with the Swedish government in particular declaring its intention to focus on structural racism and institutional discrimination as a means to tackle the problem.[79] But it could be suggested that similar attitudes also continued to inform the methods used by the Nordic authorities to collect official statistics about immigration and the ethnic composition of the population. The Norwegian statistical authorities, for example, included under the category 'immigrant' or 'immigrant background' first-generation immigrants, but also those children born in Norway to parents who had themselves immigrated. Moreover, this categorization excluded all those who were the children of mixed couples, and could therefore be considered to have 'Norwegian background'.[80] The effect of this, and possibly of the methods of statistical counting of ethnicity in general, was twofold: on the one hand it homogenized diverse groups of people under the heading 'immigrants', or even, in the case of Norway, 'Third World immigrants'; while on the other hand it reinforced the concept of the nation state as an ethno-cultural community above all.

The Nordic state where the principle of *ius sanguinis* seemed to have the biggest impact on citizenship and immigration policy was perhaps Finland. The impact of the major wave of late twentieth-century immigration came slightly later to Finland than to the other Nordic countries. Within Europe only Iceland, Ireland and Portugal absorbed fewer refugees before 1990, and the vast majority of immigrants were Finnish re-migrants returning from Sweden.[81] The number of refugees and asylum seekers arriving in Finland rose somewhat from the late 1980s, and by 1993 there were over 3,500 refugees in Finland, most of them Somalian by origin.[82]

This meant that the self-image of Finland, as a culturally and ethnically homogeneous country characterized by its relative isolation from international currents such as mass migration, persisted among politicians and the general public alike well into the 1990s.[83] A Eurobarometer poll in 1997 found that four-fifths of those surveyed described themselves as 'rather racist', and on occasion negative attitudes towards immigrants spilled over into direct hostility and even violence, such as the emergence of an overtly racist skinhead movement in the eastern town of Joensuu.[84] Moreover, there was evidence for a deterioration in attitudes during the years 1987–93. Of course, part of this period coincided, as in Sweden, with a severe economic crisis, but as in Sweden this is clearly not the whole story.[85] At government level, the perception that Finland remained untroubled by the global growth in migration also meant that as late as 1998 Finland still lacked an official refugee policy of any coherence. Government reponsibility for immigrants was split between several ministries, and there was also a tendency to disperse refugees across different municipalities, which meant that it was difficult for ethnic minority groups to maintain linguistic, cultural and religious traditions.[86]

Like the other Nordic countries, the evolution of Finnish minorities policy demonstrates a rather paradoxical position between the poles of civic and ethnic models of citizenship. Historically, Finland was the only Nordic country to give a privileged position within its constitution to its linguistic (Swedish-speaking) and religious (Orthodox) minorities, and for this reason it was even cited as an example of cultural pluralism in a UNESCO report from 1985.[87] The increase in immigration from the early 1990s, however, coincided with social and cultural changes promoting a greater degree of linguistic homogeneity in Finland. The Swedish-speaking minority had declined in numbers to the extent that it consisted of between 5 and 6 per cent of the population, and despite constitutional provisions to support the Swedish language through education and the media, for example, it seemed that there was a growing trend towards inter-marriage and thus Finnish-Swedish bilingualism among the Swedish-speaking community.[88] Moreover, the popular stereotype of the Swedish-speaking minority as a privileged and elitist group, which reflected class antagonisms dating back to the Civil War of 1918 and even earlier, persisted among the Finnish-speaking population, and even influenced the public debate on immigration. Speaking in the Eduskunta during the debate on refugee policy in 1991, the Green Party politician Paloheimo expressed his opposition to immigration in terms of an outspoken hostility to the Swedish-speaking minority and a defence of Finnishness in ethno-linguistic terms that are quite striking:

> The low self-esteem of the Finns makes them – or us – be ashamed of our own identity and to admire everything international and foreign. The motivation of Swedish-speaking Finns in the issue of immigration is logical: the more and fresher minorities, the easier it will be for an old and established minority to breathe. Our most noteworthy minority perhaps wouldn't

mind, if the present majority would gradually sink to a minority position.[89]

The debate about Finnishness was also shaped by a remarkable development in April 1990. Speaking in a television interview, the Finnish president Mauno Koivisto announced his decision to extend the rights accorded to returning Finnish migrants from Sweden to the Ingrian community. The term Ingrian (*Inkeri* in Finnish) referred to those inhabitants of the region around St Petersburg with Finnish ancestry, who were assumed both to speak Finnish and to adhere to the Lutheran faith (in practice many Ingrians did neither). Many Ingrians had been present in Finland after the end of the Second World War, from where they had been forcibly repatriated to the Soviet Union. Koivisto's announcement was thus seen partly as an acknowledgement of culpability for this, though it also reflected the romanticization of Karelia in the Finnish nationalist imagination.[90] It was also remarkable in its identification of a Finnish ethno-linguistic community stretching beyond the boundaries of the current state and in its explicit acknowledgement therefore of the *ius sanguinis* elements of the Finnish conception of citizenship. In order to claim rights to work permits and social security benefits, the would-be Ingrian returnees had to prove that at least one of their four grandparents was from Finland. Later, these requirements were tightened, but by 2002, 22,000 Ingrians had 'returned' to Finland, a migration that was without parallel in the rest of the Nordic region.

CONCLUSION

Questions of cultural difference, cultural self-determination, language and identity continued to dominate public discourse on immigration and minorities into the new millennium. The Nordic countries were not alone in this respect, of course – the debates that took place there were similar to those in most of the rest of Europe – but inevitably they were also articulated with a distinctive Nordic tone, and also revealed some important differences between the Nordic countries.

The cultural debate about the impact of immigration became particularly prominent during the 1990s, for several reasons. First, this was a period of substantial immigration to all the Nordic countries, which produced some quite profound social changes over a relatively short period of time. The experience of mass immigration in countries that – apart from Sweden – had been relatively isolated from its effects before 1990 challenged residual ideas of the Scandinavian countries as culturally homogeneous states where small groups of immigrants could be absorbed and assimilated relatively easily and rapidly. Secondly, from the early 1990s there began to emerge compelling evidence to challenge the Scandinavian self-image of being societies that were socially harmonious and tolerant. Studies of the labour market pointed to higher levels of unemployment among ethnic minority groups compared to the 'native' population, and there was a growing awareness of severe segregation within the housing sector and the rise of minority 'ghettos' in the suburbs of the larger cities. Perhaps even more influential were a number of cases of intra-ethnic tensions, sometimes violent, that received prominent coverage in the national press and broadcast media. These included the so-called laser man killings of several ethnic minority Swedes during the early 1990s, and the burning of a mosque in Trollhättan in 1993.[91] Politically, too, there were signs that immigration and multiculturalism were becoming increasingly controversial. The populist Progress Party made strong gains in the 1987 municipal elections in Norway on an anti-immigration platform, and the similar New Democracy Party won parliamentary representation in Sweden in 1991.

It is worth noting that these changes in Scandinavia were mirrored by similar events across the rest of Europe at this time, a trend that perhaps served only to underline further the erosion of the sense of Nordic 'distinctiveness' in contrast to the rest of Europe. And also, as the rest of this book has sought to demonstrate, there were many other aspects of this distinctiveness that were challenged during and after the early 1990s (whether they had ever existed is another matter) and could no longer be taken for granted. The emergence of right-wing populist parties was a challenge not only to existing immigration policy, but to the whole notion of the Nordic political model. The debates over the EU – whether conducted in terms of whether or not to espouse deeper integration after Maastricht (Denmark) or whether to join in the first place (Sweden, Norway, Finland) – were also now expressed in terms of culture above all, rather than the economic and political arguments that had dominated the discourse on European integration during the 1970s and earlier.

Not only the experience of mass immigration, but also the political, social and cultural responses to it, have thus presented serious challenges to the autostereotypes of the Scandinavian countries. This is also true for the xenostereotype, with signs that the rest of the world is no longer prepared to regard the Scandinavian countries as havens of tolerance and integration. This shift has taken some by surprise, as the geographer Allan Pred alluded to in his choice of the title *Even in Sweden* for his book on racism in 1990s Sweden. That the 2001 election campaign in Denmark attracted so much hostile coverage in the international press is partly accounted for by the perceived departure from a Scandinavian paradigm of tolerance.[92]

Conclusion: Is There a Future for the Nordic Region?

This book started from the premise that Scandinavia (or Norden) 'cannot be seen as a given fact, but is the result of discursively negotiated constructions'.[1] The concept of the nation state as an 'imagined community' is well known, but as the Finnish cultural geographer Anssi Paasi has shown, *all* political and territorial identities are fictional to some extent, including regional ones. Regions and other territories, and their symbolic representations, are thus always contingent and unstable, fluctuating in time and space.[2]

For the historian, the concept of Scandinavia can function in two ways. First, the process of writing Nordic history (instead of Finnish, Norwegian, Danish history, etc.), and of considering the similarities and differences between the Nordic countries can help to challenge the 'unconscious national understanding' that seems still to pervade historical research.[3] The closely linked histories of the Nordic countries provide an ideal framework for the exploration and analysis of long-term historical processes in comparative perspective.

Secondly, the ambition of this book was also to explore the changing meanings of the term Scandinavia. Nordic identity as a distinctive region was probably never stronger than during the period covered by this book, that is, since 1945.[4] The concept of Scandinavia as embodying a 'middle way' between capitalism and communism stemmed from the inter-war period, and above all the publication of Marquis Childs's 1936 bestseller on Sweden, but it really caught on during the post-war period, both as an external stereotype of the region and an element of self-identity within it. In the first place, even though three out of five of the Nordic states joined NATO, Scandinavia seemed to stand outside the bi-polar divisions of the Cold War. The historic legacy of neutrality, minimal engagement with the alliance in military terms, and the willingness of Nordic politicians to exploit the moral advantages of their small-state status through international organizations such as the United Nations all contributed to this view. Secondly, and more importantly, the apparent success of Scandinavian countries in overcoming poverty and economic backwardness without the sacrifice of democratic principles seemed to suggest that Scandinavia stood for a different type of politics from that which characterized much of the rest of Europe: consensual and compromise-driven, social democratic in outlook and able to combine a comprehensive and redistributive welfare state with a successful capitalist economy.

Of course, to some extent it was not Scandinavia that was distinctive but the age. The two decades between 1950 and 1970 were an unprecedented golden age for much of Europe. The economic prosperity, political stability and social consensus that defined the era stood in contrast to the disasters of the 'Age of Catastrophe' that had preceded it,[5] although many problems remained, not least the need to rebuild industry and infrastructure after three decades of conflict and upheaval, and to rehouse the millions of displaced people. Looking back, it is easy to overlook the anxieties and insecurities of the period, above all, the strains of living under the shadow of the nuclear bomb. For all their semi-aligned status, this was a threat of which the populations of the Nordic countries were acutely aware, given their proximity to the USSR.

Nevertheless, the Nordic countries were different in the eyes of many. For many on the social democratic left, the Nordic countries assumed utopian qualities as living examples of the social democratic vision of equality and prosperity for all. As Reinhart Koselleck has suggested, the term utopia implies the deferral of dreams and aspirations to the future.[6] Thus, although some might have regarded the Nordic example as a blueprint for reform, it also functioned as an example of an aspiration that was unattainable or impossible in the current context. On the Anglo-American right in particular, Scandinavia also came to assume the status of a dystopia, associated with melancholy, conformity and control. The Nordic region functioned in this way in part because it retained the image, even into the post-war period, of being cold, remote and relatively unknown. In the early twenty-first century age of cheap flights, it is worth remembering that travel in post-war Europe was still relatively expensive and thus also difficult and time-consuming. The Nordic countries were clearly less accessible by rail, and thus less familiar than the rest of central and western Europe. Helsinki, during the height of its Cold War isolation during the 1960s and 1970s, was probably more provincial and inward-looking than it had been at any time since 1809.

As this book has attempted to show, the implementation of the Nordic model in practical terms – in terms of the economic, social and foreign policies adopted – took different forms in different parts of the Nordic region. In the same way, the relevance and meaning of the Nordic model as a concept and source of identity varied across the region. The archetypal Nordic country was always Sweden, even to the extent that one may question whether the so-called Nordic model was in fact a Swedish one.[7] All the elements of the Nordic model seemed to be present unproblematically in Sweden: strong social democracy, the extensive welfare state, neutrality in foreign policy, class compromise and consensus in the labour market.

Some historians have attempted to distinguish between 'west Norden' (Denmark, Norway and the Atlantic islands) and 'east Norden' (Sweden and Finland) to take account of the legacies of early modern state development in Denmark and Sweden, and the orientation towards the north Atlantic and the Baltic respectively.[8] Despite this, for nearly all the other countries in the region, the main reference point, and the partner in the most important intra-Nordic relationship in the post-war period, was Sweden.[9] The exception was perhaps Iceland, which inevitably looked towards Denmark as the former colonial power after independence in 1944. For Denmark itself, Sweden was the 'other' whose undesirable traits – the cold climate, inhospitability and restrictions on social behaviour, especially the consumption of alcohol – reinforced the positive elements of Danish self-identity as warmer, more relaxed and more 'Continental' in its social attitudes.[10] For Norway, post-war relations were coloured by a legacy of some bitterness over Swedish inactions during the war, and a residual sense of inferiority as the younger sibling of the lopsided union relationship.[11] The influence of the Swedish model was perhaps strongest of all in Finland. In the words of the Finnish historian Max Engman, '[i]n no other land was there the same willingness to accept Swedish ideas and social innovations'.[12] For Finland, relations with Sweden continued to be coloured to some extent by class differences between the Swedish-speaking minority and the Finnish-speaking majority, but for many Finnish citizens Sweden also appeared a land of opportunity, providing employment for hundreds of thousands of Finnish labour migrants during the 1960s.

Although Scandinavia was always an important element in the self-identity of the populations of north-eastern Europe, it never amounted to more than 'a pooling of nationalisms'. In other words, it was never conceptualized as a challenge to the different Scandinavian national identities but rather as an extra layer of 'second nationhood'.[13] Scandinavianism worked to strengthen national identity in two different ways. For Sweden and Denmark it helped to provide the means of adapting to small-state status after military defeats in 1809 and 1864 respectively. More importantly, for the former colonial states that achieved national independence during the first half of the twentieth century, 'Norden' also functioned as an aspiration and was a very important means to help to cement national independence and statehood against internal and external threats. This was particularly the case for Finland, where the Nordic sphere was seen as a bulwark against the threat of the Soviet Union, during both the inter-war period and the Cold War.[14]

Finland's realignment as a Nordic country during the inter-war period helps to illustrate the flexibility of Norden as a concept, able to change and accommodate different geo-political constellations. This is especially true of the period since 1989–91. The end of the Cold War is widely understood as a formative moment for the remaking of regional identities.[15] For a while it seemed that the upheavals would bring the end of the Nordic model altogether. The new right-wing Swedish government elected in 1991 built its platform on an explicit rejection of the model. In the words of the new prime minister, Carl Bildt, 'The time for

the Nordic model has passed ... It created societies that were too monop-
olised, too expensive and didn't give people the freedom of choice that they
wanted; societies that lacked flexibility and dynamism.'[16] Elsewhere in the
region, politicians and academics alike began to refer explicitly to the
Danish, Finnish or Norwegian models, as an attempt to distance themselves from the undesirable associations of the Nordic (Swedish) model.[17]

At the same time, from the late 1980s there were also signs of a growing interest in the cultural similarities shared by the countries of the
traditional Nordic region and beyond. Within the Nordic countries
themselves this interest was expressed in the tendency, in both academic
research and public discourse, to essentialize the Nordic model in terms
of its deep historical roots stretching back to the Enlightenment or
even the sixteenth-century Reformation. But it also led to attempts to
redefine the entire region, first as a 'new Hansa' and then, more influ-
entially, as the Baltic. The collapse of communism and the removal of the
Iron Curtain had, it was suggested, re-established the traditional trade
routes across the Baltic Sea, and in doing so had led to the rediscovery of
forgotten affinities among peoples that shared close historical and
cultural ties. The Council for Baltic Sea States was founded in 1992, and
there was a flurry of activity to promote economic, cultural, educational
and personal links, especially in Finland and Sweden.[18]

The emergence of the 'Baltic' as a focus for regional identity seems to
support Samuel P. Huntington's 'clash of civilizations' thesis, where
'global politics is being reconfigured along cultural lines ... [and] alignments defined by ideology and superpower relations are giving way to
alignments defined by culture and civilization.'[19] But there is a danger
of over-stating the significance of a common Baltic identity. In the first
place, as the Finnish scholar Marko Lehti has pointed out, the process
of rethinking regional identity at the end of the Cold War was mainly
confined to the discursive level, as an attempt to rename and reorgan-
ize a world that seemed to be disintegrating.[20] Perhaps the greatest
impact was on academia, where there was a sudden rush of interest in
funding Baltic research projects and a number of attempts to write the
common history of the region.[21]

Secondly, just like Norden or Scandinavia, the notion of 'the Baltic'
was rather a fluid one, which carried different meanings in different

contexts. For the governments of Sweden and Finland (and, to a lesser extent, Denmark), interest in the Baltic states was partly motivated by a sense of moral responsibility and the need to atone for past misdeeds, notably the extradition of Estonian refugees to the Soviet Union during and after the Second World War.[22] But the Baltic also served to counteract fears of marginalization in the post-Cold War world, by demonstrating the continued relevance of the Nordic model as an exportable concept.

On the other side of the Baltic Sea, with clear parallels to the Finnish case during the inter-war period, the concept of the Nordic model became part of the new narrative of 'transition' following the collapse of the Soviet Union and independence in 1991. As the Estonian scholar and politician Marju Lauristin has pointed out, 'transition' is an explicitly teleological concept, implying development towards a stated end, in this case the 'return home' to western civilization.[23] The utopian qualities of the Nordic model could therefore serve as both the means and the end for those who sought to reintegrate their newly independent countries into Western Europe. This applied especially to Estonia, where the historical and cultural ties with Scandinavia seemed to be the strongest. Indeed, this was certainly true at the discursive level, where reformers could point to the shared Lutheran tradition, the educational and institutional legacies of seventeenth-century Swedish rule and the linguistic and cultural affinities with Finland, but it was also true in practical terms.[24] Finnish television programmes had been broadcast in northern Estonia since 1958, and contacts were facilitated by the strong similarities between the Estonian and Finnish languages. And if Lauristin suggests that '[t]he similarity with Finns became practically a national conviction for Estonians' during the Soviet period, then after 1991 at least the interest was also reciprocated, with the rediscovery in Finland of an ethno-linguistic community that united Finns, Karelians, Ingrians and Estonians.[25] Moreover, for Estonia, the stated affinity with the Nordic region provided a means to differentiate the country from Latvia and Lithuania, states that seemed to be united by the shared experience of Soviet occupation but by very little else.[26]

The idea of a Baltic region attracted widespread enthusiasm during the early 1990s, but this interest could not be sustained. More sober assessments made during the late 1990s and afterwards began to question the relevance of the Baltic for the inhabitants of the states bordering the sea, including the Nordic ones. Marko Lehti has suggested that the Baltic was always more attractive for Sweden and Finland than it was for Estonia and Latvia, where it was only at best a staging post towards the main goal of full membership of the European Union.[27] In 1997 Peeter Vihalemm found that, although fast transport links meant that 'Tallinn is on its way to become the southern outskirts of Helsinki', there was no evidence for the emergence of a shared Estonian-Finnish identity, in either Estonia or Finland.[28] Indeed, there were instead signs of cooling relations, with rather negative public images of the other in both countries. For the Estonians, this was undoubtedly helped by the popularity of Tallinn as a cheap drinking destination for residents of southern Finland, while in Finland Estonia still seems to retain its negative image as a post-Soviet transition society. Moreover, disparities in wealth contribute to the continued unevenness of relations across the Gulf of Finland.

Meanwhile, from the late 1990s some Scottish politicians were also turning to the Nordic countries in their attempts to redefine Scottish national identity and to campaign for independence. Here, as elsewhere, the Nordic model functioned on two levels. It was on the one hand a practical source of ideas and inspiration for those seeking to establish new institutions for increased national autonomy. After the devolution legislation was passed by the UK parliament in 1997 there were widespread references in Scotland to the need to create a 'new politics', where, as David Arter has shown, the Nordic 'consensual democracies' were explicitly adopted as models. The Consultative Steering Group established to set up the new Scottish parliament referred to parliamentary practices in the three Scandinavian countries throughout its 1999 report *Shaping Scotland's Parliament*.[29]

On the other hand, the Nordic model was also used rhetorically by politicians of the pro-independence Scottish Nationalist Party (SNP) to support their case for independence. For the SNP, it was above all Norway that was of interest. Norway was similar in size of population to Scotland, and the two countries had shared close historical ties over many centuries. However, Norwegian independence, the centenary of which was marked by a debate in the Scottish parliament in 2005, had made Norway 'one of the most successful social democracies in Europe, if not the world, whilst Scotland lags behind economically and socially'.[30] Norwegian life expectancy, educational achievement, GDP per capita and gender equality were all compared favourably with the same indicators for Scotland. Above all, it was claimed, Norwegian independence had enabled Norwegian society to benefit fully from North Sea oil resources, whereas 'Scotland's oil wealth ha[d] been squandered by successive UK governments'. Even without oil, however, the other Nordic countries could also function in this way, with the SNP listing Iceland, Finland and Estonia as examples of 'success stories' for small-nation independence. In this case, therefore, the utopian appeal of the Nordic model was represented not in its usual terms of 'democracy' or 'social democracy' but instead of 'independence', where Scotland was imagined as belonging to a group of small, rich, independent, northern European nations. In the SNP's words: 'Off our east coast lies Norway, the second most prosperous country in the world. Off our west coast lies Ireland, the fourth most prosperous country in the world. Off our north coast lies Iceland, the sixth most prosperous country in the world. These independent countries represent an arc of prosperity – and Scotland has every bit as much potential as them.'[31]

While Scottish nationalists looked towards the Nordic nations that had become independent in the first half of the twentieth century, they ignored the existence of demands for independence within the Nordic region itself. At the beginning of the twenty-first century the most likely candidate to swell the ranks of the Nordic states was not Scotland but one of the three autonomous regions: Åland, Greenland and the Faroe Islands. The north Atlantic territories had remained relatively isolated as colonies of Denmark until the post-war period, when they had gained the status of autonomous territories.[32] Indeed they, and Åland, had gained so great a degree of autonomy by the end of the twentieth century that it may even have become appropriate to speak of eight separate polities in the Nordic region. The Swedish-speaking Åland islanders wished to become part of Sweden after Finnish independence in 1917, but the League of Nations ruled that they should remain as a special autonomous region within Finland. A new law on self-government in 1991 gave the islanders increased economic independence, and extended their autonomy in areas such as education and social services.

Home rule was introduced on the Faroe Islands in 1948, as a compromise arrangement in response to demands for full independence. Under the terms of the agreement, the Danish state remained responsible for foreign policy, defence, law and order and some core elements of monetary policy, but decisions about tax and public expenditure were devolved. Faroese–Danish relations were badly affected by the economic crisis of the early 1990s, when Faroese unemployment rose to 20 per cent and 10 per cent of the population left the islands. The situation was perceived to have been greatly exacerbated by the Danish state bank's mishandling of funds, which resulted eventually in a court case against the bank. The resulting distrust of the Danish state fuelled demands for independence, though in 2007 both the political parties and public opinion remained divided over the matter.[33]

In Greenland, the Danish government funded a programme of economic modernization after the Second World War, but despite major changes and the growth of the shrimp fisheries in particular the Greenlandic economy remained in a position of economic dependence. Home rule was introduced in 1979, and a few years later, following a consultative referendum in 1982, Greenland negotiated withdrawal from the European Community, which it had entered as part of Denmark in 1973. By the early twenty-first century most commentators seemed to agree that home rule had been a success for Greenland, and the country was often cited as a model for recognizing the rights of indigenous people all over the world. In 2007 two new issues were starting to promote discussions about the desirability of full independence: the effects of the shrinking ice fields on traditional culture and the fragile eco-system, made prominent by the apparent popularity of Greenland as a destination for European politicians seeking to promote their own policies on climate change, and the real possibility of discovering significant oil reserves following prospecting by international companies.[34]

Although it is still perhaps too soon to assess accurately the long-term impact of the years 1989–91 as a turning point in European history, the upheavals of those years undoubtedly helped to destabilize the idea of Norden as a stable, coherent region.[35] New ways of imagining this part of northern Europe have emerged since then, and in turn have faded. The 'new Hansa' of the late 1980s soon gave way to ideas about the Baltic, but by the late 1990s this too had become fragmented into different attempts at region-building. Among these can be noted the Finnish government's attempts to construct a 'northern dimension' during its successful and high-profile EU presidency in 1999, and the launch of the Barents Euro-Arctic Region in Norway in 1993.[36] Among the more fanciful attempts at region-building was the concept of the 'Yule countries', promoted by the Estonians Lennart Meri and Toomas Hendrik Ilves, that united both Estonia and the British Isles with the Nordic countries. Beneath the apparently trivial concept of a region based on a shared word for Christmas was supposed to lie a common mentality and political culture.[37]

Parallel to these attempts to construct a new macro-regional identity, there is also evidence for a growing interest in sub-national regions within the Nordic countries. Demands for increased autonomy may even result in the emergence of new independent micro-states in Greenland and the Faroe Islands as we have seen, though the minority campaigns for increased independence in places like Skåne and Jämtland could not really be taken seriously. Nonetheless, the example of Skåne indicates the best-known transnational city region within the Nordic countries, namely the increased contacts between Malmö and Copenhagen following the opening of the Öresund bridge in 1999.

Yet, against all of this, what seems to be remarkable is the resilience and stability of *Norden* as a concept. The post-war framework for the region – five sovereign states cooperating internationally (but never supra-nationally) – seems to endure unchallenged, just as Norden or Scandinavia as a way of imagining the region's shared culture and identity seems to persist. No one seriously seems to be suggesting that Estonia, or indeed Scotland, should be admitted to the Nordic Council any time soon, although there are arrangements to recognize the autonomy of the Nordic islands. It is hard to assess the impact of the 'Baltic' on popular consciousness within the region, and it seems reasonable to conclude, therefore, that its greatest impact has been at an intellectual level. The 'Baltic' functions above all in the sense of the *Geschichtsregion* discussed in the introduction to this book, though as Stefan Troebst has suggested, it may be that 'north-eastern Europe' would be more neutral and thus function better for heuristic purposes.[38] Certainly, there is a strong justification for an historical perspective that goes beyond the framework of the present-day Nordic states to include Russia, the Baltic states, north Germany or the British Isles.[39]

Nonetheless, however compelling the evidence for strong historical links among the Nordic states and the other territories bordering the Baltic or North Seas, it can be asserted that for the period of the Cold War, that is for most of the period covered by this book, the Nordic or Scandinavian perspective seemed to remain the most valid one. Norden was never formally a geo-political entity, though the Nordic Council acted to some extent as a channel to co-ordinate the affairs of its member states. Nonetheless, as we have seen, the existence of a Nordic or Scandinavian model in politics and policy is widely accepted within the scholarly literature. Finally, although Nordic politicians may have sought to distance themselves from the concept of the Nordic model in recent years, the model – or at least elements of it – seems to retain some of its popularity and utopian functions (and less commonly its dystopian ones) among politicians and journalists from outside the region. The British journalist Robert Taylor, writing in 2005, suggested that '[w]hat Sweden and the other Nordics have achieved is of crucial importance in the much wider public policy debate of how the European left should response to ... complex challenges'.[40] In this respect, at least, not much had changed since the 1930s.

Tables & Figures

TABLE 1: The Historic Party System in Scandinavia

COUNTRY	SOCIALIST OR NON-BOURGEOIS PARTIES		BOURGEOIS OR NON-SOCIALIST PARTIES			
	Communists	Social Democrats	Liberals	Agrarians	Conservatives	Other
Denmark	Communist Party	Social Democratic Party	Radical Liberals	Agrarian Liberals	Conservative People's Party	
Finland	Communist Party	Social Democratic Party	National Progressive Party	Agrarian Party (Centre Party)	National Coalition	Swedish People's Party
Iceland	Communist Party	Social Democratic Party		Progressive Party	Independence Party	
Norway	Communist Party	Labour Party	Liberal Party	Agrarian Party (Centre)	Right Party	Christian People's Party
Sweden	Communist Party	Social Democratic Party	Liberal People's Party	Agrarian Party (Centre)	Moderate Unity Party	

TABLE 2: Growth of GDP in the Nordic countries (annual average rates of growth as percentages)

	1870–1913	1913–50	1950–73	1973–2001
Denmark	2.66	2.55	3.81	2.06
Finland	2.74	2.69	4.94	2.57
Norway	2.12	2.93	4.06	3.30
Sweden	2.17	2.74	3.73	1.83
12 country average*	2.13	1.16	4.65	2.08

*Twelve countries: Austria, Belgium, France, Germany, Italy, Netherlands, Switzerland, United Kingdom, and the four Nordic countries. For the period 1913–50, only Switzerland and the Netherlands recorded higher growth rates than the Nordic countries.
Source: Angus Maddison, *The World Economy: Historical Statistics* (Paris: OECD, 2003), p. 260.

TABLE 3: Percentage of the Nordic labour force employed in the agricultural sector, 1910–70

Year	Denmark	Finland	Norway	Sweden
1910	42.7 (1911)	71.5	39.2	45.6
1920	35.2 (1921)	70.4	36.8	40.4
1930	35.2	64.5	35.3	35.4
1940	29.9	57.4	29.5 (1946)	28.8
1950	25.6	46.0	25.9	20.3
1960	17.8	35.5	19.5	13.8
1970	10.6	20.3	11.6	8.1

Source: Peter Flora, Franz Kraus and Winifred Pfenning, *State, Economy and Society in Western Europe, 1815–1975: A Data Handbook*, vol. II (Frankfurt, 1987), pp. 471, 485, 571, 582.

TABLE 4: Government expenditure as a percentage of GDP, and government expenditure on social services as a percentage of GDP, 1950 and 1972

	Denmark	Finland	Norway	Sweden
General government expenditure as percentage of GDP, 1950	19.0	28.6	27.6	23.0
Government expenditure on social services as percentage of GDP, 1950	9.7	10.1	11.2	11.5
General government expenditure as percentage of GD, 1972	45.4	35.8	46.8	49.0
Government expenditure on social services as percentage of GDP, 1972	32.0	20.2	15.3 (1971)	27.9

Source: Peter Flora et al., *State, Economy and Society in Western Europe 1815–1975*, vol. I (Frankfurt, London and New York, 1983), pp. 362–75, 414–32.

TABLE 5: Union density in the Nordic countries, 1950–90 (percentage of labour force)

Country	1950	1960	1970	1980	1990
Denmark	56.5	60.6	60.2	76.3	74.4
Finland	31.5	32.7	51.9	70.4	71.9
Norway	48.3	57.7	55.6	55.7	53.8
Sweden	66.7	70.1	66.2	78.0	82.9
Average for eight countries[*] (weighted by size of labour force)	41.5	42.1	41.6	45.4	41.7

Source: Michael Wallerstein, Miriam Golden and Peter Lange, 'Unions, Employers' Associations and Wage-Setting Institutions in Northern and Central Europe, 1950–1992', *Industrial and Labor Relations Review*, L, 3 (1997), pp. 379–401 (382).
[*]Austria, Belgium, Germany, Netherlands and the four Nordic countries.

TABLE 6: Selected economic indicators for Finland and Sweden
during the economic crisis of the 1990s

	FINLAND				SWEDEN			
	1991	1992	1993	1994	1991	1992	1993	1994
Real GDP growth	-6.4	-3.7	-0.9	3.6	-1.1	-1.2	-2.1	3.9
Unemployment	6.7	11.6	16.4	16.8	3.1	5.6	9.0	9.4
Government net borrowing/lending	5.47	-0.99	-5.53	-7.24	3.77	-1.19	-7.57	-11.41

Sources: OECD; Statistiska centralbyrån; Tilastokeskus

TABLE 7: Net immigration to the Scandinavian countries since 1940

Net immi-gration, by decade	Sweden	Denmark	Norway	Finland	Iceland
1940–49	122,595	-19,467		-42,359[1]	
1950–59	10,024	-58,438		-76,434	
1960–69	197,812	18,671	3181[2]	-150,388	-2749[3]
1970–79	125,580	37,282	39,847	-62,972	-4870
1980–89	147,395	34,774	59,171	32,984	1066
1990–99	11,591	129,369	95,646	55,761	-682
2000–05	165,625	48,519	77,752	35,026	6664

Source: Danmarks Statistik, Sveriges officiella statistik, Statistisk Sentralbyrå
(Norway), Statistics Finland, Statistics Iceland
[1] These figures are for the period 1945–9 only. There are no statistics available for
1940–45, due to the difficulties of collecting information during the war years.
[2] This figure is for the period 1961–9.
[3] This figure is for the period 1961–9.

TABLE 8: Inflows of asylum seekers into the Nordic countries (excluding Iceland) 1993-2002 (thousands)

	1993	1994	1995	1996	1997	1998	1999	2000	2001	2002
Denmark	16.5	8.0	10.1	7.4	5.6	6.1	7.1	13.0	10.3	6.7
Finland	2.0	0.8	0.8	0.7	1.0	1.3	3.1	3.2	1.7	3.4
Norway	12.9	3.4	1.5	1.8	2.3	8.5	10.2	10.8	14.8	17.5
Sweden	37.6	18.6	9.0	5.8	9.6	12.5	11.2	16.3	23.5	33.0

Source: OECD

FIGURE 1: Annual inflation rates (consumer price index) for Iceland 1969–1990

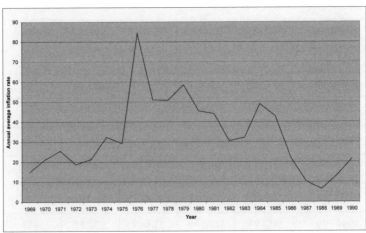

Source: Statistics Iceland

References

Introduction

1 Uffe Østergård, 'The Geopolitics of Nordic Identity: From Composite States to Nation-States', in *The Cultural Construction of Norden*, ed. Øystein Sørensen and Bo Stråth (Oslo, 1997), pp. 25–71 (31).

2 '[une] grande péninsule d'Europe, que les anciens croyoient une île, & qui comprend aujourd'hui le Danemarck, la Suede, la Norwège, la Laponie & la Finlande.'

3 The term itself was much older; the Swedish Academy gives 1689 for the first use of the term 'Norden' to denote the region. Svenska Akademiens ordbok online version (http://g3.spraakdata.gu.se/saob/index.html), accessed 18 July 2007.

4 See Gun Widmark, 'Det skandinaviska samspråket', *Nordisk Tidskrift*, LXXII/1 (1996), pp. 15–25; Ståle Løland, 'Språkforståelse og språksamarbeid i Norden', *Nordisk Tidskrift*, LXXII/1 (1996), pp. 7–13.

5 There are, however, semantic and lexical similarities between Finnish and Swedish, resulting from over six hundred years of shared history. See Max Engman, 'Är Finland ett nordiskt land?', *Den jyske Historiker*, 69–70 (1994), pp. 62–78.

6 Kenneth R. Olwig, 'In Search of the Nordic Landscape: A Personal View', in *Voices from the North: New Trends in Nordic Human Geography*, ed. Jan Öhman and Kirsten Simonsen (Aldershot, 2003), pp. 211–32 (212).

7 Harald Gustafsson, *Nordens historia: En europeisk region under 1200 år* (Lund, 1997), p. 14.

8 Patrik Hall, *Den svenskaste historien: Nationalism i Sverige under sex sekler* (Stockholm, 2000); Ottar Dahl, *Norsk historieforskning i 19. og 20. århundre* (Oslo, 1959).

9 Harald Gustafsson, 'Om Nordens historia', *Scandia*, LXVII (2001), pp. 187–92 (192). For a discussion of 'anthology comparisons', see Silke Neunsinger, 'Om nyttan att jämföra äpplen och päron: Några reflektioner kring möjligheterna av en komparation mellan Tyskland och Sverige under mellankrigstiden', in *Køn, religion og kvinder i bevægelse*, ed. Anette Warring (Roskilde, 1999), pp. 364–77 (371).

10 Norbert Götz, 'Norden: Structures That Do Not Make a Region', *European Review of History/Revue européene d'histoire*, X (2003), pp. 325–41.

11 Gustafsson, 'Om Nordens historia', pp. 187–8.

12 Stefan Troebst, 'Introduction: What's In a Historical Region?', *European Review of History/Revue européene d'histoire*, x (2003), pp. 173–88. See also Götz, 'Norden: Structures That Do Not Make a Region'.

13 Troebst, 'Introduction: What's In a Historical Region?'

14 Øystein Sørensen and Bo Stråth, 'Introduction: The Cultural Construction of Norden', in *The Cultural Construction of Norden* (Oslo, 1997), pp. 1–24. The same authors have also made similar arguments within a national context: see Bo Stråth, 'The Swedish Demarcation to Europe', in *The Meaning of Europe: Variety and Contention within and among Nations*, ed. Mikael af Malmborg and Bo Stråth (Oxford, 2002), pp. 125–47; Øystein Sørensen, *Kampen om Norges sjel* (Oslo, 2001). For an extreme version of the continuity thesis, see Carsten Selch Jensen, 'Hvad nyt? En velfærdsstat med middelalderlige rødder', in *13 historier om den danske velfærdsstat*, ed. Klaus Pererson (Odense, 2003), pp. 15–25.

15 Nina Witoszek, 'Fugitives from Utopia: The Scandinavian Enlightenment Reconsidered', in *The Cultural Construction of Norden*, ed. Sørensen and Stråth, pp. 72–90 (73).

16 Østergård, 'The Geopolitics of Nordic Identity'; Stråth, 'The Swedish Demarcation to Europe'.

17 Sven-Eric Liedman, 'Liberalism in the Nordic Context', in *Liberalism: Seminars on Historical and Political Keywords in Northern Europe*, ed. Ilkka K. Lakaniemi, Anna Rotkirch and Henrik Stenius (Helsinki, 1995), pp. 33–48.

18 Nils Elvander, 'Från liberal skandinavism till konservativ nationalism i Sverige', *Scandia*, xxvii (1961), pp. 366–86 (370).

19 Götz, 'Norden: Structures That Do Not Make a Region'.

20 Kazimierz Musiał, *Roots of the Scandinavian Model: Images of Progress in the Era of Modernisation* (Baden-Baden, 2002), pp. 42–4. For examples, see Agnes Rothery, *Denmark, Kingdom of Reason* (London, 1937); Frederic C. Howe, *Denmark: A Co-operative Commonwealth* (New York, 1921).

21 Marquis Childs, *Sweden: The Middle Way* (London, 1936); Margaret Cole and Charles Smith, ed., *Democratic Sweden: A Volume of Studies Prepared by Members of the New Fabian Research Bureau* (London, 1938); E. D. Simon, *The Smaller Democracies* (London, 1939).

22 *The Northern Countries in the World Economy*, Delegation for the Promotion of Economic Co-operation Between the Northern Countries (Copenhagen, 1937). Musiał, *Roots of the Scandinavian Model*, pp. 122–3.

23 Francis Sejersted, *Socialdemokratins tidsålder: Sverige och Norge under 1900–talet* (Nora, 2005), p. 31. See also Sverker Sörlin, *Framtidslandet Debatten om Norrland och naturresurserna under det industriella genombrottet* (Stockholm, 1988).

24 Musiał, *Roots of the Scandinavian Model*, p. 232.

25 Roland Huntford, *The New Totalitarians* (London, 1971); Frederick Hale, 'Brave New World in Sweden? Roland Huntford's *The New Totalitarians*', *Scandinavian Studies*, lxxviii/2 (2006), pp. 167–90.

26 On the towering influence of Grundtvig, see Flemming Lundgreen-Nielsen, 'Grundtvig og danskhet', in *Folkets Danmark 1848–1940*, ed. Ole Feldbæk, vol. iii of *Dansk identitetshistorie* (Copenhagen, 1991), pp. 9–187. On Linna, see John Sundholm, '"The Unknown Soldier", Film as a Founding Trauma and National Monument', in *Collective Traumas: Memories of War and Conflict in 20th-Century Europe*, ed. Conny Mithander, John Sundholm and Maria Holmgren Troy (Brussels, 2007), pp. 111–41.

27 See C. Claire Thomson, 'Incense in the Snow: Topologies of Intimacy and

Interculturality in Friðriksson's *Cold Fever* and Gondry's *Jóga'*, in *Northern Constellations: New Readings in Nordic Cinema*, ed. C. Claire Thomson (Norwich, 2006), pp. 149–74.

28 Mette Hjort, *Small Nation, Global Cinema* (Minneapolis, MN, 2005).

29 Kirsi Saarikangas, 'The Politics of Modern Home: Organization of the Everyday in Swedish and Finnish Housing Design from the 1930s to the 1950s', in *Models, Modernity and the Myrdals*, ed. Pauli Kettunen and Hanna Eskola (Helsinki, 1997), pp. 81–108 (87). See also Childs, *Sweden: The Middle Way*, pp. 44–58.

30 Saarikangas, 'The Politics of Modern Home', p. 105.

31 Sejersted, *Socialdemokratins tidsålder*, pp. 255–9.

32 Musiał, *Roots of the Scandinavian Model*, pp. 184–7

33 Kevin Davies, 'Scandinavian Furniture in Britain: Finmar and the UK Market, 1948–1952', *Journal of Design History*, X/1 (1997), pp. 39–52; see also Per H. Hansen, *Da danske møbler blev moderne – historien om dansk møbeldesigns storhedstid* (Odense, 2006).

34 Saarikangas, 'The Politics of Modern Home', p. 102.

35 The UN Human Development Report for 2007–8 placed Iceland and Norway in first and second place respectively in its Human Development Index. Sweden was ranked sixth, Finland eleventh and Denmark fourteenth.

Chapter 1: Consensual Democracies? The Nordic Political Model

1 Kazimierz Musiał, *Roots of the Scandinavian Model: Images of Progress in the Era of Modernisation* (Baden-Baden, 2002), pp. 72–3.

2 Anthony Blunt, 'Holidays Nearer Home', *The Spectator*, CLX (8 April 1938), p. 623; cited in Musiał, *Roots of the Scandinavian Model*, p. 11.

3 E. D. Simon, *The Smaller Democracies* (London, 1939), p. 175.

4 Øystein Sørensen and Bo Stråth, 'Introduction: The Cultural Construction of Norden', in *The Cultural Construction of Norden*, ed. Øystein Sørensen and Bo Stråth (Oslo, 1997), pp. 1–24 (20). See also Erik Axelsson, *Historien i politiken: Historieanvändning i norsk och svensk EU-debatt 1990–1994* (Uppsala, 2006).

5 Norbert Götz, 'Norden: Structures That Do Not Make a Region', *European Review of History*, X (2003), pp. 323–41 (330–33); Sørensen and Stråth, 'Introduction: The Cultural Construction of Norden'.

6 Neil Elder, Alastair H. Thomas and David Arter, *The Consensual Democracies? The Government and Politics of the Scandinavian States* (Oxford, 1982); Lars-Göran Stenelo and Magnus Jerneck, eds, *The Bargaining Democracy* (Lund, 1996); David Arter, *Democracy in Scandinavia: Consensual, Majoritarian or Mixed?* (Manchester, 2006), p. 6.

7 Peter Esaiasson and Knut Heidar, 'Learning from the Nordic Experience', in *Beyond Westminster and Congress: The Nordic Experience*, ed. Peter Esaiasson and Knut Heidar (Columbus, OH, 2000), pp. 409–38 (422).

8 Matti Alestalo and Stein Kuhnle, 'The Scandinavian Route: Economic, Social and Political Developments in Denmark, Finland, Norway and Sweden', in *The Scandinavian Model: Welfare States and Welfare Research*, ed. Robert Eriksen et al. (Armonk, NY, 1987), pp. 3–38 (9–10); Øyvind Østerud, *Agrarian Structure and Peasant Politics in Scandinavia: A Comparative Study of Rural Response to Economic Change* (Oslo, 1978).

9 Stein Rokkan, 'Dimensions of State Formation and Nation-Building', in *The*

Formation of National States in Western Europe, ed. Charles Tilly (Princeton, NJ, 1975); Stein Rokkan and Derek W. Urwin, Economy, Territory, Identity: Politics of West-European Peripheries (London, 1983); cited in Knut Heidar et al., 'Five Most Similar Systems', in Beyond Westminster and Congress: The Nordic Experience, ed. Peter Essaiasson and Knut Heidar (Columbus, 2000), pp. 17–47 (17–18).

10 Alestalo and Kuhnle, 'The Scandinavian Route', p. 25.

11 Berndt Schiller, 'Years of Crisis', in Sweden's Development From Poverty to Affluence, 1750–1970, ed. Steven Koblik, trans. Joanne Johnson (Minneapolis, MN, 1975), pp. 197–228 (199); cf. Nils Elvander, Skandinavisk arbetarrörelse (Stockholm, 1980), pp. 28–34.

12 See Stig Hadenius, Hans Wieslander and Björn Molin, Sverige efter 1900: En modern politisk historia [1967] (3rd edn Stockholm, 1969); Carl Göran Andræ, Revolt eller reform: Sverige inför revolutionerna i Europa 1917–1918 (Stockholm, 1998).

13 For a discussion of this point, see Henrik Horstbøll and Uffe Østergård, 'Reform and Revolution: The French Revolution and the Case of Denmark', Scandinavian Journal of History, XV (1990) pp. 155–79 (156–9); see also Ole Feldbæk, 'Denmark', in Nationalism in the Age of the French Revolution, ed. Otto Dann and John Dinwiddy (London, 1988), pp. 87–100 (96–7).

14 Niels Finn Christiansen, Klassesamfundet organiseres 1900–1925 (Copenhagen, 1990), pp. 290–99.

15 Donald R. Matthews and Henry Valen, Parliamentary Representation: The Case of the Norwegian Storting (Columbus, OH, 1999), p. 16.

16 One estimate suggests that 45.5 per cent of Norwegian men over 25 got the vote. Stein Kuhnle, 'Stemmeretten i 1814', Historisk Tidskrift [Norway] LI, (1972), pp. 373–90.

17 H. Arnold Barton, Scandinavia in the Revolutionary Era, 1760–1815 (Minneapolis, MN, 1986), pp. 29, 32–36; Bo Stråth, Union och demokrati: De förenade rikena Sverige-Norge 1814–1905 (Nora, 2005).

18 Gunnar Karlsson, Iceland's 1100 Years: History of a Marginal Society (London, 2000).

19 Guðmundur Hálfdanarson, 'Þingvellir: An Icelandic "Lieu de mémoire"', History and Memory, XII, 1 (2000), pp. 5–29; William R. Shaffer, Politics, Parties and Parliaments: Political Change in Norway (Columbus, OH, 1998), pp. 25–33.

20 Alestalo and Kuhnle, 'The Scandinavian Route'; Sørensen and Stråth, The Cultural Construction of Norden.

21 Mary Hilson, 'Pan-Scandinavianism and Nationalism in the Scandinavian States: Civic and Ethnic Nationalism in Denmark, Norway and Sweden', in What is a Nation?: Europe 1789–1914, ed. Mark Hewitson and Timothy Baycroft (Oxford, 2006), pp. 192–209; Harald Gustafsson, Nordens historia. En europeisk region under 1200 år (Lund, 1997), pp. 187–8.

22 Alestalo and Kuhnle, 'The Scandinavian Route', pp. 8–10; Karlsson, Iceland's 1100 Years, p. 262; Sørensen and Stråth, 'Introduction', pp. 5–8.

23 Eva Österberg, 'Vardagens sträva samförstånd: Bondepolitik i den svenska modellen från vasatid till frihetstid', in Tänka, tycka, tro. Svensk historia underifrån, ed. Gunnar Broberg, Ulla Wikander, Klas Åmark (Stockholm, 1993), pp. 126–46 (133–8); Eva Österberg, 'Svenska lokalsamhällen i förändring ca 1550–1850. Participation, representation och politisk kultur i den svenska självstyrelsen. Ett angeläget forskningsområde', Historisk Tidskrift (Sweden), CVII (1987), pp. 321–40.

24 Österberg, 'Vardagens sträva samförstånd', p. 144.

25 Peter Aronsson, Bönder gör politik: Det lokala självstyret som social arena i tre smålandssocknar, 1680–1850 (Lund, 1992), p. 344.

26 Barrington Moore, *Social Origins of Dictatorship and Democracy: Lord and Peasant in the Making of the Modern World* (Harmondsworth, 1969); see also Gregory M. Luebbert, *Liberalism, Fascism or Social Democracy: Social Classes and the Political Origins of Regimes in Interwar Europe* (Oxford, 1991); Alestalo and Kuhnle, 'The Scandinavian Route', pp. 8–10, 19–21; Øyvind Østerud, 'Introduction: The Peculiarities of Norway', *West European Politics*, XXVIII/4 (2005), pp. 705–20.

27 Börje Harnesk, 'Den svenska modellens tidigmoderna rötter?', *Historisk Tidskrift* [Sweden], CXXII (2002), pp. 78–90 (81–3). See also Eva Österberg, ed., *Socialt och politiskt våld: Perspektiv på svensk historia* (Lund, 2002).

28 Patrik Hall, *Den svenskaste historien: Nationalism i Sverige under sex sekler* (Stockholm, 2000), p. 109.

29 Guðmundur Hálfdanarson, 'Þingvellir'; Andrew Wawn, *The Vikings and the Victorians: Inventing the North in Nineteenth Century Britain* (Cambridge, 2000), pp. 97–8.

30 Thorkild Kjærgaard, 'The Farmer Interpretation of Danish History', *Scandinavian Journal of History*, X (1985), pp. 97–118; Claus Bjørn, 'The Peasantry and Agrarian Reform in Denmark', *Scandinavian Economic History Review*, XXV (1977), pp. 117–37.

31 Gøsta Esping-Andersen, *Politics against Markets: The Social Democratic Road to Power* (Princeton, NJ, 1985), p. 41.

32 Mary Hilson, 'Scandinavia' in *Twisted Paths: Europe 1914–45*, ed. Robert Gerwarth (Oxford, 2007), pp. 8–32.

33 The use of the term 'Red Guards' to denote the revolutionary side in the Finnish Civil War is misleading, however: ideologically, this group drew more of their inspiration from syndicalist ideas for direct democracy than from the Bolsheviks.

34 Lena Berggren, 'Den svenska mellankrigsfascismen – ett ointressant marginalfenomen eller ett viktigt forskningsobjekt?', *Historisk Tidskrift* [Sweden], CXXII (2002), pp. 427–44.

35 Angus Calder, *The People's War: Britain, 1939–45* (London, 1969); Paul Addison, *The Road to 1945: The Impact of the War on British Politics, 1939–45* (London, 1975).

36 Elder, Thomas and Arter, *The Consensual Democracies?*.

37 Seymour Martin Lipset and Stein Rokkan, 'Cleavage Structures, Party Systems and Voter Alignments: An Introduction', in *Party Systems and Voter Alignments: Cross-National Perspectives*, ed. Seymour Martin Lipset and Stein Rokkan (New York, 1967), pp. 1–64.

38 David Arter, 'Conclusion', in *From Farmyard to City Square? The Electoral Adaptation of the Nordic Agrarian Parties*, ed. David Arter (Aldershot, 2001), pp. 162–183 (162–4, 168); see also Luebbert, *Liberalism, Fascism or Social Democracy*.

39 Arter, 'Conclusion', p. 163. Though Scandinavia witnessed some attempts at right-wing organization in the countryside, as we have seen.

40 Arter, 'Conclusion', pp. 169–70.

41 Arter, 'Conclusion', pp. 174–5, 179.

42 Göran Therborn, 'Nation och klass, tur och skicklighet', in *Den svenska modellen*, ed. Per Thullberg and Kjell Östberg (Lund, 1994), pp. 59–74 (59–61).

43 Gøsta Esping-Andersen, 'Single-Party Dominance in Sweden: The Saga of Social Democracy', in *Uncommon Democracies: The One-Party Dominant Regimes*, ed. T. J. Pempel (Ithaca, NY, 1990), pp. 33–57; Therborn, 'Nation och klass', p. 67; Walter Korpi, *The Working Class in Welfare Capitalism: Work, Unions and Politics in Sweden* (London, 1978), pp. 72–5.

44 Therborn, 'Nation och klass', p. 64; Hugh Heclo and Henrik Madsen, *Policy and*

Politics in Sweden: Principled Pragmatism (Philadelphia, PA, 1987), p. 17; Francis G. Castles, The Social Democratic Image of Society: A Study of the Achievements and Origins of Scandinavian Social Democracy in Comparative Perspective (London, 1978), p. 13; Esping-Andersen, 'Single-Party Dominance in Sweden'.

45 Esping-Andersen, Politics Against Markets, p. 8.

46 Nils Elvander, Skandinavisk arbetarrörelse (Stockholm, 1980), p. 333.

47 Therborn, 'Nation och klass', p. 71; Castles, The Social Democratic Image of Society, p. 14.

48 Lars Trägårdh, 'Varieties of Volkish Identities', in Language and the Constitution of Class Identities, ed. Bo Stråth (Göteborg, 1990), pp. 25–54.

49 David Aly Redvaldsen, 'The British and Norwegian Labour Parties in the Interwar Period with Particular Reference to 1929–1936: Electoral Prospects', unpublished PhD thesis, University College London 2007.

50 Castles, The Social Democratic Image of Society; Jonas Pontusson, 'Swedish Social Democracy and British Labour: Essays on the Nature and Conditions of Social Democratic Hegemony', Cornell University, Center for International Studies: Occasional Paper no. 19 (1988). On corporatism, see Bo Rothstein, Den korporativa staten: Intresseorganisationer och statsförvaltning i svensk politik (Stockholm, 1992).

51 Leif Lewin, Ideology and Strategy: A Century of Swedish Politics, trans. Victor Kayfetz (Cambridge, 1988).

52 Pontusson, 'Swedish Social Democracy', pp. 10, 15.

53 Pontusson, 'Swedish Social Democracy'.

54 Heclo and Madsen, Policy and Politics in Sweden, pp. 23–4.

55 Heclo and Madsen, Policy and Politics in Sweden, pp. 9, 15–16, 30.

56 Shaffer, Politics, Parties and Parliaments, pp. 32–3.

57 Roland Huntford, The New Totalitarians (London, 1971); Frederick Hale, 'Brave New World in Sweden? Roland Huntford's The New Totalitarians', Scandinavian Studies, LXXVIII/2 (2006), pp. 167–90.

58 Joseph V. Femia, Gramsci's Political Thought: Hegemony, Consciousness and the Revolutionary Process (Oxford, 1981), p. 24.

59 Åsa Linderborg, Socialdemokraterna skriver historia: historieskrivning som ideologisk maktresurs 1892–2000 (Stockholm, 2001).

60 Linderborg, Socialdemokraterna skriver historia; Francis Sejerstad, Socialdemokratins tidsålder: Sverige och Norge under 1900-talet (Nora, 2005); Heclo and Madsen, Policy and Politics in Sweden, pp. 7, 27; Klas Åmark, 'Sammanhållning och intressepolitik', in Den svenska modellen, ed. Per Thullberg and Kjell Östberg (Lund, 1994), pp. 27–58 (27, 56).

61 Robert Geyer, 'Traditional Norwegian Social Democracy and the Rejection of the EU: A Troublesome Victory', Scandinavian Studies, LXIX/3 (1997), pp. 322–45 (325–30).

62 For example, David Arter, Scandinavian Politics Today (Manchester, 1999), p. 98.

63 David Arter, 'Party System Change in Scandinavia since 1970: "Restricted Change" or "General Change"?', West European Politics, XXII/3 (1999), pp. 139–58.

64 John T. S. Madeley, 'Life at the Northern Margin: Christian Democracy in Scandinavia', in Christian Democratic Parties in Europe since the End of the Cold War, ed. Steven Van Hecke and Emmanuel Gerard (Leuven, 2004), pp. 217–41.

65 See Kim O. K. Zilliacus, '"New Politics" in Finland: The Greens and the Left Wing in the 1990s', West European Politics, XXIV/1 (2001), pp. 27–54.

66 Sighrúdur Helga Sigurbjarnardóttir, '"On Their Own Premises": The Political Project of the Icelandic Women's Alliance', trans. Frødis Jaren in Is There a Nordic

Feminism? Nordic Feminist Thought on Culture and Society, ed. Drude von der Fehr et al. (London, 1998), pp. 69–89; Edward Schneier, 'Icelandic Women on the Brink of Power', *Scandinavian Studies*, LXIV/3 (1992), pp. 417–38.

67 Sven-Olof Josefsson, *Året var 1968: Universitetskris och student revolt i Stockholm och Lund* (Göteborg, 1996); Steven L. B. Jensen and Thomas Ekman Jørgensen, 'Studentoprøret i Danmark', *Historisk Tidskrift* [Denmark], CI/2 (2001), pp. 435–70.

68 Trond Bergh, 'Arbeiderbevegelsen i Norge og den kalde krigen', *Arbejderhistorie*, (2000), pp. 1–15.

69 Ole Borre, 'Alienation and Critical Issues in Denmark', *Scandinavian Political Studies*, XXIII/4 (2000), pp. 285–309 (289).

70 Castles, *The Social Democratic Image of Society*, p. 40; Therborn, 'Nation och klass', p. 62. See also Mikael af Malmborg, *Neutrality and State-Building in Sweden* (Basingstoke, 2001); Ann-Sofie Dahl, 'The Myth of Swedish Neutrality', in *Haunted by History: Myths in International Relations*, ed. Cyril Buffet and Beatrice Heuser (Oxford, 1998), pp. 28–40.

71 Geyer, 'Traditional Norwegian Social Democracy', p. 333.

72 See Jonas Hinnfors, *Reinterpreting Social Democracy: A History of Stability in the British Labour Party and Swedish Social Democratic Party* (Manchester, 2006); Philip Whyman, *Sweden and the 'Third Way': A Macroeconomic Evaluation* (Aldershot, 2003); J. Magnus Ryner, 'Neo-Liberalization of Social Democracy: The Swedish Case', *Comparative European Politics*, II (2004), pp. 97–119.

73 See chapter Five.

74 See Conclusion.

75 It should be noted, however, that in the Danish system, which requires only 2 per cent of the popular vote for a party to gain parliamentary representation, the Sweden Democrats would be seated in the Riksdag. On Finland, see Elina Kestilä, 'Is There Demand for Radical Right Populism in the Finnish Electorate?', *Scandinavian Political Studies*, XXIX/3 (2006), pp. 169–91.

76 Elder, Thomas and Arter, *Consensual Democracies?*, pp. 10–11.

77 Arter, 'Party System Change in Scandinavia'; Knut Heidar, 'Norwegian Parties and the Party System: Steadfast and Changing', *West European Politics*, XXVIII/4 (2005), pp. 804–33; Eric S. Einhorn and John Logue, *Modern Welfare States: Scandinavian Politics and Policy in the Global Age*, 2nd edn (Westport, CN, 2003), p. 42.

78 Pertti Pesonen, 'Change and Stability in the Finnish Party System', in *Party Systems and Voter Realignments Revisited*, ed. Lauri Karvonen and Stein Kuhnle (London, 2001), pp. 115–37 (115, 118, 120). For a discussion of the social roots of party change, see Diane Sainsbury, 'The Electoral Difficulties of the Scandinavian Social Democrats in the 1970s: The Social Bases of the Parties and Structural Explanations of Party Decline', *Comparative Politics*, XVIII, 1 (1985), pp. 1–19.

79 Heidar, 'Norwegian Parties and the Party System', p. 830.

80 Heidar, 'Norwegian Parties and the Party System', pp. 807–8, 817.

81 Christina Bergqvist, ed., *Equal Democracies? Gender and Politics in the Nordic Countries* (Oslo, 2000); Nina C. Raaum, 'Gender Equality and Political Representation: A Nordic Comparison', *West European Politics*, XXVIII/4 (2005), pp. 872–97. The UN Human Development Index for 2007–8 ranked Norway, Sweden, Finland, Denmark and Iceland top in the world, in that order, for empowerment of women.

82 Michele Micheletti, *Civil Society and State Relations in Sweden* (Aldershot, 1995); Peter Munk Christiansen and Hilmar Rommetvedt, *From Corporatism to Lobbyism? Parliaments, Executives and Organized Interests in Denmark and Norway*

(Oslo, 1999).

83 Heidar, 'Five Most Similar Systems', pp. 25–8 (42); Shaffer, *Politics, Parties and Parliaments*, pp. 34–5.

84 Stein Ringen, 'Wealth and Decay: Norway Funds a Massive Political Self-Examination – and Finds Trouble for All', *Times Literary Supplement* (13 February 2004), pp. 3–5.

85 For example, the Finnish prime minister Anneli Jäätteenmäki was forced out of office shortly after her election in 2003, and in 2004 the Icelandic prime minister Davíð Oddsson was caught up in a wave of popular protest against proposals for a new media bill.

86 Borre, 'Critical Issues and Political Alienation'.

Chapter 2: The Nordic Economies

1 Lasse Sonne, *Nordek: A Plan for Increased Nordic Economic Co-operation and Integration 1968–1970* (Helsinki, 2007), pp. 30–31; Nils Elvander, 'Från liberal skandinavism till konservativ nationalism i Sverige', *Scandia*, XXVII (1961), pp. 366–86. The consumer co-operative movement provided one example of successful pan-Nordic economic cooperation: see Keijo Hummelin, *Nordisk Andelsförbund* NAF *1918–1993* (Copenhagen, 1998).

2 Jonathon W. Moses, *Norwegian Catch-Up: Development and Globalization before World War* II (Aldershot, 2005). The relative backwardness of the nineteenth-century Scandinavian economies measured in terms of the basic economic indicators is disputed: see Jan Tore Klovland's review of Moses in *Economic History Review*, LX/1 (2007), pp. 224–5. Nonetheless, the popular myth of nineteenth-century Scandinavia as a backward region remains a powerful one, and it cannot be disputed that for many Scandinavian peasants (i.e., most of the population), life was very hard.

3 Marquis W. Childs, *Sweden: The Middle Way* (London, 1936).

4 However, Finland and Iceland retained protectionism until they joined EFTA in 1961 and 1971 respectively. See Tapani Paavonen, 'Finland and the Question of West European Economic Integration, 1947–1961', *Scandinavian Economic History Review*, LII/2–3 (2004), pp. 85–109.

5 See Yrjö Kaukiainen, 'Foreign Trade and Transport', in *The Road to Prosperity: An Economic History of Finland*, ed. Jari Ojala et al. (Helsinki, 2006), pp. 127–63, who suggests that Finland was already integrated into the world economy from the early modern period.

6 See chapter Six.

7 Lars Magnusson, *Den tredje industriella revolutionen – och den svenska arbetsmarknaden* (Stockholm, 2000).

8 Unemployment peaked in 1932 at 31.7 per cent in Denmark, and in 1933 at 33.4 per cent in Norway. B. R. Mitchell, *International Historical Statistics: Europe 1750–1988* (Basingstoke, 1992), Table J2; for Finland: Matti Hannikainen and Sakari Heikkinen, 'The Labour Market, 1850–2000', in *The Road to Prosperity*, pp. 165–85 (178). Recent research suggests, however, that this figure is too high for Norway: see Ola Grytten Honningdal, 'The Scale of Norwegian Interwar Unemployment in International Perspective', *Scandinavian Economic History Review*, XXXXIII/2 (1995), pp. 226–50. The average annual rate of unemployment for the years 1921–39 was 19.4 per cent for Denmark, 20.5 per cent for Norway and 14.2 per cent for Sweden (1925–39).

9 Arthur Montgomery, *How Sweden Overcame the Depression 1930–1933* (Stockholm, 1938); Brinley Thomas, *Monetary Policy and Crises: A Study of Swedish Experience* (London, 1936). See also Lars Magnusson, *An Economic History of Sweden* (London, 2000), pp. 194–9.

10 Hugh Dalton, Preface to Brinley Thomas, *Monetary Policy and Crises: A Study of Swedish Experience* (London, 1936), p. x.

11 Childs, *Sweden: The Middle Way.*

12 *The Northern Countries in World Economy: Denmark–Finland–Iceland–Norway–Sweden*, published by the delegations for the promotion of economic cooperation between the northern countries (Copenhagen, 1937). See also Kazimierz Musiał, *Roots of the Scandinavian Model: Images of Progress in the Era of Modernisation* (Baden-Baden, 2002), p. 122.

13 Lennart Schön, *En modern svensk ekonomisk historia: Tillväxt och omvandling under två sekel* (Stockholm, 2000), pp. 334, 338.

14 Gunnar Myrdal, *Varning för fredsoptimism* (Stockholm, 1944).

15 Even Lange, *Samling om felles mål*, vol. xi of *Aschehougs Norges historie*, ed. Knut Helle [1996] (Oslo 2005), p. 162.

16 Odd Aukrust and Petter Jakob Bjerve, *Hva krigen kostet Norge* (Oslo, 1945); cited in Lange, *Samling om felles mål*, p. 164.

17 Erkki Pihkala, 'The Political Economy of Post-War Finland, 1945–1952', *Scandinavian Economic History Review*, xxxxvii/3 (1999), pp. 26–47 (27); Jason Lavery, *The History of Finland* (Westport, cn, 2006), p. 135.

18 Pihkala, 'The Political Economy of Post-War Finland', p. 32.

19 Pihkala, 'The Political Economy of Post-War Finland', p. 28.

20 Fritz Hodne, *The Norwegian Economy 1920–1980* (London, 1983), p. 155.

21 Lange, *Samling om felles mål*, p. 165.

22 Hans Christian Johansen, *The Danish Economy in the Twentieth Century* (London, 1987), p. 93.

23 Hodne, *The Norwegian Economy*, p. 160.

24 See Jussi M Hanhimäki, *Scandinavia and the United States: An Insecure Friendship* (New York, 1997).

25 Pihkala, 'The Political Economy of Post-War Finland', p. 31; Mikko Majander, 'The Limits of Sovereignty: Finland and the Question of the Marshall Plan in 1947', *Scandinavian Journal of History*, xix/4 (1994), pp. 309–26. According to David Kirby, 'Finland's decision not to participate in the Marshall aid programme was widely interpreted as a further sign of the country's subjugation to the will of Moscow.' David Kirby, *A Concise History of Finland* (Cambridge, 2006), p. 240.

26 Vibeke Sørensen, *Denmark's Social Democratic Government and the Marshall Plan 1947–1950* (Copenhagen, 2001), pp. 31, 40.

27 Lange, *Samling om felles mål*, p. 219.

28 Lange, *Samling om felles mål*; Sørensen, *Denmark's Social Democratic Government*; Charles Silva, *Keep Them Strong, Keep Them Friendly: Swedish–American Relations and the Pax Americana, 1948–1952* (Stockholm, 1999).

29 Palle Schelde Andersen and Johnny Åkerholm, 'Scandinavia', in *The European Economy: Growth and Crisis*, ed. Andrea Boltho (Oxford, 1982), pp. 610–44 (617–8).

30 The growth of the Finnish economy was subject to wide fluctuations, however: its best year was 1969 when it grew 9.6 per cent, but the previous year's rate was only 2.3 per cent. The annual average rate for 1946–70 was 5.04 per cent. Riitta Hjerppe, *The Finnish Economy 1860–1985: Growth and Structural Change* (Helsinki, 1989), Appendix: Table 1. Peter Flora, Franz Kraus and Winifred Pfenning, *State,*

Economy and Society in Western Europe 1815–1975 (Frankfurt, 1987), vol. II, p. 485.

31 Andersen and Åkerholm, 'Scandinavia', p. 617.

32 Andersen and Åkerholm, 'Scandinavia', p. 615.

33 Statistics Iceland.

34 Gunnar Karlsson, Iceland's 1100 Years: The History of a Marginal Society (London, 1999), pp. 348–52.

35 Andersen and Åkerholm, 'Scandinavia', p. 620. Henrik Christoffersen, Danmarks økonomiske historie efter 1960 (Gylling, 1999).

36 Andersen and Åkerholm, 'Scandinavia', p. 622.

37 Toivo Miljan, The Reluctant Europeans: The Attitudes of the Nordic Countries Towards European Integration (London, 1977), p. 51.

38 Andersen and Åkerholm, 'Scandinavia', p. 623.

39 Karlsson, Iceland's 1100 Years, p. 358.

40 Erik Lundberg, 'The Rise and Fall of the Swedish Economic Model', in Europe's Economy in Crisis, ed. Ralf Dahrendorf (London, 1982), pp. 195–211.

41 Sørensen, Denmark's Social Democratic Government, p. 26.

42 Sørensen, Denmark's Social Democratic Government, pp. 27, 33.

43 See Myrdal, Varning för fredsoptimism.

44 Lennart Erixon, 'A Swedish Economic Policy – The Theory, Application and Validity of the Rehn-Meidner Model', Department of Economics, University of Stockholm (2000), www.ne.su.se/paper/wp00__13.pdf [accessed 1 September 2005]; Lundberg, 'The Rise and Fall of the Swedish Economic Model'.

45 Erixon, 'A Swedish Economic Policy'; see Albin Lind, Solidarisk lönepolitik och förhandsförhandlingar (Stockholm, 1938).

46 Magnusson, An Economic History, p. 237.

47 Magnusson, An Economic History, pp. 233–4.

48 Francis Sejersted, Socialdemokratins tidsålder: Sverige och Norge under 1900–talet (Nora, 2005), p. 244.

49 Andersen and Åkerholm, 'Scandinavia', p. 615.

50 Sejerstad, Socialdemokratins tidsålder, p. 247.

51 Hodne, The Norwegian Economy, p. 235.

52 Hodne, The Norwegian Economy, pp. 231, 236; Sejerstad, Socialdemokratins tidsålder, p. 247.

53 Johansen, The Danish Economy, pp. 104–5, 106–9. Note that there were very similar export constraints on Icelandic economic policy though here it was inflation that was the main problem.

54 Nils Elvander, Skandinavisk arbetarrörelse (Stockholm, 1980), p. 152.

55 Francis G. Castles, The Social Democratic Image of Society: A Study of the Achievements and Origins of Scandinavian Social Democracy in Comparative Perspective (London, 1978), pp. 14–18.

56 Michael Wallerstein, Miriam Golden and Peter Lange, 'Unions, Employers' Associations and Wage-Setting Institutions in Northern and Central Europe, 1950–1992', Industrial and Labor Relations Review, L/3 (1997), pp. 379–401 (395).

57 Johansen, The Danish Economy, p. 123.

58 Johansen, The Danish Economy, p. 150.

59 Hannikainen and Heikkinen, 'The Labour Market', p. 172.

60 Kirby, A Concise History of Finland, p. 216; Tapio Bergholm, A Short History of SAK (Helsinki, 2003), p. 31.

61 Osmo Jussila, Seppo Hentilä and Jukka Nevikivi, From Grand Duchy to a Modern State: A Political History of Finland since 1809, trans. David and Eva-Kaisa Arter

(London, 1999), p. 254.

62 Wallerstein, 'Unions, Employers' Associations and Wage-Setting Institutions',
    p. 394; Hannikainen and Heikkinen, 'The Labour Market', p. 174.

63 Lavery, *The History of Finland*, p. 147.

64 Kirby, *A Concise History of Finland*.

65 This accounted for 13–18 per cent of Norwegian investment in the period
    1950–80. Hodne, *The Norwegian Economy*, p. 242.

66 Sejerstad, *Socialdemokratins tidsålder*, pp. 254–9.

67 Åsa Linderborg, *Socialdemokraterna skriver historia: Historieskrivning som ideologisk
    maktresurs 1892–2000* (Stockholm, 2001). See chapter Two.

68 Wallerstein, 'Unions, Employers' Associations and Wage-Setting Institutions'.

69 Wallerstein, 'Unions, Employers' Associations and Wage-Setting Institutions',
    p. 390; Peter Swenson, 'Managing the Managers: The Swedish Employers'
    Confederation, Labor Scarcity and the Suppression of Labor Market
    Segmentation', *Scandinavian Journal of History*, XVI (1991), pp. 335–56.

70 Bo Rothstein, 'State Structure and Variations in Corporatism: The Swedish Case',
    Scandinavian Political Studies, XIV/2 (1991), pp. 149–71.

71 Jens Blom-Hansen, 'Still Corporatism in Scandinavia? A Survey of Recent
    Empirical Findings', *Scandinavian Political Studies*, XXIII/2 (2000), pp. 157–81; Peter
    Munk Christiansen and Hilmar Rommetvedt, 'From Corporatism to Lobbyism?
    Parliaments, Executives and Organized Interests in Denmark and Norway',
    Scandinavian Political Studies, XXII/3 (1999), pp. 195–220.

72 Klas Eklund, 'Gösta Rehn and the Swedish Model: Did We Follow the Rehn-
    Meidner Model Too Little Rather Than Too Much?', in *Gösta Rehn, the Swedish
    Model and Labour Market Policies: International and National Perspectives*, ed. Henry
    Milner and Eskil Wadensjö (Aldershot, 2001), pp. 53–72.

73 Andersen and Åkerhielm, 'Scandinavia', pp. 628, 634.

74 Andersen and Åkerhielm, 'Scandinavia', p. 635.

75 Ole Karup Pedersen, *Danmark og verden 1970–1990*, vol. XV of *Gyldendal og Politikens
    Danmarks Historie* (Copenhagen, 1991), pp. 25, 68.

76 Erixon, 'A Swedish Economic Policy', p. 29.

77 Edgeir Benum, *Overflod og fremtidsfrykt*, vol. XII of *Aschehougs Norges Historie* (Oslo,
    1996), p. 54.

78 Magnusson, *Den tredje industriella revolutionen*.

79 Schön, *En modern svensk ekonomisk historia*, p. 473.

80 Pirkko-Liisa Rauhala et al., 'Why Are Social Care Services a Gender Issue?' in
    Social Care Services: The Key to the Scandinavian Welfare Model, ed. Jorma Sipilä
    (Aldershot, 1997), pp. 131–55 (145–7).

81 See Hodne, *The Norwegian Economy*, p. 229.

82 Eklund, 'Gösta Rehn and the Swedish Model'.

83 Erixon, 'A Swedish Economic Policy', pp. 25, 30–32; Lundberg, 'The Rise and Fall of
    the Swedish Economic Model', p. 31.

84 Schön, *En modern svensk ekonomisk historia*, p. 490; James Angresano, 'The
    Swedish Economy 1932–Present', in *Comparative Economics*, ed. James Angresano,
    2nd edn (Upper Saddle River, NJ, 1996), pp. 279–328 (312).

85 J. Magnus Ryner, 'Neo-Liberalization of Social Democracy: The Swedish Case',
    Comparative European Politics, II (2002), pp. 97–119 (98–102).

86 Benum, *Overflod og fremtidsfrykt*, p. 67.

87 Brian Fullerton and Richard Knowles, *Scandinavia* (London, 1991), p. 24.

88 As an example of this critique, see Jørgen S. Dich, *Den herskande klasse*

(Copenhagen, 1973); Henrik Madsen, 'For velfærdens skyld? En analyse af de danske debatter om velfærdsstat og medlemskab af EF 1950–1972', unpublished PhD thesis, Syddansk Universitet, 2006.

89 Seppo Honkapohja and Erkki Koskela, 'The Economic Crisis in the 1990s in Finland', in *Down from the Heavens, Up from the Ashes: The Finnish Economic Crisis of the 1990s in the Light of Economic and Social Research*, ed. Jorma Kalela et al. (Helsinki, 2001), pp. 52–101 (56–7).

90 Honkopohja and Koskela, 'The Economic Crisis in the 1990s', p. 63.

91 Honkopohja and Koskela, 'The Economic Crisis in the 1990s'; Schön, *En modern svensk ekonomisk historia*, pp. 471–3.

92 Schön, *En modern svensk ekonomisk historia*, pp. 503–5.

93 Sven Jochem, 'Equality, Solidarity and the Welfare State: The Nordic Employment Performance in Comparative Perspective', in *Gösta Rehn, the Swedish Model and Labour Market Policies*, ed. Milner and Wadensjö, pp. 167–88 (174–5).

94 Erixon, 'A Swedish Economic Policy', p. 40.

95 Erixon, 'A Swedish Economic Policy', pp. 42–5.

96 Maria-Pia Boëthius, *Heder och samvete: Sverige och andra världskriget* (Stockholm, 2001). On neutrality, see chapter Four; on sterilization, see chapter Three.

97 Sakari Heikkinen and Antti Kuusterä, 'Finnish Economic Crises in the 20th Century', in *Down from the Heavens*, pp. 25–51; Antti Häkkinen and Jarmo Peltola, 'On the Social History of Unemployment and Poverty in Finland 1860–2000', in *Down from the Heavens*, pp. 309–45.

98 ILO. Pasi Huovinen and Hannu Piekkola, 'Unemployment and Early Retirements of the Finnish Aged Workers in 1989–1996', in *Down from the Heavens*, pp. 249–76.

99 Matti Peltonen, 'Between Landscape and Language: The Finnish National Self-Image in Transition', *Scandinavian Journal of History*, xxv/4 (2000), pp. 265–80.

100 OECD: export shares of high-technology industries as percentage of total manu-facturing exports.

101 The dominance of Nokia is confirmed by some recent evidence suggesting that productivity gains and growth in the rest of the ICT sector in Finland has been much slower. Francesco Daveri and Olmo Silva, 'Not Only Nokia: What Finland Tells Us About New Economy Growth', *Economic Policy*, xix/38 (2004), pp. 117–63.

102 Darius Ornston, 'Reorganising Adjustment: Finland's Emergence as a High Technology Leader', *West European Politics*, xxix/4 (2006), pp. 784–801 (786).

103 Lars Ilshammar, *Offentlighetens nya rum: teknik och politik i Sverige 1969–1999* (Örebro, 2002).

104 Ornston, 'Reorganising Adjustment', pp. 791–3.

105 OECD.

106 Ornston, 'Reorganising Adjustment', p. 794.

107 Lauri Haataja, *Suomen malli 1940–1956: Työmarkkinajärjestelmän ja poliittisen järjes-telmän vuorovaikutussuhde neuvottelujen vakiintumisesta keskityksen purkautumiseen* (Helsinki, 1993); Helka Hytti, *Varhainen eläkkeelle siirtyminen: Suomen malli* (Helsinki, 1998). I am grateful to Tapio Bergholm for these references.

108 Moses, *Norwegian Catch-Up*; Jari Ojala et al., eds, *The Road to Prosperity: An Economic History of Finland* (Helsinki, 2006).

109 Hannikainen and Heikkinen, 'The Labour Market', p. 180.

Chapter 3: The Nordic Model of Welfare

1 Henrik Stenius, 'The Good Life Is a Life of Conformity: The Impact of the Lutheran Tradition on Nordic Political Culture', in *The Cultural Construction of Norden*, ed. Øystein Sørensen and Bo Stråth (Oslo, 1997), pp. 161–71 (171).

2 Richard M. Titmuss, *Essays on 'The Welfare State'* (London, 1958); Harold Wilensky and Charles Lebeaux, *Industrial Society and Social Welfare* (New York, 1965); Diane Sainsbury, 'Analysing Welfare State Variations: The Merits and Limitations of Models Based on the Residual–Institutional Distinction', *Scandinavian Political Studies*, XIV (1991), pp. 1–30.

3 Gøsta Esping-Andersen, *The Three Worlds of Welfare Capitalism* (Cambridge, 1990).

4 Evelyne Huber and John D. Stephens, 'The Social Democratic Welfare State', in *Social Democracy in Neo-Liberal Times: The Left and Economic Policy since 1980*, ed. Andrew Glyn (Oxford, 2001), pp. 276–311 (276); Walter Korpi and Joakim Palme, 'The Paradox of Redistribution and Strategies of Equality: Welfare State Institutions, Inequality and Poverty in the Western Countries', *American Sociological Review*, LXIII/5 (1998), pp. 661–87 (666).

5 David Arter, *Scandinavian Politics Today* (Manchester, 1999); Eric S. Einhorn and John Logue, *Modern Welfare States: Scandinavian Politics and Policy in the Global Age*, 2nd edn (Westport, CT, 2003); Kåre Hagen and Jon M Hippe, 'The Norwegian Welfare State: From Post-War Consensus to Future Conflicts?', in *Continuity and Change: Aspects of Contemporary Norway* (Oslo, 1993), pp. 85–105; Mikko Kautto et al., 'Introduction: How Distinct Are the Nordic Welfare States?', in *Nordic Welfare States in the European Context*, ed. Mikko Kautto et al. (London, 2001), p. 6; Klaus Petersen and Niels Finn Christiansen, 'Preface' to 'The Nordic Welfare States 1900–2000', *Scandinavian Journal of History*, XXVI/3 (2001), pp. 153–6; Huber and Stephens, 'The Social Democratic Welfare State'; Korpi and Palme, 'The Paradox of Redistribution', p. 670.

6 See Kautto et al., 'Introduction', p. 10, for the distinction between welfare states and welfare regimes.

7 Bo Rothstein, 'The Universal Welfare State as a Social Dilemma', *Rationality and Society*, XIII (2001), pp. 213–33 (218); Andreas Bergh, 'The Universal Welfare State: Theory and the Case of Sweden', *Political Studies*, LII (2004), pp. 745–66; Torben M. Andersen, 'Challenges to the Scandinavian Welfare Model', *European Journal of Political Economy*, XX (2004), pp. 743–54 (745); Niels Finn Christiansen and Pirjo Markkola, 'Introduction', in *The Nordic Model of Welfare: A Historical Reappraisal*, ed. Niels Finn Christiansen et al. (Copenhagen, 2006); Kautto et al., 'Introduction', p. 6.

8 Huber and Stephens, 'The Social Democratic Welfare State', table 1, pp. 280–81. In Finland taxation as a percentage of GDP was only 35 per cent.

9 Jenny Andersson, *Mellan tillväxt och trygghet: Idéer om produktiv socialpolitik i social-demokratisk socialpolitisk ideologi under efterkrigstiden* (Uppsala, 2003).

10 Klas Åmark, *Hundra år av välfärdspolitik: Välfärdsstatens framväxt i Norge och Sverige* (Umeå, 2005), p. 299; Niels Finn Christiansen and Klaus Petersen, 'Den nordiske modellen - myte og realitet', *Humaniora*, XVI/1 (2001), pp. 16–19 (18); Pirkko-Liisa Rauhala et al., 'Why Are Social Services a Gender Issue?', in *Social Care Services: The Key to the Scandinavian Welfare Model*, ed. Jorma Sipilä (Aldershot, 1997), pp. 131–55.

11 Bergh, 'The Universal Welfare State', pp. 749–50; Korpi and Palme, 'The Paradox of Redistribution', p. 669.

12 Christiansen and Markkola, 'Introduction', p. 14; Peter Abrahamson, 'The Scandinavian Model of Welfare', in *Comparing Social Systems in Nordic Europe and France*, ed. Denis Bouget and Bruno Palier (Paris, 1999); Peter Abrahamson, 'The Welfare Modelling Business', *Social Policy and Administration*, XXXIII/4 (1999), pp. 349–415.

13 Christiansen and Markkola, 'Introduction', p. 13; Åmark, *Hundra år av välfärdspolitik*, pp. 274–5; Pekka Kosonen, 'The Finnish Model and the Welfare State in Crisis', in *The Nordic Welfare State as a Myth and as Reality*, ed. Pekka Kosonen (Helsinki, 1993), pp. 45–66 (55).

14 Hagen and Hippe, 'The Norwegian Welfare State'; Urban Lundberg and Klas Åmark, 'Social Rights and Social Security: The Swedish Welfare State, 1900–2000', *Scandinavian Journal of History*, XXVI/3 (2001), pp. 157–76; Niels Finn Christiansen and Klaus Petersen, 'The Dynamics of Social Solidarity: The Danish Welfare System, 1900–2000', *Scandinavian Journal of History*, XXVI/3 (2001), pp. 177–96; Christiansen and Markkola, 'Introduction', p. 15.

15 Esping-Andersen, *The Three Worlds of Welfare Capitalism*, p. 30. See also Søren Kolstrup, 'Forskning i velfærdsstatens rødder: Forskningsstrategier, resultater, huller', *Historisk Tidskrift* [Denmark], LXXXIV (1994), pp. 315–36 (325–6); Gregory M. Luebbert, *Liberalism, Fascism or Social Democracy: Social Classes and the Political Origins of Regimes in Interwar Europe* (Oxford, 1991), p. 11.

16 See chapter One. Esping-Andersen, *The Three Worlds of Welfare Capitalism*; Gøsta Esping-Andersen, *Politics Against Markets: The Social Democratic Road to Power* (Princeton, NJ, 1985), pp. xv, 314, 319; Walter Korpi, *The Democratic Class Struggle* (London, 1983); Luebbert, *Liberalism, Fascism or Social Democracy*; Per Thullberg and Kjell Östberg, 'Introduction', in *Den svenska modellen*, ed. Per Thullberg and Kjell Östberg (Lund, 1994), pp. 5–9 (6).

17 Peter Baldwin, 'The Scandinavian Origins of the Social Interpretation of the Welfare State', *Comparative Studies in Society and History*, XXXI (1989), pp. 3–24; Peter Baldwin, *The Politics of Social Solidarity: Class Bases of the European Welfare State 1875–1975* (Cambridge, 1990), pp. 65–76; Jørn Henrik Petersen, 'Gårdmandsvenstre – velfærdsstatens far', in *13 historier om den danske velfærdsstat*, ed. Klaus Petersen (Odense, 2003), pp. 81–93.

18 Nils Edling, 'Limited Universalism: Unemployment Insurance in Northern Europe 1900–2000', in *The Nordic Model of Welfare*, ed. Christiansen et al., pp. 99–143 (102, 107, 110).

19 Baldwin, 'The Scandinavian Origins'; Øyvind Bjørnson and Inger Elisabeth Haavet, *Langsomt ble landet et velferdssamfunn: Trygdens historie 1894–1994* (Oslo, 1994), p. 22.

20 Åmark, *Hundra år av välfärdspolitik*, p. 46; Stein Kuhnle, 'Growth of Social Insurance Programs in Scandinavia: Outside Influences and Internal Forces', in *The Development of Welfare States in Europe and America*, ed. Peter Flora and Arnold J. Heidenheimer (London, 1981), pp. 125–50 (126–31).

21 Bjørnson and Haavet, *Langsomt ble landet et velferdssamfunn*, p. 16; Benny Carlsson, *Ouvertyr till folkhemmet: Wagnerska tongångar i förra sekelskiftets Sverige* (Lund, 2002).

22 Klaus Petersen and Klas Åmark, 'Old Age Pensions in the Nordic Countries 1880–2000', in *The Nordic Model of Welfare*, ed. Christiansen et al., pp. 145–88 (152).

23 Tim Knudsen, 'Tilblivelsen af den universalistiske velfærdsstat', in *Den nordiske protestantisme*, ed. Tim Knudsen (Århus, 2000), pp. 20–64; Dag Thorkildsen,

'Religious Identity and Nordic Identity', in *The Cultural Construction of Norden*, ed. Sørensen and Stråth, pp. 138–60; Uffe Østergaard, 'Lutheranism, danskheden og velfærdsstaten', in *13 historier om den danske velfærdsstaten*, ed. Petersen, pp. 27–46.

24 Stenius, 'The Good Life Is a Life of Conformity'; Øyvind Bjørnson, 'The Social Democrats and the Norwegian Welfare State: Some Perspectives', *Scandinavian Journal of History*, XXVI/3 (2001), pp. 197–223 (198); Søren Kolstup, 'Kommunen – velfærdsstatens spydspids', in *13 historier om den danske velfærdsstaten*, ed. Petersen, pp. 95–111.

25 Bjørnson, 'The Social Democrats and the Norwegian Welfare State', pp. 198–205; Bjørnson and Haavet, *Langsomt ble landet et velferdssamfunn*, pp. 18, 21; Christiansen and Markkola, 'Introduction'.

26 See Nils Edling, *Det fosterländska hemmet: Egnahemspolitik, småbruk och hemideologi kring sekelskiftet 1900* (Stockholm, 1996), pp. 95–7 (373).

27 Petersen and Åmark, 'Old Age Pensions in the Nordic Countries', p. 183.

28 Åmark, *Hundra år av välfärdspolitik*, p. 50.

29 Anne-Lise Seip, *Veien til velferdsstaten: Norsk sosialpolitikk 1920–1975* (Oslo, 1994), pp. 198ff; cited in Åmark, *Hundra år av välfärdspolitik*, p. 53.

30 Baldwin, 'The Scandinavian Origins'.

31 Petersen and Åmark, 'Old Age Pensions in the Nordic Countries', pp. 161–6.

32 Bjørnson, 'The Social Democrats and the Norwegian Welfare State', p. 206.

33 Åmark, *Hundra år av välfärdspolitik*, p. 83.

34 Edling, 'Limited Universalism', p. 99.

35 Edling, 'Limited Universalism', pp. 105, 110. On respectability, see Ronny Ambjörnsson, *Den skötsamme arbetaren: Idéer och ideal i ett norrländskt sågverkssamhälle 1880–1930* [1988] (Stockholm).

36 Åmark, *Hundra år av välfärdspolitik*, p. 109.

37 Åmark, *Hundra år av välfärdspolitik*, pp. 125, 137–8, 143, 156; Francis Sejersted, *Socialdemokratins tidsålder: Sverige och Norge under 1900-talet* (Nora, 2005), p. 273.

38 Bent Greve, *Historical Dictionary of the Welfare State* (Lanham, MD, 1998), p. 103.

39 A partial exception was Denmark, where the flat-rate universal pension scheme was accompanied by private supplementary schemes. See Klaus Petersen, 'Fordelningspolitik, samfundsøkonomi og organisationsinteresser: Den danske arbejderbevægelse og spørgsmålet om tillægspension 1963–1990', *Historisk Tidskrift* [Denmark], CII/1 (2002), pp. 126–69.

40 For this view: Walter Korpi, *The Working Class in Welfare Capitalism* (London, 1978); Walter Korpi, *The Democratic Class Struggle* (London, 1983), esp. pp. 196–9, 208–9.

41 Åmark, *Hundra år av välfärdspolitik*; see also Petersen and Åmark, 'Old Age Pensions in the Nordic Countries', pp. 163–5; Bjørnson and Haavet, *Langsomt ble landet et velferdssamfunn*, pp. 24–5.

42 Åmark, *Hundra år av välfärdspolitik*, pp. 109–10, 266.

43 Åmark, *Hundra år av välfärdspolitik*, pp. 138, 145; Bjørnson, 'The Social Democrats and the Norwegian Welfare State'.

44 Åmark, *Hundra år av välfärdspolitik*, pp. 194, 269; Sejersted, *Socialdemokratins tidsålder*, p. 279; Edling, 'Limited Universalism', pp. 110, 138.

45 Åmark, *Hundra år av välfärdspolitik*, pp. 277–9. See also Hugh Heclo and Henrik Madsen, *Policy and Politics in Sweden: Principled Pragmatism* (Philadelphia, PA, 1987); Urban Lundberg and Klaus Petersen, 'Social Democracy and the Welfare State in Denmark and Sweden' (Arbejdspapirer fra Institut for Historie, Købehavns universitet, 1999), p. 5.

46 Gudmundur Jonsson, 'The Icelandic Welfare State in the Twentieth Century', *Scandinavian Journal of History*, XXVI/3 (2001), pp. 249–67 (266).

47 Jonsson, 'The Icelandic Welfare State', pp. 258, 262, 265, 267.

48 Kosonen, 'The Finnish Model and the Welfare State in Crisis'.

49 Kosonen, 'The Finnish Model and the Welfare State in Crisis', p. 52.

50 Pauli Kettunen, 'The Nordic Welfare State in Finland', *Scandinavian Journal of History*, XXVI/3 (2001), pp. 225–47 (235).

51 Kettunen, 'The Nordic Welfare State in Finland', p. 253; Jonsson, 'The Icelandic Welfare State', pp. 258–60.

52 Sejersted, *Socialdemokratins tidsålder*, pp. 278–80.

53 Bjørnson and Haavet, *Langsomt ble landet et velferdssamfunn*.

54 Tim Knudsen, 'Tilblivelsen af den universalistiske velfærdsstat', in *Den nordiske protestantisme og velfærdsstaten*, ed. Tim Knudsen (Århus, 2000), pp. 20–64.

55 Christiansen and Petersen, 'The Dynamics of Social Solidarity'.

56 Klaus Petersen, 'Constructing Nordic Welfare? Nordic Social and Political Co-operation 1919–1955', in *The Nordic Model of Welfare*, ed. Christiansen et al., pp. 67–98; Bjørnson, 'The Social Democrats and the Norwegian Welfare State', p. 208.

57 Kettunen, 'The Nordic Welfare State in Finland', pp. 232–4; Petersen, 'Constructing Nordic Welfare', p. 94; Mikko Majander, 'Tillbaka till den nordiska gemenskapen: De finska socialdemokraterna och Norden 1944–48', *Historisk Tidskrift för Finland*, LXXXII/1 (1997), pp. 45–76.

58 Teresa Kulawik, 'The Nordic Model of the Welfare State and the Trouble with a Critical Perspective', address to 'Norden at the Crossroads' conference, Helsinki 2002; republished in Netværk for nordisk velfærdsstatshistorie, Nyhedsbrev 21 (December 2002).

59 Knudsen, 'Tilblivelsen af den universalistiske velfærdsstat'; Stenius, 'The Good Life Is a Life of Conformity'; Ambjörnsson, *Den skötsamme arbetaren*.

60 Marika Hedin, *Ett liberalt dilemma: Ernst Beckman, Emilia Broomé, G. H. von Koch och den sociala frågan* (Stockholm, 2002); Caroline Sutton, *Swedish Alcohol Discourse: Constructions of a Social Problem* (Uppsala, 1998).

61 Knudsen, 'Tilblivelsen af den universalistiske velfærdsstat'; Daniel Levine, 'Conservatism and Tradition Danish Social Welfare Legislation 1890–1933: A Comparative View', *Comparative Studies in Society and History*, XX/1 (1978), pp. 54–69.

62 Sejersted, *Socialdemokratins tidsålder*, p. 264; Christiansen and Petersen, 'The Dynamics of Social Solidarity', p. 182.

63 Alva Myrdal and Gunnar Myrdal, *Kris i befolkningsfrågan* (Stockholm, 1934). The Myrdals' work appeared in English as Alva Myrdal, *Nation and Family: The Swedish Experiment in Democratic Family and Population Policy* (London, 1945).

64 Sejersted, *Socialdemokratins tidsålder*, p. 269. See also Kari Melby et al., *Inte ett ord om kärlek: Äktenskap och politik i Norden ca 1850–1930* (Gothenburg, 2006).

65 Bent Sigurd Hansen, 'Something Rotten in the State of Denmark: Eugenics and the Ascent of the Welfare State', in *Eugenics and the Welfare State: Sterilization Policy in Denmark, Sweden, Norway and Finland*, ed. Gunnar Broberg and Nils Roll-Hansen (East Lansing, 1995), pp. 9–76 (10).

66 Maija Runcis, *Steriliseringar i folkhemmet* (Stockholm, 1998), p. 277; Gunnar Broberg and Mattias Tydén, 'Eugenics in Sweden: Efficient Care', in *Eugenics and the Welfare State*, ed. Broberg and Roll-Hansen, pp. 77–147 (110).

67 Broberg and Tydén, 'Eugenics in Sweden', pp. 110, 112.

68 Broberg and Tydén, 'Eugenics in Sweden', p. 118.

69 Runcis, *Steriliseringar i folkhemmet*, p. 252; Broberg and Tydén, 'Eugenics in Sweden', pp. 118–19.

70 Alberto Spektorowski and Elisabet Mizrachi, 'Eugenics and the Welfare State in Sweden: The Politics of Social Margins and the Idea of a Productive Society', *Journal of Contemporary History*, xxxIX/3 (2004) pp. 333–52 (334, 349); Runcis, *Steriliseringar i folkhemmet*, p. 170.

71 Broberg and Tydén, 'Eugenics in Sweden', p. 120.

72 Runcis, *Steriliseringar i folkhemmet*, pp. 137–8.

73 See Maciej Zaremba, *De rena och de andra: Om tvångssteriliseringar, rashygien och arvsynd* (Stockholm, 1999).

74 Hansen, 'Something Rotten in the State of Denmark', pp. 44, 52; Nils Roll-Hansen, 'Conclusion: Scandinavian Eugenics in the International Context', in *Eugenics and the Welfare State*, ed. Broberg and Roll-Hansen, p. 262.

75 Hansen, 'Something Rotten in the State of Denmark', p. 29; Timothy Tilton, *The Political Theory of Swedish Social Democracy: Through the Welfare State to Socialism* (Oxford, 1990), pp. 150–52.

76 Cited in Tage Kaarsted, *Krise og krig 1925–1950*, vol. XIII of *Gyldendal og Politikens Danmarkshistorie* (Copenhagen, 1991), p. 98.

77 Allan Pred, *Recognizing European Modernities: A Montage of the Present* (London, 1995), pp. 97–173; Tilton, *The Political Theory of Swedish Social Democracy*, p. 146; Arthur Gould, *Developments in Swedish Social Policy: Resisting Dionysus* (Basingstoke, 2001), pp. 17–18.

78 Andersson, *Mellan tillväxt och trygghet*; Christiansen and Markkola, 'Introduction', p. 21.

79 Andersson, *Mellan tillväxt och trygghet*, p. 22.

80 And to some extent in Norway as well; less in the other Scandinavian countries. Edling, 'Limited Universalism', pp. 117–18. See chapter Two. On Denmark: Niels Wium Olesen, 'Planer for velfærd: Sammenlignende studie af de nordvesteuropæiske socialdemokratiers efterkrigsprogrammer', *Jyske Historiker*, LXXXII (1998), pp. 62–91.

81 Hans Dahlqvist, 'Folkhemsbegreppet: Rudolf Kjellén vs Per Albin Hansson', *Historisk Tidskrift* [Sweden], CXXII, (2002), pp. 445–65 (447, 454–5, 464). See also Norbert Götz, *Ungleiche Geschwister: Die konstruktion von nationalsozialistischer Volksgemeinschaft und schwedischem Volksheim* (Baden-Baden, 2000), pp. 206–18.

82 Per Albin Hansson, 'Folkhemmet, medborgarhemmet', in *Från Fram till folkhemmet: Per Albin Hansson som tidningsman och talare*, ed. Anna Lisa Berkling (Solna, 1982), p. 227; quoted in Dahlqvist, 'Folkhemsbegreppet', pp. 459–60.

83 Andersson, *Mellan tillväxt och trygghet*, p. 123.

84 Ole Karup Pedersen, *Danmark og verden 1970–1990*, vol. XV of *Gyldendal og Politikens Danmarkshistorie* (Copenhagen, 1991), pp. 56–7.

85 See chapter One. Lundberg and Petersen, 'Social Democracy and the Welfare State', pp. 21–2.

86 Christiansen and Petersen, 'The Dynamics of Social Solidarity', p. 189; Bjørnson, 'The Social Democrats and the Norwegian Welfare State', p. 219.

87 Huber and Stephens, 'The Social Democratic Welfare State', p. 289.

88 Esping-Andersen, *The Three Worlds of Welfare Capitalism*, p. 28; Lars Trägårdh, 'Statist Individualism: On the Culturality of the Nordic Welfare State', in *The Cultural Construction of Norden*, ed. Sørensen and Stråth, pp. 253–85 (253–4).

89 Klas Åmark, 'Women's Labour Force Participation in the Nordic Countries during the Twentieth Century', in *The Nordic Model of Welfare*, ed. Christiansen et

al., pp. 299–333 (324).

90 Melby, *Inte ett ord om kärlek*; Barbara Hobson, 'Feminist Strategies and Gendered Discourses in Welfare States: Married Women's Right to Work in the United States and Sweden', in *Mothers of a New World: Maternalist Politics and the Origins of Welfare States*, ed. Seth Koven and Sonya Michel (New York, 1993), pp. 396–429.

91 Lena Sommestad, 'Welfare State Attitudes to the Male Breadwinning System: The United States and Sweden in Comparative Perspective', *International Review of Social History*, XXXXII (1997) Åmark, *Hundra år av välfärdspolitik*, p. 228.

92 Kettunen, 'The Nordic Welfare State in Finland', pp. 239–40.

93 Bjørnson, 'The Social Democrats and the Norwegian Welfare State', p. 220. Sejersted, *Socialdemokratins tidsålder*, pp. 269–72.

94 See, pp. 153–74; Jane Lewis and Gertrude Åström, 'Equality, Difference and State Welfare: Labor Market and Family Policies in Sweden', *Feminist Studies*, XVIII/1 (1992), pp. 49–87; Yvonne Hirdman, *Att lägga livet till rätta: Studier i svensk folkhemspolitik* (Stockholm, 1989).

95 Åmark, 'Women's Labour Force Participation', p. 322; Randi Kjeldstad, 'Gender Policies and Gender Equality', in *Nordic Welfare States*, ed. Kautto et al., pp. 66–97 (91).

96 Åmark, *Hundra år av välfärdspolitik*, p. 226.

97 Åmark, 'Women's Labour Force Participation', pp. 321, 323–4.

98 Hirdman, *Att lägga livet till rätta*.

99 Lewis and Åström, 'Equality, Difference and State Welfare'; Kjeldstad, 'Gender Policies and Gender Equality', pp. 77–8.

100 See chapter One.

101 For Sweden, see Leif Lewin, *Ideology and Strategy: A Century of Swedish Politics*, trans. Victor Kayfetz (Cambridge, 1988); on Denmark, see Henrik Madsen, *For velfærdens skyld? En analyse af de danske debatter om velfærdsstat og medlemskab af EF 1950–1972*, unpublished PhD thesis, Syddansk University, 2006.

102 Roland Huntford, *The New Totalitarians* (London, 1971); Frederick Hale, 'Brave New World in Sweden? Roland Huntford's *The New Totalitarians*', *Scandinavian Studies*, LXXVIII/2 (2006), pp. 167–90.

103 See chapter Two.

104 Andersson, *Mellan tillväxt och trygghet*, p. 126.

105 Huber and Stephens, 'The Social Democratic Welfare State', p. 282.

106 One possible exception to this is Swedish pension reform: see Urban Lundberg, *Juvelen i kronan: Socialdemokraterna och den allmänna pensionen* (Stockholm, 2003).

107 Virpi Timonen, *Restructuring the Welfare State: Globalization and Social Policy Reform in Finland and Sweden* (Cheltenham, 2003), pp. 183–6.

108 Huber and Stephens, 'The Social Democratic Welfare State', p. 296; Stein Kuhnle, 'The Scandinavian Welfare State in the 1990s: Challenged But Still Viable', *West European Politics*, XXIII/2 (2000), pp. 209–28 (211–16, 225); Anders Lindbom, 'Dismantling the Social Democratic Welfare Model? Has the Swedish Welfare State Lost Its Defining Characteristics?', *Scandinavian Political Studies*, XXIV/3 (2001), pp. 171–93 (179, 182–3, 186).

109 Klas Åmark, 'Trygghet och tvång – två teman i aktuell nordisk välfärdsstatshistorisk forskning', *Arkiv för studier i arbetarrörelsens historia*, LXXXXI (2004), pp. 1–18. See also Hirdman, *Att lägga livet till rätta*; Bo Rothstein, *Vad bör staten göra? Om välfärdsstatens moraliska och politiska logik* (Stockholm, 1994).

110 See Zaremba, *De rena och de andra*.

111 Lindbom, 'Dismantling the Social Democratic Welfare Model?' pp. 187–8.

112 Torben M. Andersen, 'Challenges to the Scandinavian Welfare Model', *European Journal of Political Economy*, XX (2004), pp. 743–54 (746).

113 'Flexicurity', *The Economist*, 7 September 2006.

114 See chapter Five.

115 Henrik Berggren and Lars Trägårdh, *Är svensken människa? Gemenskap och oberoende i det moderna Sverige* (Stockholm, 2006).

116 Kautto, 'Introduction', p. 4.

117 *The Nordic Welfare States 1900–2000*, ed. Klaus Petersen and Niels Finn Christiansen, *Scandinavian Journal of History* themed issue, XXVI, 3 (2001).

118 Christiansen and Markkola, 'Introduction', p. 21.

119 See, for example, Robert Taylor, 'Sweden's New Social Democratic Model: Proof That a Better World Is Possible', (London, 2005), p. 10. www.compassonline.org.uk/publications/compass_sweden.pdf.

Chapter 4: Between East and West? The Nordic Countries in International Relations

1 Norbert Götz, 'On the Origins of "Parliamentary Diplomacy": Scandinavian "Bloc Politics" and Delegation Policy in the League of Nations', *Cooperation and Conflict*, XXXX/3 (2005), pp. 263–79 (271).

2 Clive Archer, 'Introduction', in *The Nordic Peace*, ed. Clive Archer and Pertti Joenniemi (Aldershot, 2003), pp. 1–23 (7–8); Neil Elder, Alastair H. Thomas and David Arter, *The Consensual Democracies? The Government and Politics of the Scandinavian States* (Oxford, 1982). For the concept of the security community, see Emmanuel Adler and Michael Barnett, 'Security Communities in Theoretical Perspective', in *Security Communities*, ed. Emmanuel Adler and Michael Barnett (Cambridge, 1998), pp. 3–28.

3 Karl Deutsch, *Political Community and the North Atlantic Area* (Princeton, NJ, 1957), pp. 22–3 (64–9).

4 Pertti Joenniemi, 'Norden Beyond Security Community', in *The Nordic Peace*, ed. Archer and Joenniemi, pp. 198–212.

5 See, however, Barry Turner with Gunilla Nordquist, *The Other European Community: Integration and Co-operation in Nordic Europe* (London, 1982).

6 Francis Sejersted, *Socialdemokratins tidsålder: Sverige och Norge under 1900-talet*, trans. Lars Andersson and Per Lennart Månsson (Nora, 2005).

7 Sejerstad, *Socialdemokratins tidsålder*, p. 191.

8 Norbert Götz, '"Blue-Eyed Angels" at the League of Nations: The Genevese Construction of Norden', in *Regional Co-operation and International Organisation: Advances and Setbacks in Nordic Bloc Politics*, ed. Norbert Götz and Heidi Haggrén (forthcoming).

9 Patrick Salmon, *Scandinavia and the Great Powers, 1890–1940* (Cambridge, 1997), pp. 198–9.

10 See Leena Kaukiainen, 'From Reluctancy to Activism: Finland's Way to the Nordic Family During 1920s and 1930s', *Scandinavian Journal of History*, IX/3 (1984), pp. 201–19.

11 In Johannes Lehmann, ed., *Nordisk Samarbejde: Tre taler i idrætshuset 5 december 1934 af Per Albin Hansson, Johan Nygaardsvold, Thorvald Stauning* (Copenhagen, 1934), p. 17; cited and translated in Barbara G. Haskel, *The Scandinavian Option: Opportunities and Opportunity Costs in Post-War Scandinavian Foreign Policies* (Oslo, 1976), p. 23.

12 Salmon, *Scandinavia and the Great Powers*, p. 320.

13 Alf W. Johansson and Torbjörn Norman, 'Sweden's Security and World Peace: Social Democracy and Foreign Policy', in *Creating Social Democracy: A Century of the Social Democratic Labor Party in Sweden*, ed. Klaus Misgeld, Karl Molin and Klas Åmark, trans. Jan Teeland (University Park, PA, 1992), pp. 339–73 (351–2).

14 Sejersted, *Socialdemokratins tidsålder*, p. 200.

15 Sejersted, *Socialdemokratins tidsålder*, p. 199.

16 Ole Kristian Grimnes, 'Occupation and Collective Memory in Norway', in *War Experience, Self Image and National Identity: The Second World War as Myth and History*, ed. Stig Ekman and Nils Edling (Stockholm, 1997), pp. 130–44 (132–4).

17 Henning Poulsen, 'Denmark at War? The Occupation as History', in *War Experience, Self Image and National Identity*, ed. Ekman and Edling, pp. 98–113 (104).

18 This was in contrast to much of the rest of Europe, where, as Tony Judt has pointed out, many European countries in 1945 turned to men of an older generation: Konrad Adenauer, Alcide de Gaspari, Clement Attlee, Charles de Gaulle and Léon Blum. See Tony Judt, *Postwar: A History of Europe since 1945* (London, 2005), p. 81. Finland too followed this pattern when J. K. Paasikivi, born 1870, became president in 1946.

19 Sejersted, *Socialdemokratins tidsålder*, p. 206.

20 Stig Ekman, 'Sverige under andra världskriget: Presentation av ett forskningsprojekt', *Historisk Tidskrift* [Sweden], XXXIII (1970), pp. 310–26 (307).

21 Åsa Linderborg, *Socialdemokraterna skriver historia. Historieskrivning som ideologisk maktresurs 1892–2000* (Stockholm, 2001), p. 181.

22 David Kirby, *A Concise History of Finland* (Cambridge, 2006), p. 154.

23 Gunnar Karlsson, *Iceland's 1100 Years: History of a Marginal Society* (London, 2000), p. 316.

24 Guðmundur Háldanarson, 'Discussing Europe: Icelandic Nationalism and European Integration', in *Iceland and European Integration*, ed. Baldur Thorhallsson (London, 2004), pp. 128–44 (131–6).

25 Cited in Sejersted, *Socialdemokratins tidsålder*, p. 207.

26 Haskel, *The Scandinavian Option*, pp. 43, 85–6.

27 Toivo Miljan, *The Reluctant Europeans: The Attitudes of the Nordic Countries towards European Integration* (London, 1977), p. 16.

28 Poulsen, 'Denmark at War?' p. 106.

29 Sejersted, *Socialdemokratins tidsålder*, p. 208; Haskell, *The Scandinavian Option*, pp. 44–5.

30 Haskel, *The Scandinavian Option*, pp. 59–60.

31 Trond Bergh, 'Arbeiderbevegelsen i Norge og den kalde krigen', *Arbejderhistorie*, (2000), pp. 1–15.

32 Vibeke Sørensen, *Denmark's Social Democratic Government and the Marshall Plan 1947–1950* (Copenhagen, 2001), p. 47.

33 Baldur Thorhallsson and Hjalti Thor Vignisson, 'The Special Relationship Between Iceland and the United States of America', in *Iceland and European Integration*, ed. Thorhallsson, pp. 103–27.

34 Elder, Thomas and Arter, *The Consensual Democracies?* p. 203.

35 Juhana Aunesluoma, Magnus Petersson and Charles Silva, 'Deterrence or Reassurance? Nordic Responses to the First Détente, 1953–1956', *Scandinavian Journal of History*, XXXII/2 (2007), pp. 183–208.

36 Osmo Jussila, Seppo Hentilä and Jukka Nevakivi, *From Grand Duchy to a Modern State: A Political History of Finland since 1809*, trans. David and Eva-Kaisa Arter

(London, 1999), p. 249.

37 In Swedish, vsb-fördraget (Fördraget om vänskap, samarbete och bistånd).

38 Seppo Hentilä, 'Living Next to the Bear: How Did Finland Survive the Cold War?'
    Historiallinen Aikakauskirja, lxxxxvi/2 (1998), pp. 129–36 (131).

39 Kirby, A Concise History of Finland, pp. 144, 158; Jussila et al., From Grand Duchy to a
    Modern State, p. 232.

40 Walter Lacqueur, 'Europe: The Spectre of Finlandization', Commentary, lxiv
    (1977), pp. 37–41; Fred Singleton, 'The Myth of "Finlandisation"', International
    Affairs, lvii/2 (1981), pp. 270–85.

41 Timo Vihavainen, 'Finlandiseringens uppkomst', Historisk Tidskrift för Finland,
    lxxxii/1 (1997), pp. 112–16.

42 The debate is summarized in Jason Lavery, 'All of the President's Historians: The
    Debate over Urho Kekkonen', Scandinavian Studies, lxxv/3 (2003), pp. 375–98.

43 Lavery, 'All of the President's Historians'.

44 Esko Salminen, 'The Struggle Over Freedom of Speech in the North',
    Scandinavian Journal of History, xxiii/3–4 (1998), pp. 239–51 (242).

45 Hentilä, 'Living Next to the Bear', p. 135.

46 Ann-Sofie Dahl, 'The Myth of Swedish Neutrality', in Haunted by History: Myths in
    International Relations, ed. Cyril Buffet and Beatrice Heuser (Oxford, 1998), pp.
    28–40 (33); Miljan, The Reluctant Europeans, pp. 36, 38; Mikael af Malmborg,
    Neutrality and State-Building in Sweden (Basingstoke, 2001), p. 164; Christine Agius,
    The Social Construction of Swedish Neutrality: Challenges to Swedish Identity and
    Sovereignty (Manchester, 2006), pp. 6–8.

47 Bo Huldt, 'Svensk neutralitet – historia och framtidsperspektiv', in Svensk neutra-
    litet, Europa och eg, ed. Ulla Nordlöf-Lagercranz (Stockholm, 1990), pp. 7–26; af
    Malmborg, Neutrality and State-Building; Bo Stråth, Folkhemmet mot Europa: Ett
    historiskt perspektiv på 90-talet (Stockholm, 1993).

48 Miljan, The Reluctant Europeans, p. 48.

49 See, for example, Hans Hederborg, Svensk roulett. Den farliga vägen mellan öst och
    väst (Stockholm, 1989); Wilhelm Agrell, Den stora lögnen. Ett säkerhetspolitiskt
    dubbelspel i alltför många akter (Stockholm, 1991); Olof Kronvall and Magnus
    Petersson, Svensk säkerhetspolitik i supermakternas skugga 1945–1991 (Stockholm,
    2005).

50 Af Malmborg, Neutrality and State-Building; Dahl, 'The Myth of Swedish
    Neutrality', pp. 33–4, 37.

51 Statens Offentliga Utredningar (sou) 2002: 93: Övervakningen av 'skp-komplexet':
    Forskarrapport till Säkerhetstjänstkommissionen.

52 Archer, 'Introduction'; Deutsch, Political Community and the North Atlantic Area;
    Adler and Barnett, 'Security Communities in Theoretical Perspective'.

53 Hans Mouritzen, 'The Nordic Model as a Foreign Policy Instrument: Its Rise and
    Fall', Journal of Peace Research, xxxii/1 (1995), pp. 9–21.

54 Elder, Thomas and Arter, The Consensual Democracies? pp. 195, 207.

55 Øystein Østerud, 'Introduction: The Peculiarities of Norway', West European
    Politics, xxviii/4 (2005), pp. 705–20 (705, 713).

56 Christine Ingebritsen, 'Norm Entrepreneurs: Scandinavia's Role in World
    Politics', Co-operation and Conflict, xxxvii/1 (2002), pp. 11–23.

57 Martin Grass, '...Den starkest brygga mellan Nordens folk för fredligt arbete...',
    Arbeiderhistorie (1988), pp. 76–105.

58 Af Malmborg, Neutrality and State-Building, p. 169.

59 Jussila, Hentilä and Nevakivi, From Grand Duchy to a Modern State, pp. 312–13.

60 Elder, *The Consensual Democracies?* p. 194.

61 Joenniemi, 'Norden Beyond Security Community', pp. 204–6.

62 Joenniemi, 'Norden Beyond Security Community', pp. 204–6.

63 Nils Andrén, 'Nordic Integration', *Co-operation and Conflict*, II (1967), pp. 1–25 (8–10).

64 Miljan, *The Reluctant Europeans*, pp. 280, 283.

65 Jukka Nevakivi, 'Kekkonen, the Soviet Union and Scandinavia: Aspects of Policy in the Years 1948–1965', *Scandinavian Journal of History*, XXII/2 (1997), pp. 65–81 (69–72).

66 Indeed, for Denmark it served this function: see Michael Bruun Andersen, 'Dansk europapolitik og nordisk samarbejde', *Historisk Tidskrift* [Denmark], CIV/1 (2004), pp. 86–121.

67 Lasse Sonne, *Nordek: A Plan for Increased Nordic Economic Co-operation and Integration 1968–1970* (Helsinki, 2007).

68 Jan Heckler-Stampehl, 'Finland och förhandlingarna om Nordek 1968–1970. En fallstudie i det nordiska samarbetets begränsningar och Finlands ställning i Norden', *Historisk Tidskrift för Finland*, LXXXX/3 (2005), pp. 358–90 (370–71).

69 Sejersted, *Socialdemokratins tidsålder*, p. 199; Andrén, 'Nordic Integration', p. 14.

70 Elder, Thomas and Arter, *The Consensual Democracies?* p. 195.

71 Miljan, *The Reluctant Europeans*, p. 97.

72 Andrén, 'Nordic Integration', p. 11.

73 Ståle Løland, 'Språkforståelse og språksamarbeid i Norden', *Nordisk Tidskrift*, LXXII/1 (1996), pp. 7–13 (9).

74 Svein Olav Hansen, *Drømmen om Norden: Den norske Foreningen Norden og det nordiske samarbetet 1919–1994* (Oslo, 1994); Kersti Blidberg, 'Ideologi och pragmatism. Samarbetet inom nordisk socialdemokratiska arbetarrörelse 1930–1955', *Den jyske Historiker*, LXIX–LXX (1994), pp. 132–50.

75 For practical purposes the Cold War really ended at the Reagan–Gorbachev summits held in Reykjavík in 1986 and Washington, DC, in 1987. See Eric Hobsbawm, *Age of Extremes: The Short Twentieth Century, 1914–1991* (London, 1994), p. 250.

76 See chapter Two.

77 Tony Judt, 'The Past is Another Country: Myth and Memory in Postwar Europe', in *The Politics of Retribution in Europe: World War II and its Aftermath*, ed. István Deak, Jan T. Gross and Tony Judt (Princeton, NJ, 2000), pp. 293–323 (315). See also R.J.B. Bosworth, *Explaining Auschwitz and Hiroshima: History Writing and the Second World War 1945–1990* [1993] (London, 1994), pp. 3–4; Claus Bryld and Anette Warring, *Besættelsetiden som kollektiv erindring. Historie og traditionsforvaltning af krig og besættelse 1945–1997* (Frederiksberg, 1998).

78 Guðmundur J. Guðmundsson, 'The Cod and the Cold War', *Scandinavian Journal of History*, XXXI/2 (2006), pp. 97–118; Gudni Th. Jóhannesson, 'How "Cod War" Came: The Origins of the Anglo-Icelandic Fisheries Dispute, 1958–61', *Historical Research*, LXXVII/198 (2004), pp. 543–74.

79 See chapter Five.

80 Miljan, *The Reluctant Europeans*, pp. 238–40.

81 Ole Wæver, 'Norden Rearticulated', in *Nordic Security in the 1990s: Options in the Changing Europe*, ed. Jan Øberg (London, 1992), pp. 135–64 (135, 141–3).

82 Christine Ingebritsen, *The Nordic States and European Unity* (Ithaca, NY, 1998), pp. 96–7.

83 Ingebritsen, *The Nordic States and European Unity*, pp. 107–8; Østerud, 'Introduc-

tion: The Peculiarities of Norway', p. 718.

84 Roger Buch and Kasper M Hansen, 'The Danes and Europe: From EC 1972 to Euro 2000 – Elections, Referendums and Attitudes', *Scandinavian Political Studies*, XXV/1 (2002), pp. 1–26 (7).

85 See chapter Two.

86 Ingebritsen, *The Nordic Countries and European Unity*, pp. 184–5.

87 Lars Trägårdh, 'Sweden and the EU: Welfare State Nationalism and the Spectre of "Europe"', in *European Integration and National Identity: The Challenge of the Nordic States*, ed. Lene Hansen and Ole Wæver (London, 2002), pp. 130–81 (158–63).

88 Sejersted, *Socialdemokratins tidsålder*, p. 500; Trägårdh, 'Sweden and the EU', p. 170.

89 Ingebritsen, *The Nordic States and European Unity*.

90 Ingebritsen, *The Nordic States and European Unity*, pp. 157–60.

91 The exception here is Denmark, because until the 1990s the regions (especially Jutland) were more likely to vote in favour of European integration than Copenhagen. See Buch and Hansen, 'The Danes and Europe', p. 13.

92 Baldur Thorhallsson, 'Approaching the Question: Domestic Background and Conceptual Framework', in *Iceland and European Integration*, ed. Thorhallsson, pp. 1–18.

93 Thorhallsson, 'Approaching the Question'.

94 Trägårdh, 'Sweden and the EU'; Lene Hansen, 'Sustaining Sovereignty: The Danish Approach to Europe', in *European Integration and National Identity*, ed. Hansen and Wæver, pp. 50–87; Bo Stråth, 'The Swedish Demarcation to Europe', in *The Meaning of Europe: Variety and Contention within and among Nations*, ed. Mikael af Malmborg and Bo Stråth (Oxford, 2002), pp. 125–47; Guðmundur Hálfdanarsson, 'Discussing Europe: Icelandic Nationalism and European Integration', in *Iceland and European Integration*, ed. Thorhallsson, pp. 128–44.

95 Cited in Even Lange, *Samling om felles mål*, vol. XI of *Aschehougs Norges historie*, ed. Knut Helle [1996] (Oslo, 2005), p. 216.

96 Judt, *Postwar*, p. 158.

97 Miljan, *The Reluctant Europeans*, p. 80.

98 Øystein Sørensen and Bo Stråth, 'Introduction: The Cultural Construction of Norden', in *The Cultural Construction of Norden* (Oslo, 1997), pp. 1–24 (20).

99 Trägårdh, 'Sweden and the EU'; Hansen, 'Sustaining Sovereignty'.

100 David J. Smith, 'Nordic Near Abroad or New Northern Europe? Perspectives on Post-Cold War Regional Co-operation in the Baltic Sea Area', in *Post-Cold War Identity Politics: Northern and Baltic Experiences*, ed. Marko Lehti and David J. Smith (London, 2003), pp. 50–77 (70).

101 The CBSS was not the first pan-Baltic organization; it was pre-dated by the Helsinki Commission established in 1974 to tackle pollution in the Baltic.

102 Marko Lehti, 'Possessing a Baltic Europe: Retold National Narratives in the European North', in *Post-Cold War Identity Politics*, ed. Lehti and Smith, pp. 11–49 (25–6).

103 Lehti, 'Possessing a Baltic Europe'; Smith, 'Nordic Near Abroad or New Northern Europe?'

104 Lee Miles, *Fusing with Europe? Sweden in the European Union* (Aldershot, 2005).

105 Cf., however, Mouritzen, 'The Nordic Model as a Foreign Policy Instrument', for a more pessimistic assessment of the continued ability of the Nordic countries to influence foreign policy.

106 Peter Lawler, 'Janus-Faced Solidarity: Danish Internationalism Reconsidered', *Co-operation and Conflict*, XXXXII (2007), pp. 101–26 (117–20).

Chapter 5: Scandinavian Society: Equality, Ethnicity and Multiculturalism

1 Øystein Sørensen and Bo Stråth, 'Introduction: The Cultural Construction of Norden', in *The Cultural Construction of Norden* (Oslo, 1997), pp. 1–24.
2 Øystein Sørensen, *Kampen om Norges sjel* (Oslo, 2001), pp. 69ff.
3 Harald Runblom, 'Immigration to Scandinavia after World War II', in *Ethnicity and Nation Building in the Nordic World*, ed. Sven Tägil (London, 1995), pp. 282–324 (313).
4 Allan Pred, 'Memory and the Cultural Reworking of Crisis: Racisms and the Current Moment of Danger in Sweden, or Wanting It Like Before', *Environment and Planning D: Society and Space*, XVI/6 (1998), pp. 635–64 (638–40); Allan Pred, *Even in Sweden: Racisms, Racialized Spaces and the Popular Geographical Imagination* (Berkeley, CA, 2000); Maaria Ylänkö, *La Finlande, pays d'accueil: approche historique et anthropoligique. Le cas des immigrés d'Afrique noire* (Helsinki, 2002), p. 139.
5 Karen Wren, 'Cultural Racism: Something Rotten in the State of Denmark?', *Social and Cultural Geography*, II/2 (2001), pp. 141–62.
6 Hanna Hodacs, *Converging World Views: The European Expansion and Early Nineteenth-Century Anglo-Swedish Contacts* (Uppsala, 2003).
7 Juha Pentikäinen, 'Finland as a Cultural Area', in *Cultural Minorities in Finland: An Overview Towards Cultural Policy*, ed. Juha Pentikäinen and Marja Hiltunen (Helsinki, 1995), pp. 11–27 (18).
8 Marja Nylund-Oja et al., 'Finnish Emigration and Immigration', in *Cultural Minorities in Finland*, ed. Pentikäinen and Hiltunen, pp. 173–225 (185–6).
9 Ylänkö, *La Finlande, pays d'accueil*, p. 162.
10 Lenard Sillanpää, 'A Comparative Analysis of Indigenous Rights in Fenno-Scandia', *Scandinavian Political Studies*, XX (1997), pp. 197–271 (215), n. 1.
11 Einar Niemi, 'Sami History and the Frontier Myth: A Perspective on the Northern Sami Spatial and Rights History', in *Sami Culture in a New Era*, ed. Harald Gaski (Kárášjohka, 1997), pp. 62–85 (69).
12 Sverker Sörlin, *Framtidslandet: Debatten om Norrland och naturresurserna under det industriella genombrottet* (Stockholm, 1988); Niemi, 'Sami History and the Frontier Myth', pp. 62–3; Ottar Brox, *Nord-Norge: Fra allmenning til koloni* (Oslo, 1984); Irja Seurujärvi-Kari et al., 'The Sami People in Finland', in *Cultural Minorities in Finland*, ed. Pentikäinen, pp. 101–45.
13 Tove Skovedt, 'Sami: The Indigenous Peoples of Norway', in *Continuity and Change: Aspects of Contemporary Norway*, ed. Anne Cohen Kiel (Oslo, 1993), pp. 85–105.
14 Trong Berg Eriksen, Andreas Hompland and Eivind Tjønneland, *Et lite land i verden* (Oslo, 2003), p. 188.
15 Eriksen, Hompland and Tjønneland, *Et lite land i verden*, p. 184.
16 Harald Eidheim, 'Ethno-Political Development among the Sami after World War II', in *Sami Culture in a New Era*, ed. Gaski, p. 46.
17 Eriksen, Hompland and Tjønneland, *Et lite land i verden*, p. 188.
18 Eriksen, Hompland and Tjønneland, *Et lite land i verden*, p. 190.
19 Sven Lundkvist, 'The Saamis and the Swedish State in the Twentieth Century', in *States and Minorities*, ed. Veniamin Alekseyev and Sven Lundkvist (Stockholm, 1997), pp. 117–22 (120).
20 Seurujärvi-Kari, 'The Sami People in Finland'.
21 Nylund-Oja, 'Finnish Emigration and Immigration', pp. 188–9; Pär Stenbäck, 'Finlands flyktningpolitik', *Nordisk Tidskrift*, LXIII/6 (1987), pp. 487–94 (488–9).

22 Kirk Scott, *The Immigrant Experience: Changing Employment and Income Patterns in Sweden, 1970–1993* (Lund, 1999), pp. 37, 40. The anomaly in the early 1970s was accounted for by high levels of return migration associated with the downturn in the international economy. Most of the immigration during the 1930s was accounted for by the return of Swedish Americans.

23 Runblom, 'Immigration to Scandinavia after World War II', p. 289.

24 See, for example, Susanna Alakoski, *Svinalångorna* (2006) for a fictional, semi-autobiographical account of this phenomenon.

25 See chapter Two.

26 Peder J. Pedersen and Nina Smith, 'International Migration and Migration Policy in Denmark', Working Paper 01-05, Centre for Labour Market and Social Research, Aarhus School of Business (February 2001).

27 Francis Sejersted, *Socialdemokratins tidsålder. Sverige och Norge under 1900-talet* (Nora, 2005), pp. 419–20.

28 Edgeir Benum, *Overflod og fremtidsfrykt 1970–97* (Oslo, 2005), p. 264.

29 Statistics Finland, Statistics Iceland.

30 Sejersted, *Socialdemokratins tidsålder*, p. 420; Pedersen and Smith, 'International Migration and Migration Policy'; Peter Lawler, 'Janus-Faced Solidarity: Danish Internationalism Reconsidered', *Co-operation and Conflict*, XXXII (2007), pp. 101–26 (113).

31 Sejersted, *Socialdemokratins tidsålder*, p. 421.

32 Hans Jørgen Nielsen, *Er danskerne fremmedfjendske? Udlandets syn på debatten om indvandrere 2000–2002* (Århus, 2004), p. 47.

33 Nielsen, *Er danskerne fremmedfjendske?* p. 45.

34 Sejersted, *Socialdemokratins tidsålder*, p. 418; Mary Hilson, 'Pan-Scandinavianism and Nationalism in the Scandinavian States: Civic and Ethnic Nationalism in Denmark, Norway and Sweden', in *What is a Nation? Europe 1789–1914*, ed. Mark Hewitson and Timothy Baycroft (Oxford, 2006), pp. 192–209.

35 Harald Runblom, 'Swedish Multiculturalism in a Comparative European Perspective', in *Language, Minority, Migration*, ed. Sven Gustavsson and Harald Runblom (Uppsala, 1995), pp. 199–228.

36 Martin Bak Jørgensen, 'Dansk realisme og svensk naivitet? En analyse av den danske og svenske integrationspolitik', in *Bortom stereotyperna? Invandrare och integration i Danmark och Sverige*, ed. Ulf Hedetoft, Bo Petersson and Lina Sturfelt (Lund, 2006), pp. 266–98 (270).

37 Jørgensen, 'Dansk realisme og svensk naivitet?', pp. 271–2; Pedersen and Smith, 'International Migration and Migration Policy', pp. 16–17.

38 Jørgensen, 'Dansk realisme og svensk naivitet?', p. 274.

39 Ulf Hedetoft, 'Divergens eller konvergens? Perspektiver i den dansk-svenske sammenstilling', in *Bortom stereotyperna?* ed. Hedetoft, Petersson and Sturfelt, pp. 390–407 (393).

40 Jørgensen, 'Dansk realisme og svensk naivitet?', p. 278.

41 Hedetoft, 'Divergens eller konvergens?' pp. 395–6.

42 Dag Blanck and Mattias Tydén, 'Becoming Multicultural? The Development of a Swedish Immigrant Policy', in *Welfare States in Trouble: Historical Perspectives on Canada and Sweden* (Umeå, 1995), pp. 57–70 (57, 63).

43 Runblom, 'Immigration to Scandinavia after World War II', p. 315.

44 Sejersted, *Socialdemokratins tidsålder*, p. 422.

45 Sejersted, *Socialdemokratins tidsålder*, p. 422.

46 Jørgensen, 'Dansk realisme og svensk naivitet?', p. 284.

47 Bo Petersson, 'Invandring och integration i Danmark och Sverige: Likt och olikt i debatt och politisk praxis', in *Bortom stereotyperna?* ed. Hedetoft, Petersson and Sturfelt, pp. 7–25 (14); Hedetoft, 'Divergens eller konvergens?' p. 391.

48 Mads Qvortrup, 'The Emperor's New Clothes: The Danish General Election 20 November 2001', *West European Politics*, xxv (2002), pp. 205–11. One of the most notorious examples of Venstre's controversial campaigning methods was its use of a campaign poster depicting a recent court case where three ethnic minority men were acquitted for group rape. The poster carried the slogan, 'This will not be tolerated once Venstre gets in.'

49 Sasha Polakow-Suransky, 'Fortress Denmark?' *American Prospect*, xiii/10, (3 June 2002). Nielsen, *Er danskerne fremmedfjendske?* p. 148.

50 Roger Boye, 'Denmark ready to adopt strictest asylum law in EU', *The Times*, 30 May 2002. The new laws also abolished the concept of de facto refugee status, first introduced in 1983, and lengthened the periods of residency required for elibility for benefits, for permanent residency and for full citizenship. See Nielsen, *Er danskerne fremmedfjendske?* p. 55. For the UN criticism, see Claus Blom Thomsen, 'FN vil overvåge dansk flygtningepolitik', *Politiken*, 20 June 2002. This followed early criticism of the Danish treatment of immigrants and ethnic minorities by the Council of Europe's European Commission Against Racism and Intolerance (ECRI). See Nielsen, *Er danskerne fremmedfjendske?* pp. 64–6, 79–81.

51 Anders Westgårdh, 'Någonting är ruttet i staten Danmark', *Aftonbladet*, 23 November 2001.

52 Nielsen, *Er danskerne fremmedfjendske?* p. 17.

53 For the Mohammed cartoons affair, see Mary Hilson, entry on the Nordic countries in *The Annual Register: World Events*, ccxxxxviii (2007), pp. 53–8.

54 The foreign minister, Laila Freivalds, initially denied knowing anything about this intervention, but was later forced to resign when it became clear that she had indeed sanctioned it.

55 Kristina Olsson, 'Danskjävlar!', *Politiken* 19 February 2006; Niklas Johansson, 'Sverige og Danmark: Nu svider sandheden i Sverige', *Politiken*, 31 March 2006.

56 Stefan Jonsson, 'En kulturjournalist i reservat', *Dagens Nyheter*, 18 November 2006; Kristian Lindberg, 'Det han siger, er han selv'; Jakob Høyer, 'Svenskerhår'; Kristian Lindberg, 'I er alt for overfladiske', *Berlingske Tidende*, 15 November 2006.

57 Jonathan Friedman and Kajsa Ekholm Friedman, 'Sverige: från nationalstat till pluralt samhälle', in *Bortom stereotyperna?* ed. Hedetoft, Petersson and Sturfelt, pp. 66–92 (74–6).

58 Friedman and Friedman, 'Sverige', pp. 85–7; Hedetoft, 'Divergens eller konvergens?' pp. 398–9. This was also the foreign perception: see Christopher Caldwell, 'Islam on the Outskirts of the Welfare State', *New York Times*, 5 February 2006.

59 Pred, 'Memory and the Cultural Reworking of Crisis', p. 647. On neo-Nazism in Sweden, see Tore Bjørgo, '"The Invaders", "The Traitors" and "The Resistance Movement": The Extreme Right's Conceptualisation of Opponents and Self in Scandinavia', in *The Politics of Multi-Culturalism in the New Europe: Racism, Identity and Community*, ed. Tariq Modood and Pnina Werbner (London, 1997), pp. 54–72.

60 Hedetoft, 'Divergens eller konvergens?'

61 Even before the 2001 election there were signs that the success of the Danish People's Party was forcing changes of policy among the mainstream parties, for example the Social Democrats' appointment of the outspoken Karen Jespersen as Minister of the Interior in 2000. See Lawler, 'Janus-Faced Solidarity', p. 112.

62 Eva Østergaard-Nielsen, 'Counting the Cost: Denmark's Changing Migration Policies', *International Journal of Urban and Regional Research*, XXVII/2 (2003), pp. 448–54 (449).

63 Bjørgo, "The Invaders", pp. 55–9.

64 Pred, 'Memory and the Cultural Reworking of Crisis', p. 647.

65 Jens Rydgren, 'Varför inte i Sverige? Den radikala högerpopulismens relativa misslyckande', *Arkiv för studier i arbetarrörelsens historia*, LXXXVI–VII (2002), pp. 1–34.

66 Qvortrup, 'The Emperor's New Clothes'. Compare Nielsen, *Er danskerne fremmedfjenske?* who suggests that the coverage of the 2001 election campaign in the international media was one-sided and excluded most other issues apart from immigration.

67 Jørgensen, 'Dansk realisme og svensk naivitet?', p. 289.

68 Qvortrup, 'The Emperor's New Clothes'. They did the same in 2005 and increased their percentage share of the vote significantly, doing especially well in the more multi-ethnic districts of inner Copenhagen.

69 Lars Halskov, 'Kandidaten', *Politiken*, 18 November 2001.

70 Magnus Dahlstedt and Fredrik Hertzberg, 'Democracy the Swedish Way? The Exclusion of Immigrants in Swedish Politics', *Scandinavian Political Studies*, XXX (2007), pp. 175–203 (176).

71 Katarina Mattsson, 'Ekonomisk rasism: Föreställningar om de Andra inom ekonomisk invandrarforskning', in *Sverige och de Andra: Postkoloniala perspektiv*, ed. Michael McEachrane and Louis Faye (Stockholm, 2001), pp. 243–64 (260).

72 Wren, 'Cultural Racism', p. 147.

73 The first recorded use was in 1993: see Pia Jarvad, *Nye ord. Ordbog over nye ord i dansk 1955–1998* (Copenhagen, 1999), p. 605. I am grateful to Tom Lundskær-Nielsen for this reference.

74 Nielsen, *Er danskerne fremmedfjenske?*, p. 48; Lawler, 'Janus-Faced Solidarity', p. 116.

75 Kåre Vessenden, *Innvandrere i Norge: Hvem er de, hva gjør de og hvordan lever de?* (Oslo, 1997), p. 117.

76 Henry Bäck and Maritta Soinenen, 'Immigrants in the Political Process', *Scandinavian Political Studies*, XXI/1 (1998), pp. 29–50.

77 Martin Klinthäll, *Return Migration from Sweden 1968–1996: A Longitudinal Analysis* (Stockholm, 1993), pp. 19–21; Scott, *The Immigrant Experience*, pp. 201–3; Pedersen and Smith, 'International Migration and Migration Policy', pp. 16–17.

78 Mattsson, 'Ekonomisk rasism', pp. 245–6; Wren, 'Cultural Racism', p. 152.

79 Jørgensen, 'Dansk realisme og svensk naivitet?', p. 285.

80 Vessenden, *Innvandrere i Norge*, pp. 37–40.

81 Nylund-Oja, 'Finnish Emigration and Immigration', p. 214; Ylänkö, *La Finlande, pays d'accueil*, pp. 7, 144; Jouni Korkiasaari and Ismo Söderling, 'Finland: From a Country of Emigration into a Country of Immigration', in *A Changing Pattern of Migration in Finland and Its Surroundings*, ed. Ismo Söderling (Helsinki, 1998), pp. 7–28 (14).

82 Nylund-Oja, 'Finnish Emigration and Immigration', pp. 202–3.

83 Outi Laati, 'Immigrants in Finland: Finnish-to-be or Foreigners Forever? Conceptions of Nation-State Debate on Immigration Policy', in *A Changing Pattern of Migration in Finland* ed. Söderling, pp. 29–49 (31); Stenbäck, 'Finlands flyktningpolitik', pp. 489–90.

84 Ylänkö, *La Finlande, pays d'accueil*, p. 6.

85 M. Jaakkola, *Suomalaisten suhtautuminen ulkomaalaisin ja ulkomaalaispolitiikkaan*

(Helsinki, 1989); M. Jaakkola, *Suomalaisten kiristyvåt ulkomaalaisasenteet* (Helsinki, 1995); both cited in Korkiasaari and Söderling, 'Finland', pp. 23–4.

86 Ylänkö, *La Finlande, pays d'accueil*, pp. 6, 215; Korkiasaari and Söderling, 'Finland', p. 21.

87 Ylänkö, *La Finlande, pays d'accueil*, pp. 139, 150

88 Ylänkö, *La Finlande, pays d'accueil*, p. 158.

89 Cited in Laati, 'Immigrants in Finland', p. 45.

90 Ylänkö, *La Finlande, pays d'accueil*, p. 194.

91 Pred, *Even in Sweden*, pp. 203–23.

92 Nielsen, *Er danskerne fremmedfjenske?*

Conclusion

1 Jan Hecker-Stampehl, 'Finland och förhandlingarna om Nordek 1968–1970: En fallstudie i det nordiska samarbetets begränsningar och Finlands ställning i Norden', *Historisk Tidskrift för Finland*, III (2005), pp. 358–90 (365).

2 Anssi Paasi, *Territories, Boundaries and Consciousness: The Changing Geographies of the Finnish-Russian Border* (Chichester, 1996), p. 12.

3 Harald Gustafsson, 'Om Nordens historia', *Scandia*, 67 (2001), pp. 187–92 (189).

4 Norbert Götz, 'Norden: Structures That Do Not Make a Region', *European Review of History*, X (2003), pp. 323–41 (324).

5 E. J. Hobsbawm, *Age of Extremes: The Short Twentieth Century, 1914–1991* (London, 1995).

6 Reinhart Koselleck, *The Practice of Conceptual History: Timing History, Spacing Concepts*, trans. Todd Samuel Presner et al. (Stanford, CA, 2002), pp. 84–99.

7 Olof Petersson, *The Government and Politics of the Nordic Countries*, trans. Frank Gabriel Perry (Stockholm, 1994), pp. 28–9.

8 E.g., Dag Thorkildsen, 'Religious Identity and Nordic Identity', in *The Cultural Construction of Norden*, ed. Øystein Sørensen and Bo Stråth (Oslo, 1997), pp. 138–60.

9 Hans Mouritzen, 'The Nordic Model as a Foreign Policy Instrument: Its Rise and Fall', *Journal of Peace Research*, XXXI/1 (1995), pp. 9–21 (11).

10 Hanne Sanders, *Nyfiken på Danmark – klokare på Sverige* (Göteborg, 2006).

11 Francis Sejersted, *Socialdemokratins tidsålder. Sverige och Norge under 1900-talet* (Nora, 2005).

12 Max Engman, 'Är Finland ett nordiskt land?', *Den Jyske Historiker*, LXVIX–LXX (1994), pp. 62–78 (72).

13 Götz, 'Norden: Structures That Do Not Make a Region', p. 340.

14 Mikko Lagerspetz, 'How Many Nordic Countries? Possibilities and Limits of Geopolitical Identity Construction', *Co-operation and Conflict*, XXXVIII/1 (2003), pp. 49–61 (54–5); Jan Hecker-Stampehl, 'Finland och förhandlingarna om Nordek', p. 365; Jukka Nevakivi, 'Kekkonen, the Soviet Union and Scandinavia: Aspects of Policy in the Years 1948–1965', *Scandinavian Journal of History*, XXII/2 (1997), pp. 65–81.

15 Marko Lehti, 'Possessing a Baltic Europe: Retold National Narratives in the European North', in *Post-Cold War Identity Politics: Northern and Baltic Experiences*, ed. Marko Lehti and David J. Smith (London, 2003), pp. 11–49 (13); Paasi, *Territories, Boundaries and Consciousness*, p. 6.

16 *International Herald Tribune*, 24 February 1992; cited in Mouritzen, 'The Nordic Model as a Foreign Policy Instrument', p. 14.

17 Jan-Otto Andersson, Pekka Kosonen and Juhana Vartianen, *The Finnish Model of Economic and Social Policy: From Emulation to Crash* (Åbo, 1993); Terje Tvedt, *Utviklingshjelp, utenrikspolitikk og makt: Den norske modellen* (Oslo, 2003), cited in Øystein Østerud, 'Introduction: The Peculiarities of Norway', *West European Politics*, XXVIII/4 (2005), pp. 705–20 (713–4).

18 Marko Lehti and David J. Smith, 'Introduction: Other Europes', in *Post-Cold War Identity Politics*, pp. 1–10 (4); Lehti, 'Possessing a Baltic Europe'.

19 Samuel P. Huntington, *The Clash of Civilizations and the Remaking of World Order* [1996] (London, 2002), p. 125.

20 Lehti, 'Possessing a Baltic Europe', p. 14.

21 D. G. Kirby, *Northern Europe in the Early Modern Period: The Baltic World 1492–1772* (London, 1990); D. G. Kirby, *The Baltic World 1772–1993: Europe's Northern Periphery in an Age of Change* (London, 1995); Matti Klinge, *The Baltic World*, trans. Timothy Binham (Helsinki, 1995); Kristian Gerner and Klas-Göran Karlsson with Anders Hammarlund, *Nordens Medelhav: Östersjöområdet som historia, myt och projekt* (Stockholm, 2002). As the title of the last volume suggests, the authors refer explicitly to Fernand Braudel's celebrated history of the Mediterranean.

22 Lehti, 'Possessing a Baltic Europe', p. 22.

23 Marju Lauristin, 'Contexts of Transition', in *Return to the Western World: Cultural and Political Perspectives on the Estonian Post-Communist Transition*, ed., Marju Lauristin and Peeter Vilhalemm (Tartu, 1997), pp. 26–40 (26–7).

24 Helmut Piirimäe, 'Historical Heritage: The Relations between Estonia and Her Nordic Neighbours', in *Return to the Western World*, ed. Lauristin and Vilhalemm, pp. 43–72.

25 Lauristin, 'Contexts of Transition', p. 35. The most prominent example of this was President Mauno Koivisto's decision to offer returning migrant status to the Ingrians of the St Petersburg district. See chapter Five.

26 Peeter Vihalemm, 'Changing National Spaces in the Baltic Area', in *Return to the Western World*, ed. Lauristin and Vihalemm, pp. 129–62.

27 Lehti, 'Possessing a Baltic Europe', p. 41.

28 Vihalemm, 'Changing National Spaces in the Baltic Area', pp. 160–62.

29 Consultative Steering Group, *Shaping Scotland's Parliament* (Edinburgh, 1999); cited in David Arter, *Democracy in Scandinavia: Consensual, Majoritarian or Mixed?* (Manchester, 2006), p. 2. See also David Arter, *The Scottish Parliament: A Scandinavian-Style Assembly?* (London, 2004).

30 Alex Neil MSP, '100 Years of Norwegian Independence: A Study and Comparison with Scotland'. SNP press release, 8 June 2005: www.snp.org/press-releases/2005/snp_press_release [accessed 29 October 2007].

31 Scottish National Party website, www.snp.org/independence/benefits [accessed 5 November 2007].

32 Petersson, *The Government and Politics*, pp. 28–9.

33 Lise Lyck, 'The Faroe Islands: The Birth of a New Microstate', in *The Nordic Peace*, ed. Clive Archer and Pertti Joeniemi (Aldershot, 2003), pp. 66–80.

34 Lise Lyck, 'Greenland and the Challenges for the Danish Realm', in *The Nordic Peace*, ed. Archer and Joeniemi, pp. 81–87; Greenland Home Rule (official site of Greenland's home rule government): www.nanoq.gl/English.aspx [accessed 5 November 2007].

35 Pirjo Jukarainen, 'Norden is Dead – Long Live the Eastwards Faced Euro-North. Geopolitical Re-Making of Norden in a Nordic Journal', *Co-operation and Conflict*, XXXIV/4 (1999), pp. 355–82.

36 The Norwegian Barents Secretariat: www.barents.no/index.php?cat=41098 [accessed 5 November 2007].

37 Lagerspetz, 'How Many Nordic Countries?'.

38 Stefan Troebst, 'Nordosteuropa: Geschichtsregion mit Zukunft', *Scandia*, LXV (1999), pp. 153–68; Ralph Tuchtenhagen, 'The Best (and the Worst) of Several Worlds: The Shifting Historiographical Concept of Northeastern Europe', *European Review of History*, X (2003), pp. 361–74.

39 David Kirby, *The Baltic World: Europe's Northern Periphery in an Age of Change* (London, 1995); Klinge, *The Baltic World*, Nina Witoszek and Lars Trägårdh, *Culture and Crisis: The Case of Germany and Sweden* (Oxford, 2002); Maria Ågren and Amy Louise Erickson, *The Marital Economy in Scandinavia and Britain, 1400–1900* (Aldershot, 2005).

40 Robert Taylor, 'Sweden's New Social Democratic Model: Proof That a Better World Is Possible', (London, 2005), p. 10. www.compassonline.org.uk/publications/compass_sweden.pdf.

Select Bibliography

General histories

Benum, Edgeir, *Overflod og fremtidsfrykt*, vol. XII of Aschehougs Norges Historie, ed. Knut Helle (Oslo, 1996)

Einhorn, Eric S., and John Logue, *Modern Welfare States: Scandinavian Politics and Policy in the Global Age*, 2nd edn (Westport, CA, 2003)

Elvander, Nils, *Skandinavisk arbetarrörelse* (Stockholm, 1980)

Engman, Max, 'Är Finland ett nordiskt land?', *Den jyske Historiker*, LXIX–LXX (1994), pp. 62–78

Eriksen, Trong Berg, Andreas Hompland and Eivind Tjønneland, *Et lite land i verden* (Oslo, 2003)

Gerner, Kristian, and Klas-Göran Karlsson with Anders Hammarlund, *Nordens Medelhav: Östersjöområdet som historia, myt och projekt* (Stockholm, 2002)

Gustafsson, Harald, *Nordens historia: En europeisk region under 1200 år* (Lund, 1997)

Götz, Norbert, 'Norden: Structures That Do Not Make a Region', *European Review of History*, X (2003), pp. 323–41

Jespersen, Knud J. V., *A History of Denmark*, trans. Ivan Hill (Basingstoke, 2004)

Jussila, Osmo, Seppo Hentilä and Jukka Nevikivi, *From Grand Duchy to a Modern State: A Political History of Finland since 1809*, trans. David and Eva-Kaisa Arter (London, 1999)

Kaarsted, Tage, *Krise og krig 1925–1950*, vol. XIII of *Gyldendal og Politikens Danmarkshistorie* (Copenhagen, 1991)

Karlsson, Gunnar, *Iceland's 1100 Years: The History of a Marginal Society* (London, 1999)

Kirby, David, *A Concise History of Finland* (Cambridge, 2006)

—, *The Baltic World 1772–1993: Europe's Northern Periphery in an Age of Change* (London, 1995)

Lange, Even, *Samling om felles mål* [1996], vol. XI of *Aschehougs Norges historie*, ed. Knut Helle (Oslo, 2005)

Lavery, Jason, *The History of Finland* (Westport, CA, 2006)

Musiał, Kazimierz, *Roots of the Scandinavian Model: Images of Progress in the Era of Modernisation* (Baden-Baden, 2002)

Pedersen, Ole Karup, *Danmark og verden 1970–1990*, vol. XV of *Gyldendal og Politikens Danmarkshistorie* (Copenhagen, 1991)

Sejersted, Francis, *Socialdemokratins tidsålder: Sverige och Norge under 1900-talet*, trans. Lars Andersson and Per Lennart Månsson (Nora, 2005)

Sørensen, Øystein, and Bo Stråth, eds, *The Cultural Construction of Norden* (Oslo, 1997)

Stråth, Bo, 'The Swedish Demarcation to Europe', in *The Meaning of Europe: Variety and Contention within and among Nations*, ed. Mikael af Malmborg and Bo Stråth (Oxford, 2002), pp. 125–47

Politics

Arter, David, *Democracy in Scandinavia: Consensual, Majoritarian or Mixed?* (Manchester, 2006)

—, *Scandinavian Politics Today* (Manchester, 1999)

Bergqvist, Christina, ed., *Equal Democracies? Gender and Politics in the Nordic Countries* (Oslo, 2000)

Castles, Francis G., *The Social Democratic Image of Society: A Study of the Achievements and Origins of Scandinavian Social Democracy in Comparative Perspective* (London, 1978)

Elder, Neil, Alastair H. Thomas and David Arter, *The Consensual Democracies? The Government and Politics of the Scandinavian States* (Oxford, 1982)

Esaiasson, Peter, and Knut Heidar, ed., *Beyond Westminster and Congress: The Nordic experience* (Columbus, OH, 2000)

Esping-Andersen, Gøsta, *Politics Against Markets: The Social Democratic Road to Power* (Princeton, NJ, 1985)

Hadenius, Stig, Hans Wieslander and Björn Molin, *Sverige efter 1900: En modern politisk historia* [1967], 3rd edn (Stockholm, 1969)

Heclo, Hugh, and Henrik Madsen, *Policy and Politics in Sweden: Principled Pragmatism* (Philadelphia, PA, 1987)

Heidar, Knut, 'Norwegian Parties and the Party System: Steadfast and Changing', *West European Politics*, XXVIII/4 (2005), pp. 804–33

—, ed. *Nordic Politics: Comparative Perspectives* (Oslo, 2004)

Lewin, Leif, *Ideology and Strategy: A Century of Swedish Politics*, trans. Victor Kayfetz (Cambridge, 1988)

Linderborg, Åsa, *Socialdemokraterna skriver historia: Historieskrivning som ideologisk maktresurs 1892–2000* (Stockholm, 2001)

Lipset, Martin, Seymour Rokkan and Stein Rokkan, 'Cleavage Structures, Party Systems and Voter Alignments: An Introduction', in *Party Systems and Voter Alignments: Cross-National Perspectives*, ed. Seymour Martin Lipset and Stein Rokkan (New York, 1967), pp. 1–64

Matthews, Donald R., and Henry Valen, *Parliamentary Representation: The Case of the Norwegian Storting* (Columbus, OH, 1999)

Misgeld, Klaus, Karl Molin and Klas Åmark, eds, *Creating Social Democracy: A Century of the Social Democratic Labor Party in Sweden*, trans. Jan Teeland (University Park, PA, 1992)

Østerud, Øystein, 'Introduction: The Peculiarities of Norway', *West European Politics*, XXVIII/4 (2005), pp. 705–20

Petersson, Olof, *The Government and Politics of the Nordic Countries*, trans. Frank Gabriel Perry (Stockholm, 1994)

Raaum, Nina C., 'Gender Equality and Political Representation: A Nordic Comparison', *West European Politics*, XXVIII/4 (2005), pp. 872–97

Shaffer, William R., *Politics, Parties and Parliaments: Political Change in Norway* (Columbus, OH, 1998)

Tilton, Timothy, *The Political Theory of Swedish Social Democracy: Through the Welfare State to Socialism* (Oxford, 1990)

Economic history

Andersen, Palle Schelde, and Johnny Åkerholm, 'Scandinavia', in *The European Economy: Growth and Crisis*, ed. Andrea Boltho (Oxford, 1982), pp. 610–44

Andersson, Jenny, *Mellan tillväxt och trygghet. Idéer om produktiv socialpolitik i social-demokratisk socialpolitisk ideologi under efterkrigstiden* (Uppsala, 2003)

Christoffersen, Henrik, *Danmarks økonomiske historie efter 1960* (Gylling, 1999)

Daveri, Francesco, and Olmo Silva, 'Not Only Nokia: What Finland Tells Us About New Economy Growth', *Economic Policy*, XIX/38 (2004), pp. 117–63

Eklund, Klas, 'Gösta Rehn and the Swedish Model: Did We Follow the Rehn-Meidner Model Too Little Rather Than Too Much?', in *Gösta Rehn, the Swedish Model and Labour Market Policies: International and National Perspectives*, ed. Henry Milner and Eskil Wadensjö (Aldershot, 2001)

Hjerppe, Riitta, *The Finnish Economy 1860–1985: Growth and Structural Change* (Helsinki, 1989)

Hodne, Fritz, *The Norwegian Economy 1920–1980* (London, 1983)

Johansen, Hans Christian, *The Danish Economy in the Twentieth Century* (London, 1987)

Kalela, Jorma et al., eds, *Down from the Heavens, Up from the Ashes: The Finnish Economic Crisis of the 1990s in the Light of Economic and Social Research* (Helsinki, 2001)

Lundberg, Erik, 'The Rise and Fall of the Swedish Economic Model', in *Europe's Economy in Crisis*, ed. Ralf Dahrendorf (London, 1982)

Magnusson, Lars, *An Economic History of Sweden* (London, 2000)

Ojala, Jari et al., eds, *The Road to Prosperity: An Economic History of Finland* (Helsinki, 2006)

Ornston, Darius, 'Reorganising Adjustment: Finland's Emergence as a High Technology Leader', *West European Politics*, XXIX/4 (2006), pp. 784–801

Schön, Lennart, *En modern svensk ekonomisk historia: Tillväxt och omvandling under två sekel* (Stockholm, 2000)

Thullberg, Pers and Kjell Östberg, eds, *Den svenska modellen* (Lund, 1994)

Whyman, Philip, *Sweden and the 'Third Way': A Macroeconomic Evaluation* (Aldershot, 2003)

Welfare state

Åmark, Klas, *Hundra år av välfärdspolitik. Välfärdsstatens framväxt i Norge och Sverige* (Umeå, 2005)

Baldwin, Peter, 'The Scandinavian Origins of the Social Interpretation of the Welfare State', *Comparative Studies in Society and History*, XXXI (1989), pp. 3–24

Berggren, Henrik, and Lars Trägårdh, *Är svensken människa? Gemenskap och obero-ende i det moderna Sverige* (Stockholm, 2006)

Bjørnson, Øyvind, 'The Social Democrats and the Norwegian Welfare State: Some Perspectives', *Scandinavian Journal of History*, XXVI/3 (2001), pp. 197–223

—, and Inger Elisabeth Haavet, *Langsomt ble landet et velferdssamfunn: Trygdens historie 1894–1994* (Oslo, 1994)

Broberg, Gunnar, and Nils Roll-Hansen, eds, *Eugenics and the Welfare State: Sterilization Policy in Denmark, Sweden, Norway and Finland* (East Lansing, MI, 1995)

Christiansen, Niels, Finn et al., eds, *The Nordic Model of Welfare: A Historical Reappraisal* (Copenhagen, 2006)

—, and Klaus Petersen, 'The Dynamics of Social Solidarity: The Danish Welfare System, 1900–2000', *Scandinavian Journal of History*, XXVI/3 (2001), pp. 177–96

Esping-Andersen, Gøsta, *The Three Worlds of Welfare Capitalism* (Cambridge, 1990)

Gould, Arthur, *Developments in Swedish Social Policy: Resisting Dionysus* (Basingstoke, 2001)

Hirdman, Yvonne, *Att lägga livet till rätta: Studier i svensk folkhemspolitik* (Stockholm, 1989)

Jonsson, Gudmundur, 'The Icelandic Welfare State in the Twentieth Century', *Scandinavian Journal of History*, XXVI/3 (2001), pp. 249–67

Kautto, Mikko et al., eds, *Nordic Welfare States in the European Context* (London, 2001)

Kettunen, Pauli, 'The Nordic Welfare State in Finland', *Scandinavian Journal of History*, XXVI/3 (2001), pp. 225–47

Kolstrup, Søren, 'Forskning i velfærdsstatens rødder: Forskningsstrategier, resultater, huller', *Historisk Tidskrift* [Denmark], XCIV (1994), pp. 315–36

Korpi, Walter, and Joakim Palme, 'The Paradox of Redistribution and Strategies of Equality: Welfare State Institutions, Inequality and Poverty in the Western Countries', *American Sociological Review*, LXIII/5 (1998), pp. 661–87

Kosonen, Pekka, 'The Finnish Model and the Welfare State in Crisis', in *The Nordic Welfare State as a Myth and as Reality*, ed. Pekka Kosonen (Helsinki, 1993), pp. 45–66

Kuhnle, Stein, 'The Scandinavian Welfare State in the 1990s: Challenged but Still Viable', *West European Politics*, XXIII/2 (2000), pp. 209–28

Lundberg, Urban, and Klas Åmark, 'Social Rights and Social Security: The Swedish Welfare State, 1900–2000', *Scandinavian Journal of History*, XXVI/3 (2001), pp. 157–76

Petersen, Klaus, ed., *13 historier om den danske velfærdsstat* (Odense, 2003)

Runcis, Maija, *Steriliseringar i folkhemmet* (Stockholm, 1998)

Seip, Anne-Lise, *Veien til velferdsstaten: Norsk sosialpolitikk 1920–1975* (Oslo, 1994)

Timonen, Virpi, *Restructuring the Welfare State: Globalization and Social Policy Reform in Finland and Sweden* (Cheltenham, 2003)

Foreign policy

af Malmborg, Mikael, *Neutrality and State-Building in Sweden* (Basingstoke, 2001)

Agius, Christine, *The Social Construction of Swedish Neutrality: Challenges to Swedish Identity and Sovereignty* (Manchester, 2006)

Andrén, Nils, 'Nordic Integration', *Co-operation and Conflict*, II (1967), pp. 1–25

Archer, Clive, and Pertti Joenniemi, eds, *The Nordic Peace* (Aldershot, 2003)

Guðmundsson, Guðmundur J., 'The Cod and the Cold War', *Scandinavian Journal of History*, XXXI, 2 (2006), pp. 97–118

Hanhimäki, Jussi M., *Scandinavia and the United States: An Insecure Friendship* (New York, 1997)

Hansen, Lene, and Ole Wæver, eds, *European Integration and National Identity: The Challenge of the Nordic States* (London, 2002)

Haskel, Barbara G., *The Scandinavian Option: Opportunities and Opportunity Costs in*

Post-War Scandinavian Foreign Policies (Oslo, 1976)

Ingebritsen, Christine, The Nordic States and European Unity (Ithaca, NY, 1998), pp. 96–7

—, 'Norm Entrepreneurs: Scandinavia's Role in World Politics', Co-operation and Conflict, XXXVII/1 (2002), pp. 11–23

Lawler, Peter, 'Janus-Faced Solidarity: Danish Internationalism Reconsidered', Cooperation and Conflict, XXXII (2007), pp. 101–26

Miles, Lee, Fusing with Europe? Sweden in the European Union (Aldershot, 2005)

Miljan, Toivo, The Reluctant Europeans: The Attitudes of the Nordic Countries Towards European Integration (London, 1977)

Mouritzen, Hans, 'The Nordic Model as a Foreign Policy Instrument: Its Rise and Fall', Journal of Peace Research, XXXII/1 (1995), pp. 9–21

Nevakivi, Jukka, 'Kekkonen, the Soviet Union and Scandinavia: Aspects of Policy in the Years 1948–1965', Scandinavian Journal of History, XXII/2 (1997), pp. 65–81

Thorhallsson, Baldur, ed., Iceland and European Integration (London, 2004)

Turner, Barry with Gunilla Nordquist, The Other European Community: Integration and Co-operation in Nordic Europe (London, 1982)

Wæver, Ole, 'Norden Rearticulated', in Nordic Security in the 1990s: Options in the Changing Europe, ed. Jan Øberg (London, 1992), pp. 135–64

Immigration and integration

Hedetoft, Ulf, Bo Petersson and Lina Sturfelt, eds, Bortom stereotyperna? Invandrare och integration i Danmark och Sverige (Lund, 2006)

Nielsen, Hans Jørgen, Er danskerne fremmedfjendske? Udlandets syn på debatten om indvandrere 2000–2002 (Århus, 2004)

Pentikäinen, Juha, and Marja Hiltunen, eds, Cultural Minorities in Finland: An Overview Towards Cultural Policy (Helsinki, 1995)

Pred, Allan, Even in Sweden: Racisms, Racialized Spaces and the Popular Geographical Imagination (Berkeley, CA, 2000)

Runblom, Harald, 'Immigration to Scandinavia after World War II', in Ethnicity and Nation Building in the Nordic World, ed. Sven Tägil (London, 1995), pp. 282–324

Sillanpää, Lenard, 'A Comparative Analysis of Indigenous Rights in Fenno-Scandia', Scandinavian Political Studies, XX (1997), pp. 197–271

Söderling, Ismo, ed., A Changing Pattern of Migration in Finland and Its Surroundings (Helsinki, 1998)

Vessenden, Kåre, Innvandrere i Norge: Hvem er de, hva gjør de og hvordan lever de? (Oslo, 1997)

Wren, Karen, 'Cultural Racism: Something Rotten in the State of Denmark?', Social and Cultural Geography, II/2 (2001), pp. 141–62

Ylänkö, Maaria, La Finlande, pays d'accueil: Approche historique et anthropoligique. Le cas des immigrés d'Afrique noire (Helsinki, 2002)

Acknowledgements

Many people have helped me in the preparation of this book. I would like to thank Jeremy Black for encouraging me to write it and Michael Leaman at Reaktion for his patience. In particular I wish to thank Henrik Stenius and colleagues at the Centre for Nordic Studies (CENS), Renvall Institute, University of Helsinki, for providing a congenial atmosphere in which to finish writing the book during the summer of 2007. An earlier version of chapter Three was presented to a CENS seminar. Some research expenses were met by a grant from the Dean's Research Fund, UCL Faculty of Arts and Humanities. Most importantly, I would like to thank those colleagues and friends who have read and commented on drafts, answered queries and suggested references, including Jenny Andersson, Tapio Bergholm, Norbert Götz, David Harvey, Titus Hjelm, Jason Lavery, Thomas Munch-Petersen and Stefan Nyzell. Any remaining errors are my own.

Finally, my warmest personal thanks to my partner David Harvey, and to Veli-Matti Tiainen and Asbjørn Nybo for good times in Helsinki/Savitaipale and Copenhagen respectively.

Index